Handling Edna

Also By Barry Humphries

Tid (a novel)
The Blue Lamington (a novel)
Chinese Drama on the Goldfields (a treatise)
The Treasury of Australian Kitsch (a survey)
Neglected Poems (an anthology)
More Please (autobiography)
Women in the Background (a novel)
My Life as Me (autobiography)

Handling Edna

The Unauthorised Biography

BARRY HUMPHRIES

Weidenfeld & Nicolson

LONDON

First published in Great Britain in 2010
by Weidenfeld & Nicolson

1 3 5 7 9 10 8 6 4 2

© Barry Humphries 2010

A CIP catalogue record for this book
is available from the British Library.

ISBN HB 978 0 297 86083 9
ISBN TPB 978 0 297 86084 6

Typeset by Input Data Services Ltd, Bridgwater, Somerset

Printed in Great Britain by CPI Mackays, Chatham ME5 8TD

Weidenfeld & Nicolson
The Orion Publishing Group Ltd
Orion House
5 Upper Saint Martin's Lane
London, WC2H 9EA

An Hachette Livre UK Company

The Orion Publishing Group's policy is to use papers that
are natural, renewable and recyclable products and
made from wood grown in sustainable forests. The logging
and manufacturing processes are expected to conform to
the environmental regulations of the country of origin.

www.orionbooks.co.uk

In homage to

Emily Perry
and
Edith Nesbit

Contents

List of Illustrations

Singing with Jerry Hall (Barry Humphries's personal collection)

Sharing a joke backstage (Syndication International/Photo Trends)

Edna – the spectacle (Newpix)

A radiant Edna (Andrew Ross)

Transported by Sir Richard Branson (Barry Humphries' personal collection/David Koppel)

Edna posing (Lewis Morley)

The Kiwi help (Barry Humprhies' personal collection)

Showbiz Dame (Greg Gorman)

With two gorgeous Ednaettes (Barry Humphries' personal collection)

Dancing Dame (Branco Gaica)

Sir Les Patterson – diplomat at large (Andrew Ross)

A hard act to follow (Greg Gorman)

Edna composes herself (Arts Centre, Performing Arts Collection, Melbourne)

A trusting relationship (Barry Humphries' personal collection)

Disillusioned (Barry Humphries' personal collection)

Mutual admiration (Photograph by Lichfield by courtesy of the Mandarin Oriental Hotel Group)

Note to the Reader

Hitherto the public has been confused, and in some cases deceived, by divergent accounts of Dame Edna's life and origins. Some of these accounts and wild speculations have been verbally diffused and rumour and hearsay have been transmuted into 'fact'. Many have been published in books and academic theses, and there is now a considerable apocrypha bearing Edna's name.

It should be said that the author of this memoir has himself contributed to these legends and obfuscations for reasons, largely indefensible, which are set out in the text that follows.

The reader is exhorted to ignore all other accounts, withal bearing the weight and authority of Academe, and accept what follows as the 'onlie true historie'.

A mask tells us more than a face

OSCAR WILDE

Within every man there is the reflection of a woman, and within every woman there is the reflection of a man. Within every man and woman there is also the reflection of an old man and an old woman, a little boy and a little girl.

HYEMEYOHSTS STORM

No one is unknown except for me

FRANCIS PICABIA

Nothing ages a man like living always with the same woman

NORMAN DOUGLAS

Beginning with Proteus and on through the 'Metamorphoses' of Ovid, down to the wisest and most dearly beloved of Caliphs, Haroun-al-Raschid, everybody worth mentioning has delighted in the sensation of trying to be somebody else.

EDGAR SALTUS

At last — the truth!

PIETRO ARETINO

1

A Passion Play

I wish I had never met Edna Everage. It happened at a time in my youth when many paths were open to me. I had barely left university (having failed to take a degree) but I was considered to be a person of promise and I believe that I could have pursued any number of artistic professions, that of a painter holding the strongest appeal. With a small group of waggish suburban subversives I had already held two exhibitions of paintings and 'objects' satirising, it is true, pretty standard targets like the late King of England, the Pope, Winston Churchill, and the Prime Minister of Australia, but they were demonstrations of a vigorous and even ferocious gift which I foolishly chose to set aside. Now, as my days grow shorter and the worms that will devour me have already hatched, I wonder how I could ever have allowed one seemingly shy and uneducated woman to ruin my life.

The change in her personality from a painfully reticent young housewife, barely able to conduct a conversation, to a terrifying monster looming over her theatre audiences like a vulture disguised as a bird of paradise, and a woman whose advice is today sought by world leaders, and whose clothes are shamelessly copied by First Ladies the planet over, is a transformation I could never in my most extravagant dreams have imagined when first we met.

I wish that I had kept the postcard she sent me in June 1955 – fifty-four years ago! But why should I have kept it? What early scrap of which collectors now call 'Ednabilia' was worth preserving in those far-off days, before Fame unwisely smiled upon her? This was just a stage-struck young Melbourne mother writing to a young actor seeking his advice.

Her handwriting, if I recall, was studied but childish, as though painstakingly written by a girl frowning with concentration, tongue-tip protruding from the corner of her mouth. The fact that it was written in green ink with circles over the 'i's should have alerted me immediately to the serious danger of an ensuing correspondence. Had she been writing today she might well have concluded her letter with a smiley face, a sure sign of psychopathology. The card, which bore a rather bad, out-of-register reproduction of Van Gogh's *Sunflowers*, was probably purchased at the Primrose Potterie Shoppe in Little Collins Street, Melbourne's foremost purveyor of artistic knick-knacks.

'Dear Mr Humphrey,' she had begun . . . Since the green ink had not alerted me to impending danger, my misspelt name should have been sufficiently premonitory. If only, then and there, I had chucked that postcard in the waste paper basket I might have changed the course of theatrical history, and liberated myself.

Dear Mr Humphrey, you don't know me from a bar of soap, but I am a prematurely young housewife from the dress circle suburb of Moonee Ponds . . .

Moonee Ponds was a drab working-class suburb on the 'wrong side of the tracks', as my mother would have described it. Originally the home of the Wurundjeri people, it has the only place name in Australia which combines an Aboriginal word with an English word. It was low lying and swampy and in no way deserved the fashionable fifties epithet 'dress circle', usually applied by estate agents to suburbs on higher ground and commanding panoramic views, or even 'glimpses'. Many houses in Sydney are advertised as having 'harbour glimpses' and it is true that between forlorn trees and hideous apartment blocks can sometimes be discerned a two-centimetre strip of blue.

As for not knowing my correspondent 'from a bar of soap', I should inform some readers that there was a time in Australia's history when soap was not the variously coloured and scented toiletry that it is now, but came in long tablets which were broken up into anonymous chunks. Even today I am occasionally accosted by older ladies who challenge me with the same saponacious phrase.

The postcard continued:

> *. . . I read a write-up about you in* The Argus *doing some of your skits at Melbourne Uni and I am desirous of teeing up a meeting because my girlfriends say I've got real talent . . .*

I paraphrase slightly but the enthusiasm, one might even say *chutzpah*, of this young woman's letter somehow engraved it in my memory, and in the light of what has happened since then it would certainly be of interest to the modern reader. I definitely remember her using the description 'teeing up', derived from the game of golf. It is an expression which took off like wildfire in the Melbourne of this distant age, filtering down from the middle classes who actually *played* golf to Edna Everage, who possibly had no idea where the phrase came from.

> *. . . At the moment, although I have three young youngsters, my bridesmaid is babysitting while I am in a church production of a Passion Play playing the role of Mary Magdalene which is one of the leads along with God and Jesus. I am meant to be excellent though it is not for me to say. You can see it in* The Holy Trinity *Hall, behind the church, Puckle Street, Moonee Ponds until next Saturday. I look forward to meeting you. Yours truly, Edna Everage (Mrs)*

It is an unedifying confession but I was intrigued by this missive for snobbish reasons. Witnessing a suburban passion play starring my new correspondent would surely be one for the scrapbook and most likely enjoyed with the help of a handkerchief stuffed in my mouth. But why had this deluded creature sought *my* advice? Melbourne was teeming with actors far better known than I. There was Frank Thring for example, who was world famous in South Melbourne for his performances at the avant-garde Arrow Theatre. He had even been to that mysterious place called 'Overseas' to which all Australians were drawn like salmon to the spawning ground.

Frank Thring had even been in films with Laurence Olivier and lived, it was said, a rather *louche* life in Toorak – another Aboriginal place name, and indisputably a dress circle suburb. You could sometimes see him in person sauntering down the nicer end of Collins Street wearing a black turtleneck sweater, a silver chain medallion, corduroy 'slacks' and that incontrovertible proof of effeminacy: suede shoes. Could she not have written to Frank, or even Max Oldaker, the ageing matinee idol and star of so many Gilbert and Sullivan revivals? But I was probably slightly flattered to be singled out as a mentor by this silly person since my career had been so short; just a couple of student revues and a little flurry of publicity in *The Argus* and the *Sun News-Pictorial*.

I didn't reply to Edna's letter, but that evening I took myself down to Moonee Ponds on the tram which bore the euphonious name of this almost mythical suburb. There seemed to be a different type of person on this ill-omened tram ride, not at all like the passengers on the Toorak tram, or on the Burwood, or on the Riversdale. There were men in greasy brown trilbies, open-necked shirts and fawn half-Norfolk jackets in cheap fabrics. They carried collapsed Gladstone bags from which, not seldom, issued the clink of beer bottles. In the open section of the tram I saw them rolling their own cigarettes, a generous pinch of Havelock ready-rubbed tobacco in a gnarled palm and a Boomerang cigarette paper fluttering from a cracked lip.

I had never been to this part of Melbourne before and for all my precocity in other things I had been quite unadventurous in exploring my own city. I was brought up in the new suburb of Camberwell in a two-storey Georgian house built in the mid-thirties by my recently prosperous father. It was a suburb which celebrated everything English. Many of the houses were in a mock Tudor style with imitation half-timbering. Pin oaks and liquid ambers flourished on the trim grass verges and the new gardens were invariably planted with phlox, ranunculi, zinnias and rhododendrons. In the early 1950s, weedy white-barked silver birches struggled for survival, but survive they did in this alien soil and can still be found, gnarled and deformed, on the front lawns of the now venerable cream brick villas.

The recent war had done little to change the tranquillity of our street though, for the duration of the war, windows had been pasted over with cellophane to protect us from bomb-blasted glass and some back gardens had been dug up to accommodate air raid shelters, which invariably filled up with khaki-coloured water. After the war the nicer Melbourne suburbs quickly returned to normal; but for a while, there was still some horse-drawn traffic in the quiet streets – the Milkman, the Dustman and even the Bottle-o. The latter was a hunched figure in an old army greatcoat and a battered digger's slouch hat, whose hoarse ululation 'bottle-o' rang through the morning air, as curtains twitched and prim teetotallers peeped out to see how many empties an intemperate neighbour might be discarding. In working-class suburbs there was also the Iceman, serving households too poor to own a Frigidaire, and in remoter districts as yet unsewered, there was, we were told, a sinister nocturnal personage known as 'the Nightman' with his horse-drawn cart and its cloacal burden.

Melbourne was bisected by a class barrier as immutable as the *Limes Germanicus*, which the Romans constructed as a barrier against the unsubdued barbarian tribes. In Melbourne a corresponding boundary was the River Yarra. Nice people lived south of it. North of it, beyond the commercial centre, dwelt nobody we knew or wished to know. Bluntly expressed in sanitary terms, we flushed the toilet and they pulled the chain.

Now, on the tram to Moonee Ponds, I saw that other Melbourne where the Bottle-o would have trawled with greater success: parades of Victorian shops with wide awnings supported by cast-iron columns, bristling with what is now called 'signage' . . . *Four'n Twenty Pies*, *Cerebos Salt*, *Penfolds Wine*, and *Brooke's Lemos* – a giant Michelin Man made of lemons striding across a blue hoarding. Sometimes, even today, when an old building is demolished, briefly exposing the wall of its neighbour, a hermetically preserved advertisement for that mysterious panacea *Dr Morse's Indian Roots Pills* is revealed in pristine condition, like the 50,000-year-old 'Bradshaw' paintings from the northern Kimberley, or the erotic frescoes of Herculaneum.

I alighted from the tram in Puckle Street and there, sure enough, but one hundred yards away, was a rather ugly red brick ecclesiastical building with a cluster of people outside. The women all wore floral dresses, hats and gloves, and the men, who were fewer, wore double-breasted wide-lapelled suits of a pre-war cut. No doubt they were all friends or family of the cast. I had arrived in the nick of time it seemed, and I joined the small crowd which filed down beside the church to the posterior hall, faithfully following signs which read 'Passion Play this way' like the Stations of the Cross.

From the hall came the shrill whinny of a reed organ, and on entering I was surprised to find it already quite full and furnished with extra pews and chairs to accommodate the overflow. It was an unseasonably warm evening in April and there was a strong odour of talcum powder, Faulding's Old English Lavender Water and, ever and anon, a sharp whiff of perspiration, for there were present a few recently arrived Italian parishioners who, by some accidental apostasy, had abandoned their traditional place of worship. They must have assumed that all roads led to Rome, even Puckle Street, Moonee Ponds.

A limp red curtain hung athwart the small stage and occasionally certain bumps and billowings indicated that behind it

vigorous preparations were taking place. The small but insistent organ stood on the left, close to where I had found the
uncomfortable corner of a pew, and it was being pumped and
manipulated by a large thyroid woman whose jowl and forelip
were cocooned in fine grey hair. She seemed more interested
in catching the eye of a friend in the audience than in striking
even the most approximately correct note. As the lights con-
vulsively dimmed, Miss Godkin, as I later learnt to be the
organist's name, modulated from a sketchy rendition of 'Que
Sera Sera' to a more devotional hymn. It was thus, to the tune
of 'What a Friend We Have in Jesus', that the red curtain,
after a few preliminary tugs, parted to reveal a bustling square
in old Jerusalem.

If there was a rudimentary set I don't remember it now, but
the stage swarmed with people and effective use had been
made of bath towels, dressing gowns and burnt cork. Some of
the older players threw themselves enthusiastically into the
roles of beggars, rabbis and non-specific Arabs, but the younger
actors often stood staring into the audience in search of their
proud parents. I recall a Roman soldier in cardboard armour
strutting onto the stage and bullying a crone which rather
diverted our attention from the entrance of Jesus, impersonated by a young curate, the Reverend Tony Morphett, a
handsome fellow resembling a distant relation of Leonardo
DiCaprio. He was clad anachronistically in a toga, and behind
his head, fixed to his ears with elastic bands (which had possibly
been components of his parents' Fowlers Vacola fruit bottling
equipment) was a large cardboard disc painted gold.

Unfortunately, at his first barely audible utterance, 'Peace be with you', one of the elastic bands sprang loose from its auricular mooring and for the rest of the performance Christ's halo flapped distractingly against his neck.

The production dragged on except for those moments, and they were many, when the principal players forgot their words and when Saint John's beard detached itself from his chin in the middle of a particularly moving affirmation of faith. Where was Edna? I wondered. Which one of those capering Arab urchins or veiled virgins could be my correspondent? The audience had grown a little restless and there was already quite a clatter of cups, saucers and plates as the Ladies Guild began to lay out supper on the lace-flanked trestle tables at the back of the hall. They were even chatting quite loudly as they deposited asparagus rolls, Velveeta sandwiches, cocktail frankfurters and butterfly cakes in readiness for the eschatological banquet to take place in the intermission.

At last there was a change of scene, or at least the announcement of one, as an Arab abruptly stepped forward to the footlights with a large sign which read:

THE HOUSE OF SIMON THE LEPPER

Leprosy held at that time a powerful thrall over the inhabitants of Melbourne. A boat had recently arrived with a cargo of coconut which was impounded and destroyed because a Lascar seaman suffering from leprosy had been discovered on board. Desiccated coconut was the principal constituent of the Lamington, Australia's indigenous cake, and it was also essential in the manufacture of Coconut Ice, the pink and white confectionery which every Australian child loved to make. Leprosy, that dreaded biblical infirmity, had dealt a death blow to two of the staples of the Australian diet.

An impressive leper (played, I learnt later, by an attractive Sunday School teacher) tottered around on her knees and then, gesticulating with ingenious three-fingered gloves, exhibited her malady to the great enjoyment of the audience. Notwithstanding, throughout this grim cameo she snorted with suppressed laughter at her own antics. She was presumably 'corpsing', as they say in showbiz circles.

Then Simon himself trundled on stage on something resembling a modern skateboard, wrapped in a blanket and wearing a turban which already threatened to unravel.

The warmth of the hall, the aroma of hot sausage rolls and the effluvium of talc and cologne was having a soporific effect and I may have nodded off for a few seconds, only to be jolted back to consciousness by the irruption to the stage of a striking personage. A tall, angular young woman in a scarlet and biblically inauthentic muu-muu delivered her opening line, drawn no doubt from some Apocrypha of her own:

'Christ, your feet look awful. Let me give them a bit of TLC.'

It was at once the worst and yet the most audible performance of the evening. The audience was suddenly galvanised by a presence on stage in sharp contrast to the drab, shuffling amateurs around her. However, the most conspicuous feature of this shrill and gawky interloper was her hair, which was the colour of *wisteria floribunda*. This, presumably, was my correspondent Edna impersonating Mary Magdalene fifties-style. She marched purposefully across the stage and flung herself at the big brown feet of the Reverend Tony Morphett, who meanwhile discarded his halo.

'Peace be with you,' feebly intoned Christ. Apart from his barely perceptible speech about suffering little children earlier in the production he interposed that exhortation whenever there was a hiatus in the action. Edna retrieved from a string bag – yet another scriptural anachronism – a jar of Vick's VapoRub, with which she generously embrocated Jesus's pedal extremities. In a later grandiose account of this incident, 'Dame' Edna claimed that she employed a combination of Vick's and Nivea Cream in lieu of the biblically correct spike-nard which, then as now, is not easily obtained at Melbourne pharmacies, but I can assure historians reading this eyewitness account that the unguent used by Edna–Magdalene was the much humbler emollient.

There was a gasp when, after a few brief and precocious attempts at amateur reflexology, she released her mauve chignon and proceeded to expunge the mentholated ointment from her Saviour's feet. The audience watched in astonishment at this modern re-creation of such a celebrated New Testament episode, but the Reverend Tony Morphett was obviously very ticklish, for he writhed uncomfortably in his throne on the brink, one feared, of hysteria.

As Edna rose at length from her task, her hair matted and

viscid, Jesus stiffly raised his left arm and intoned, 'What this woman has done will also be told as a memorial to her.'

Smirking rather inappropriately, Edna rose and curtsied to the assembled towels and blankets as the curtain twitched to a close.

There was a stampede to the supper tables. I realised that since this was only intermission, the audience needed to be well fed before the Crucifixion, an event I preferred to imagine. Slipping out of the hall I felt a tug on my sleeve and noticed a small, bird-like woman of indeterminate age at my side.

'Excuse I,' she said, 'are you Mr Humphrey?'

I nodded in affirmation.

'I'm Marjory Allsop, Edna's wee frind.' I realised I was being accosted by an inhabitant of the Commonwealth's most remote dominion. 'Wasn't she choice?'

I had forgotten this popular New Zealand epithet, but before I could agree or not, Mrs Allsop continued, 'I'm worried about her poor he-ah with all that muck in it. Are you staying for the Crucifixion? That's her wee big scene.'

I invented a later appointment but gave the woman my card. 'Please apologise and ask her to give me a ring.'

'But what did you *really* think of her?' pursued Edna's importunate friend.

I hesitated, seeking a form of words that would be at once encouraging yet truthful. 'Marvellous isn't the word,' I replied. As I hurried out to the lights of Puckle Street I imagined I could still hear Mrs Allsop's Kiwi lament, 'Her poor he-ah, her poor he-ah.'

Twenty minutes later and still on the tram, I realised that a rather silly triumphant smile remained on my lips. This woman was a 'natural', I thought. If I could hire her for next to nothing to appear in one of my satirical stage shows she would be hilarious, even if she only read the telephone directory. She was, in a sense, a 'primitive' like the American singer Florence Foster Jenkins, who used to rent Carnegie Hall and give recitals of famous songs and arias which she rendered with a profound seriousness and grotesque ineptitude before an audience convulsed with laughter. This Edna could be the Eliza Doolittle to my Henry Higgins.

2

Russell Collins

I was in love with Pat Casimir. She sat at her typewriter about twenty feet away from where I worked at a wholesale recorded music warehouse. I stood behind a small counter supplying the new and revolutionary LPs to Melbourne retailers. Among them the best sellers were *The Glenn Miller Story*, *The Student Prince*, *Satchmo at Pasadena*, *Mantovani Magic*, and very occasionally a classical title. It was a job that my desperate father had arranged with his golfing friend, the warehouse manager, after my promising university career had foundered.

Having to punch a clock every morning at 8 a.m. after a night of black coffee and black Sobranie cigarettes in Melbourne's only bohemian coffee lounge felt like a terrible comedown, as indeed it was. I was drawn to the theatrical life but my family had persuaded me that this was an impractical pipe dream and that I should at least, in the popular parental exhortation of the time, 'get something solid behind me' or 'have something to fall back on'. Already everyone seemed certain that I would be falling backwards sooner or later, if I hadn't done so already.

In numb despair I toiled behind my counter, occasionally sneaking behind the high metal racks of vinyl recordings to puff on a Garrick or a Du Maurier. The fags were theatrical, in name at least.

On the other side of what seemed like a vast expanse of brown linoleum, the door to Mr Miniken's outer office stood ajar and there, at her typewriter, and always with a vase of daffodils or some other seasonal bloom, sat the delectable Pat with her June Allyson bob, bathed in muted light like a painting by Vermeer. She always arrived after me and left before I had to clock off, and she always wore smart tailored suits and high-heeled shoes, perhaps from the exclusive shop of Mr Kurt Geiger.

As she passed my miserable counter each morning she would toss her golden locks and give me a heart-stopping smile which usually sustained me until lunchtime. Such was my demoralised state that I never once invited her to join me for that staple snack of the period, a cappuccino and a slice of toasted raisin bread. Indeed, in all the time I worked for that company I never once had a conversation with Pat except for a mumbled greeting, yet she was probably my only reason for staying in the job.

Now, when I reread the diary I kept at about this time and see the entry describing my first visit to Moonee Ponds – the passion play, the encounter with Mrs Allsop and, above all, my impressions of the young Edna – I am deeply ashamed of my snobbery and priggishness. What a fraud I was! I, whose theatrical credits amounted to a few university romps, a couple of bit parts in some amateur Shakespearian productions, and a minor reputation as a provincial iconoclast was, in reality, a callow young man who still lived with his parents, had dropped out of university, and was obliged to toil obscurely and resentfully in a city warehouse. What right had I to sneer patronisingly at a brave young actress who, with misplaced confidence, had politely asked me to be her mentor?

Then came another postcard. This time it was an Australian outback landscape by Albert Namatjira; a white gum tree against some red eroded hills. No green ink this time, for it seemed Edna was employing one of the new biros which the advertisements asserted could write underwater – though it was hard to imagine the circumstances under which this might be accomplished, or to what purpose. This time I kept the postcard.

'Dear Mr Humphrey', it began.

My friend Madge told me you left before the Crucifixion and I hope it wasn't because you thought I was awful.

I was backstage during interval trying to get our Lord's stickiness out of my hair, and I'm glad she didn't tell me then that you had gone.

I hope I haven't mixed you up with some other actor who I've heard on the wireless in the Kool Mint Theatre of the Air, but I would still like to talk about my career. Could I buy you a nice lunch at Russell Collins under the T&G building next Tuesday at 1 p.m.? They do a nice sweet corn on toast in the continental style. Don't look for the girl with the mauve hair as I've dyed it brown, though it looks less natural I'm afraid. Yours faithfully, Edna (Mrs)

She had written her telephone number under her address which, I had noted with a smirk, was Humoresque Street. In my lunch hour I walked down the hill to the Cathedral Hotel on the corner of Swanston Street and used the public telephone. A child answered, and when I asked for Edna I heard the vulcanite clunk of the receiver as it dropped to the floor. There ensued a long interlude of domestic noise, the sound of a radio and unidentifiable thumps and crashes.

At last a voice (was it Edna's?) came down the line: 'Who is this please?'

I announced myself and heard a muffled voice reproaching a child. 'Kenny, how many times have I told you that when someone rings up for Mummy you go and get her quick sticks.'

Then, in what struck me as a slightly la-di-da tone, she said, 'Look, Mr Humphrey, excuse I, but my little boy is always doing that. He's a real little Turk. I hope you got my postcard.'

Our foe at Gallipoli had now been subsumed into the vernacular of the nursery. I replied, 'Yes, Edna, it arrived on my desk this morning. A little lunch at Russell Collins would be perfect. I could squeeze it in between meetings this Friday if that suits you.'

Why was I suddenly pretending that I had an office, or that I attended meetings, when I was, it seemed, a total failure with no real prospects and, moreover, in no position to offer this young woman anything resembling a theatrical opportunity?

'Look, I'd love that,' said Edna. 'And Madge can babysit the nippers. Could we meet at Russell Collins at half past twelve? I'll be in a nice frock.'

When I replaced the receiver I sought refuge in the small private bar of the Cathedral with its elaborate Victorian mahogany backfitting and engraved glass, long since buried beneath the Westin Hotel. Why Edna thought her 'nice frock' was going to distinguish her from every other woman in the restaurant I could not imagine, but I felt I would know her anyway; Mary Magdalene was not easily forgotten, even if she had changed her hair colouring.

As I hacked at the T-bone steak and peas which constituted my counter lunch, I wondered if I should abandon my feeble hopes of becoming an actor and go into management. I still had the feeling that if this young woman, gawky and amateurish as she was, could appear in the right vehicle, a star might be born.

Russell Collins was not a person but a large restaurant on the corner of Russell and Collins streets. It occupied the basement of the T&G building where, years before, in the dental surgery of Doctor Morris, my 'slightly prominent' front teeth had been corrected. 'Buck teeth' was a dental affliction only tolerated north of the Yarra. The rendezvous suited me because it was just around the corner from the EMI warehouse and it was entered by passing through Melbourne's, and perhaps Australia's, first photoelectric cell: a beam of light between two chromium pillars which, when interrupted, whooshed open the doors.

It was a crowded lunch hour in the large restaurant, which was divided into nooks and alcoves in a debased antipodean version of the 'Arts and Crafts' style. There were doilies pressed beneath the glass table tops and nickel vases from which poppies drooped (and in September, jonquils diffused their fresh astringent scent). I was immediately accosted by my luncheon guest: a tall, young woman, nearly as tall as me, but instead of those memorable mauve waves, her hair was now lank and brown and clung unappealingly to the sides of her rather sallow face.

She wore glasses of the newly fashionable kind, 'the butterfly' with upswept corners, hers decorated with blue enamel and small diamantes. Her dress was cyclamen and of the 'ballerina' style, and she wore a pert hat in a similar colour, and aqua gloves. Aqua was the new colour of the fifties, the colour of kitchens and cleanliness, and it went nicely with everything, including those old favourites maize, fawn and maroon, hues which can now only be seen in any profusion in a thrift shop.

'Excuse I,' she said, 'but I was here early and I got us a nice inglenook so we can hear each other speak.'

The restaurant was indeed noisy with the sound of chatter and cutlery. As we took our seats I noticed a few people staring at us, and even grinning furtively as they observed my companion's outfit which was 'over the top', long before the epithet had been coined. Although Edna's career had barely begun, her very presence in a public place provided an opportunity for eleemosynary entertainment.

Apart from the fact that she had a child, or children, I knew nothing about the young woman across the table who was shyly removing her gloves and peering at herself in a compact mirror.

'I hope I haven't got lippy on my teeth,' she exclaimed. 'I like Forbidden Fruit, but it doesn't like me.'

Forbidden Fruit, I remember, was the latest shade of lipstick then widely advertised. It was, of course, cyclamen.

My cream of asparagus soup arrived as promptly as Edna's cream of tomato and I presumed that the cans had been opened simultaneously. I was just about to enquire about her theatrical experience, which could not have been much more extensive than my own, when an elderly woman with a sweet smile and a large prickly mole, which crouched over the corner of her mouth like a threatened echidna, approached our table.

'You don't know me from a bar of soap, Edna,' she began, 'and I suppose you get this all the time, but would you mind signing my menu?'

Rather coolly Edna withdrew a mottled green Platignum fountain pen from her handbag and inscribed the proffered card with a flourish.

'Good on you, Edna,' said the old lady, hastening back to her table of rubber-necking crones.

The incident astonished me. It was a case of mistaken identity, surely. Edna must resemble some well-known person. 'That was nice,' was all that I could say.

'I'm surprised that she recognised me,' Edna exclaimed disingenuously. 'I dyed my hair brown yesterday. It was nearly ruined in that church show and besides, I'm sick of people teasing me about my mauve mop. That's what they used to call me at school – "mauve mop"!'

Was this woman pulling my leg, I wondered? The old dears across the restaurant were still smiling and waving at us.

'Ever since I won the "Lovely Mother" contest and got all that publicity, people feel they know me,' said my companion, ordering Russell Collins' signature dish: creamed sweet corn on toast. 'I suppose it's a compliment, and it makes them proud to think that I helped to put Australia on the map.'

Somehow I had never heard of this contest but then I didn't read the women's magazines to which my mother avidly subscribed. I used to get the airmail edition of the *New Statesman* and occasionally copies of *The Listener* from faraway London. The two periodicals rarely, if ever, mentioned Australia and would certainly pay scant attention to a beauty contest for housewives.

'How wonderful!' I exclaimed. 'What was the prize?'

'An overseas trip,' Edna trilled, elocuting and extending the word 'overseas' in a manner which only a nice Melbourne person who had been overseas would employ. 'It's made me a bit restless actually,' she added, blotting a little cream of tomato off her Forbidden Fruit with the corner of a serviette.

When our sweet corn arrived, looking just like one of those very red, yellow and brown out-of-register food illustrations in the *Women's Weekly*, and garnished with tomatoes and lettuce leaves stained with beetroot, Edna was telling me excitedly about her trip and the night she went to *My Fair Lady* at the Theatre Royal in Drury Lane. The show had made a big impact on the timid Melbourne prize-winner and I realised that she saw herself as the incarnation of Eliza Doolittle, destined for grandeur.

With a shiver I recalled that I had actually cast myself, albeit facetiously, in the role of Professor Higgins on the tram on the way home from the church hall in Moonee Ponds. Was I lunching with my nemesis?

3

A Good Idea at the Time

Two stupendous events were about to change life in Melbourne forever: Television and the Olympic Games. The Games were going to put Melbourne on the world map, from which hitherto it had been conspicuously absent. Already one man, 'Whelan the Wrecker', with the blessing of the City Council, was demolishing every opulent Victorian building in town – every major hotel, bank and suburban mansion he could find – so that when the first Olympic visitors arrived they would not be affronted by the sight of ugly, old-fashioned buildings.

By 1956, when the first Olympians stepped off their planes at Melbourne's aerodrome – a few short miles from Moonee Ponds – they found a city still hazy with the dust of pulverised masonry. What had been the best preserved and most mag-nificent Victorian city, rivalling Calcutta and pre-war Glasgow, was blitzed out of recognition.

As Edna and I sat over our creamed sweet corn, it was possible to hear the distant thud of Mr Whelan's iron ball as what had been rather optimistically called the 'Paris' end of Collins Street yielded to Progress. It was as if we were warily lunching in a bunker as the barbarians closed in. Over dessert, which consisted of a segment each of lemon cream pie, Edna relaxed a little and spoke of her domestic life: her husband Norman – older, I gathered, and in fragile health – her three young children, and a companion of some sort called Madge who must have been the ill-favoured woman with a New Zealand accent I met at the passion play, the woman who was so worried about Edna's 'he-ah'.

Edna was obsessively house-proud and, unbidden, described the décor of her home in great detail. It seemed the colour scheme was predominantly fawn and burgundy, and she somehow got to describe her wedding dress and those of her bridesmaids: apricot and oyster. As I sat listening to this catalogue of niceness I apprehended that this garrulous young woman was disproving Voltaire, who defined a bore as someone who leaves nothing out. By putting everything in, everything and more, Edna's discourse became hypnotic.

Furtively I looked at my watch. I was already due back at the warehouse and I had, God knows why, pretended that I had 'a rehearsal'.

Pushing her dessert plate aside and draining her coffee cup,

Edna exclaimed rather loudly, 'That was lovely. I'm full up to dolly's wax.'

It was an announcement of repletion, which I later discovered referred to the rag dolls of yesteryear with their wax necks and heads.

'Would you like the docket now?' interrupted the waitress, wearing a white apron, a black dress, and a whiff of BO.

The bill was seven and six and Edna quickly fished a russet-coloured ten shilling note out of her clutch bag. 'I'm paying for this, Mr Humphrey,' she insisted firmly, adding somewhat archly, 'your turn next time.'

I wondered at what point in our acquaintance I would be able to tactfully correct her spelling of my name; better sooner than later.

We ascended to Collins Street, to the iron rumble of the trams and the dangerous proximity of Mr Whelan's relentless ball.

'I have an idea for something you might do in the theatre,' I lied. 'Not much money but a little prestige.'

Edna beamed and shook my hand. 'Look, I'd love that,' she said. I saw that there was quite a bit of lippy on her front teeth. 'A career has to start somewhere,' she added.

She was right, of course, and had I but known it, her career had started already. She had just bought more than lunch.

Back at the drudgery of my job in the warehouse I found myself thinking more and more about this very ordinary, yet curiously confident young woman who, with touching *naïveté*, thought I could help her career. My job had worsened. The change-over from 78 shellac records to LPs, or microgrooves as they were called, required that the large stock of obsolete discs be destroyed for obscure reasons of copyright.

I have described in another tome the terrible task to which I was assigned. It entailed spending days, and sometimes weeks, in a windowless basement room, below Flinders Lane, literally smashing records with a hammer. Hundreds and thousands of records, popular and classical: Bing Crosby, Beethoven, Sibelius and Whispering Jack Smith were all shattered and flung in boxes which were carted off to some remote furnace. I felt that my university activities as a ferocious dadaist had caught up with me and I was performing a supreme act of cultural espionage without an audience. It was karma. I was imprisoned in my subterranean cell, a grey dustcoat over the double-breasted suit which my father had paid his tailor to make for me as a reward for doing 'a real job'.

Lunchtime always provided a brief respite. I would skulk upstairs to the showroom level, stealing a furtive look at Pat at her typewriter and the golden nimbus that seemed to surround her. She always smiled, but was there a trace of contempt? I had, after all, the lowliest job in the company.

Sometimes I would perch on one of the steps of our building, reading and eating sandwiches. It was here that a wedge of sunlight could occasionally be found, for it was freezing cold in my record breaking crypt. Not seldom Pat's shapely ankles brushed past me as she stepped out for lunch in her provocative slingbacks, no doubt at some smart little coffee lounge like Raffles or 96A Collins Street. There was always a smudge of grime on her naked heels and I realised that she must drive to work in a nice car like a Vauxhall Velox.

One question haunted me. Why was I offering to help Edna's career when I could not help my own? I did not dare to think of a theatrical career for myself. Perhaps I had enjoyed a few brief moments of notoriety during my short-lived university experience; the rest was going to be downhill. And it wasn't as though I found Edna even faintly attractive: my promise of professional assistance was not part of a strategy of seduction. She was, in fact, one of the least attractive young women I had ever met, but she reminded me of someone.

That evening I went back to the university campus for rehearsal. Our little company was putting together a Christmas variety show. Appearing in university productions gave me the illusion that I was still a student, even if I had been kicked off my course. I had written a few sketches and lyrics to a couple of songs, but Ray, the director, wanted me to do something about the forthcoming Olympic Games. There have been many accounts of this period in my life and at least one from my own pen, but all of them are wildly inaccurate. The truth was that I was stumped, blocked, void of ideas. Edna kept jumping into my mind, for I had told my fellow actors about her and she had become something of a company joke. I even impersonated her, and Edna's gaucheries and genteelisms became the subject of much snobbish raillery. 'When are we going to meet your girlfriend?' was the usual taunt, and the thought suddenly struck me with the force of a thunderbolt that this was the perfect opportunity to produce my 'find' and fill a lacuna in the show.

I reached my parents' place late that night, having taken Monica, a fellow cast member, home in my mother's car. Monica was the daughter of the headmaster of a famous Presbyterian ladies college, and so I had to park the car in the damp penumbra of a venerable elm, some distance from the school's gothic portal, in order to perform an act of cramped concupiscence in the steamy confines of the car. Moreover, without attracting the curiosity of the Doctor and Mrs McAlister who maintained an anxious vigil in the headmaster's lodge.

Melbourne was at this time filled with parents waiting up for their children, and probably still is. All that has changed is the curfew. I wonder if the youth of today, returning home late after some guilty dalliance, are still greeted by the words 'Do you realise what time it is?' or 'This isn't a hotel, you know', uttered by some haggard parent in a dressing gown.

My mother and father were understandably worried that I was burning the candle at both ends: rehearsing for a show at night and punching a clock the next morning at 8 a.m. If they had also known that I was making all kinds of promises to the recent winner of the 'Lovely Mother' contest, who was also a resident of Moonee Ponds, they would have gone out of their minds with worry.

Casually I asked my mother if she had heard of Edna Everage. She thought for a while and then, as recollection dawned, she said, 'Oh yes, there was a write-up in the *Weekly* a while ago.'

It was the *Women's Weekly* that she referred to, the house-wives' bible, until *Woman's Day* came along like the New Testament. It was the Rosetta Stone of Australian culture.

'How they judge these things heaven only knows,' my mother continued. 'In the *Weekly* I thought she was a bit *ordinary* '.

'Ordinary' was my mother's favourite epithet of opprobrium. It was a nuanced way of saying 'common', and it sounded a lot less common than saying common. 'Slightly ordinary' was the ultimate condemnation.

'Where does she live, I wonder?' asked my mother with her characteristic prescience.

'I think . . . well, I'm pretty sure it's Moonee Ponds.'

My mother gave a short, almost gay, laugh. 'Near the race track probably. I'm disappointed in the *Women's Weekly*.'

My mother was a complicated woman to whom disappointment came easily, which is surprising in view of her low expectations of others. Paradoxically she encouraged me, behind my father's back, in many of my pursuits. She paid for painting classes, surreptitious driving lessons, and hire cars when I was late for work at the warehouse; which was almost every day. She also paid the subscription for a glossy American magazine called *Art News*, but if any show with which I was involved received a bad or even equivocal notice in the *The Sun* or *The Argus* she was the first to point it out.

'The man on *The Sun* didn't like it much, Barry,' she would say. 'I've just had Ada Scott on the phone and she told me that *The Argus* wasn't much better.'

My father was always too busy to involve himself in these complicated transactions between mother and son, though she would often invoke his name in expressing paternal disapproval. 'You're killing that man' was one of her favourite and most melodramatic observations, usually made at dinner in my father's presence and that of the maid. There was no answer to that, though the man at the end of the table tucking heartily into a nice juicy steak seemed to give my mother's dire announcement the lie.

I had written a two-handed sketch about the forthcoming Olympic Games in which a housewife offered to billet an Olympic visitor. Edna would be perfect for the role if I could persuade our company director to engage someone who was not a regular member of the company; who was in fact, the *real thing*. It was to be a Christmas show anyway, around which the rules were more relaxed. I telephoned Edna with an invitation to attend what amounted to an audition the following evening.

All day at work I waited nervously for the moment when I would introduce my protégé to the company. Would anyone, I wondered, be able to keep a straight face?

Edna arrived punctually at seven in a Silver Top Taxi and I noticed that her hair was still dyed brown and hung rather limply beneath a yellow conical felt hat of a type briefly fashionable. It was a clown's hat. She was almost defiantly flat chested and wore a blue twin-set, blue floral skirt and flat shoes.

As I paid the driver, she said, 'I look awful, don't I, Barry?

But I want to look the part. You've seen me in my nice frock anyway.'

I realised she was very nervous but as I presented her to the grinning cast I knew somehow that she was going to be a hit. If only I had foreseen how big a hit that was to be.

The rest, as they say, is history.

On first night Edna got the biggest laughs of the evening, merely by describing the furnishings and appointments of her Moonee Ponds residence, and even though she strayed far from the written text she seemed to strike a note which had, hitherto, not been sounded in an Australian theatre. It was a note of verisimilitude; a relentlessly prosaic litany of suburban ordinariness too dull to have ever found its way onto the stage before. Its effect on a cosy middlebrow Melbourne audience was nothing short of cathartic.

At the cast party afterwards Edna was in a triumphant mood, wearing the cyclamen dress I had seen at lunch a few weeks before. She had brought her husband Norman, a slight, ill-looking man several years her senior. He seemed discomforted by the momentum of his young wife's ascent and I tried, without success, to strike up a conversation with him.

Perhaps it was a mistake for me to praise Edna's performance and imply that she had a future as an actress, for he said, rather poignantly, 'She's got to go her own way, Mr Humphrey. I don't want to hold her back. Ed's probably told you I've been enjoying pretty poor health lately, but if you reckon she's got what it takes, I don't want to stand in her way.'

Norman Everage was an almost tragic figure as he stood before me in his brown double-breasted suit, with a small blood-stain on the collar of his shirt and a glass of Abbots Lager in his gnarled and sun-freckled hand. 'Ed tells me you're an actor too, Mr Humphrey. Don't you find it cuts in to your evenings?'

Looking down on this small, khaki-faced man who wore a glinting Returned Serviceman's badge on his lapel, I once again felt like a fraud. Was I really an actor, I asked myself, with only a few semi-amateur performances in the theatre to my credit? Now, for my own selfish amusement, and in the unlikely role of impresario, I was snatching a young wife and mother from her family and her invalid husband with the promise of a theatrical career which I was in no position to fulfil. It suddenly seemed dishonourable to lead this family on. I was an artist only in the sense that I had already, in the name of Art, begun to claim exemption from the laws and rules of life.

Edna, however, was revelling in her theatrical success. As I left that evening I saw her, well into her second Pimm's, laughing uproariously with Zoe Caldwell, who was already a big star in Melbourne and would later take her gifts to Broadway and the West End.

The following day the newspapers seemed to confirm Edna's success. But *The Age* of Melbourne, the only Australian paper to contain a 'literary supplement', headed its slightly equivocal review with the words 'Are Houses Funny?' and the critic questioned whether the mere description of a lower middle-class residence counted as authentic comedy. Was it perhaps unfair, he hinted, and even unpatriotic, to make fun of something we had never hitherto thought to be faintly amusing? It was a scruple which, over succeeding years, became a paranoid howl, and the time would come when the mature Edna would be rebuked in Parliament for her unsporting franknesses.

Naturally my mother had read the reviews, or had already had them relayed to her by Ada Scott. 'You don't get much of a mention, Barry,' she declared at breakfast the next day. If it had not been my mother, I might have detected a note of mild triumph in her voice.

The word 'majority' had recently entered the Australian vocabulary, along with 'approximately', and as was our custom with a new word we employed it relentlessly. 'This Edna woman seems to have stolen the majority of your thunder,' she continued, 'though Norman Banks said she is probably just a flash in the pan.'

Norman Banks was a popular 'radio personality' and a guru before that word had entered the vocabulary. He broadcast every morning and pontificated on all possible subjects. He was possibly the first broadcaster in Australia to succeed in persuading his listeners to share his own estimation of himself as an omniscient being. Apart from being a know-all, Norman had what women described as 'a lovely speaking voice'. The only other person in Australia to share this honour was the Prime Minister, Robert Gordon Menzies, himself. Much later this silver-tongued paragon of the radio was revealed to have feet of clay, and there was a nasty story in *The Truth*, a scrofulous publication, imputing everything from alcoholism, shoplifting and sexual unorthodoxy to the Banks family.

'You'll have your hands full with that woman,' added my mother with a gnomic smile. 'Your father always says you'll learn the hard way.'

Whatever the future held for me, I knew that I had to quit my job with the record company, and that it would be harder to tell my parents than to announce my resignation to Mr Miniken.

Then Providence struck. I was invited to join a theatrical company in Sydney which presented topical revues in a small theatre in Phillip Street. There was even a financial offer of £15 a week. It was too good to be true. So at the age of twenty-one I was suddenly to become a professional actor. It would be a blow to my parents, and one from which they would never quite recover.

4

Edna's Big Decision

The nice people at EMI – Tom, Stan, Derek, Dick, Elsie and Betty – all gave me a send-off and a pewter mug, long since lost, inscribed with their names. The gorgeous Pat did not appear at this valedictory event and I sometimes wonder where she is today. Perhaps it is better that she resides ever-young in my memory, at her typewriter in the morning sunshine in Flinders Lane. My workmates (these days they would be called colleagues) all seemed to brighten up at the prospect of my departure. Some of them might have liked me but most, quite rightly, took me for an anomaly, a square peg in a round hole, and were probably relieved that they were no longer required to treat me with polite acceptance.

The prospect of going to Sydney, the big, bad city to the

north, had many advantages. I would no longer be punching a clock in a record warehouse or be obliged to live at home in the flat my father had built for me in an attempt to immobilise me with domestic comfort. But the chief bonus of this unexpected relocation was that I could shake off Edna. She had already become importunate; ringing me up at all hours wanting to rehearse audition pieces for some of the new musicals that were coming to Melbourne.

There had, indeed, been roles in recent shows that she might have effectively taken. There was a part in Irving Berlin's *Call Me Madam* which would have suited her if she could sing, and auditions were already being held for the Australian production of *Tea and Sympathy*, which was a perfect vehicle for Edna in the Deborah Kerr role if the author of this tender and sensitive play had no objections to it being transformed into a farce. The other show for which Edna auditioned was *Teahouse of the August Moon*, an immensely popular play of the period, though unlikely to receive a modern revival.

Nothing seems to date more, and to sink more quickly into obscurity, than the work of the fashionable dramatist, though the caprices of popular taste yield some surprises: today the work of Terence Rattigan seems more 'relevant' than the turgid sermons of Bertolt Brecht. But it would be a daring producer who revived the plays of Christopher Fry, or Stephen Phillips, or Edward Knoblock, or William Douglas Home, or Clemence Dane, whose reputations once seemed so assured. We watched their boom, their apotheosis, and then their disposal and banishment to Limbo.

Edna's chances of a major part in any forthcoming commercial production were slim since, in the Australia of that time, leading roles were always assigned to English stars, not seldom at the end of their careers.

My parents were not even remotely theatrical, though on a Sunday evening after the corned beef and salad and the scones and apricot jam, we would often settle down within the warm bakelite-scented propinquity of our Radiola wireless set and listen to the Lux Radio Theatre, just in case my mother's old Sunday School friend, Thelma Scott, popped up in the cast. My mother exhibited great excitement and vicarious pride if Thelma, or her other friend, Coral Browne, starred in one of these radio melodramas.

I was frequently taken to the theatre to see the musical comedies of the day. With my mother, I attended several performances of her favourite operetta, *The Desert Song.* My mother took a sardonic delight in risibly bad performances and she was particularly entertained by a belly dance – or was it a dance of seven veils? – performed by a somewhat overweight actress called Stephanie Deste, a Helena Rubinstein lookalike who later set up 'Beauty Lodge', a famous Melbourne cosmetic and depilation salon.

A memorable moment in *The Desert Song* is the entrance of the Red Shadow on the back of a magnificent white horse. On the afternoon we attended, the horse was not well behaved and, as the Americans say with excruciating coyness, 'went to the bathroom' copiously and pungently during one of the show's most stirring and moving moments. The Red Shadow was played by my mother's favourite star, the Tasmanian matinee idol Max Oldaker, who had by then seen better days. Max still had a huge following amongst his ageing female fans, though a more sophisticated audience might have easily discerned that his own romantic inclinations excluded the feminine sex. My mother would always lean towards me and, in a whisper which must surely have been audible on stage, say, 'Isn't it pathetic at his age!' Today, if from the stage I ever see a mother and son seated in the front row at any of my theatrical offerings, I am always fearful that a similar observation might be made about me.

But before I left Melbourne and, I hoped, Edna forever, I agreed to make another trip to Moonee Ponds to meet her family.

'Look!' she had said on the phone, always beginning her sentences with the same adjuration to pay attention. 'We don't live in a mansion, Barry, but it's a clean, comfortable home and my littlies are longing to meet you.'

Humoresque Street was a dull and shabby thoroughfare, and was even drabber in the light rain which had begun to fall. I was glad I had brought a raincoat. However, Number 36 somehow stood out from its neighbours. Built in the early 1920s, it was probably a War Service home; a debased version of a Californian bungalow with roughcast walls and a small front garden. It was this garden which identified it as unmistakably Edna's. There was a bird bath at its centre, and scattered around were at least six brightly painted gnomes. Some resembled the seven dwarfs of Snow White but others were in the form of Aborigines wielding boomerangs or holding spears. They were of a type of garden ornament no longer favoured today, but in that perished age, Aboriginal 'gnomes' were popular and not seldom the object of nocturnal theft: precursors, perhaps, of the Stolen Generation, as Edna later observed. The lawn was planted with tough, scratchy buffalo grass, a variety unknown on our side of the Yarra where we preferred soft English lawns on which to plant our pin oaks and silver birches. There were a few flowers, notably gladioli, a flower I particularly disliked for I always associated it with weddings and funerals – there was something disagreeably optimistic and insensitive about its thrusting spears embellished with scentless flesh-pink florets. Little did I know then that my distrust of this flower would, over the years, grow into a burning hatred, and yet I would be purchasing thousands of gladioli a week in order to sustain Edna's priapic finale routine when audiences, infantilised, would be encouraged to wave gladioli in time to some childish anthem.

Standing on the small terrazzo porch I rang the doorbell. Moments later Edna stood before me drying her somewhat large hands on a Venomous Spiders of Tasmania apron worn over a pink seersucker frock.

'Look, Barry,' she predictably began, 'come in, and please excuse Kenny and Valmai's mess. I can't shake hands because I've just been running up a batch of lovely sponge fingers.

I must look like the Wild Man from Borneo! Make yourself comfortable in the lounge room.'

We Australians never allude simply to the 'lounge' for we always, rather quaintly, like to tack on the superfluous 'room'.

Edna then disappeared, presumably to shed her apron and check on her sponge fingers. It is true that I had arrived a little early and I had caught the young actress–housewife on the hop, no doubt preparing an indigestible afternoon tea. There was a pervasive pong of coal gas in the house but I did not immediately identify it. We, and everyone we knew, belonged to the modern, all-electric community of Frigidaires, Sunbeam Mixmasters and Electrolux vacuum cleaners. Only a great-aunt of mine – on my father's side, as my mother pointedly observed – still possessed a smelly gas stove and a primitive ice chest, which certainly did not have a light that went on when you opened the door.

I seated myself on a prickly couch of uncut moquette in a fawn colour, with chubby armrests and an enervated cubist pattern of chevrons and trapezoids which, in the thrift shops and antique bazaars of today, might earn it that all-encompassing epithet 'art deco'. In a corner beside a chair of the same design stood a smoker's companion: a chrome and bakelite standard lamp with a candlewick trimmed shade, to the stem of which was affixed an adjustable round bakelite tray with a chrome ash receptacle. Underfoot stretched a burgundy Axminster carpet. I was clearly in the 'best' room and it smelled unused like most 'best' rooms. The general colour scheme was indeed burgundy and fawn, a hue soon to be displaced in popular taste by mushroom.

Above the fireplace, shielded by a 'galleon' firescreen in *repoussé* brass, and resting on the knick-knack infested mantelpiece was a peach-tinted mirror with a scalloped edge, and on the opposite wall, in a cream frame, was a reproduction of Van Gogh's *Sunflowers*. If only Edna had known that the uni-auricular Dutch artist had also once painted a vase of gladioli! But prints of this were sadly not obtainable at the Primrose Potterie Shoppe. I noticed that the picture was crooked as if hung hurriedly, and perhaps in my honour, as a sign of the householder's sophistication. At the far end of the room were double doors leading, I presumed, to the dining room. They would originally have contained leadlight panels but these had been replaced in more recent years by frosted glass, etched with the silhouettes of reindeer and gazelle.

Edna had not taken my coat so I wandered back into the small front hallway in search of a closet. There was no sign of my hostess, who was probably somewhere towards the back of the house eradicating her resemblance to the legendary Bornean tatterdemalion. I opened what seemed to be a cupboard but had to step back hurriedly to avoid a slithering avalanche of framed pictures which had been hastily stacked therein. Down on my knees I tried to hide the evidence, noticing that they were framed prints of bluebell woods, kitschy interiors with country squires smoking pipes and, in the largest frame of all, Tretchikoff's celebrated portrait of the Chinese lady with the green face. Just as I was attempting to force the door shut on this pictorial landslide, Edna bustled into the hallway.

'What on earth are you doing, Barry?' she exclaimed tartly. 'Don't look at those silly old prints, they were all wedding presents and not my taste at all. I have always been a Van Gogh person. I'm sorry but I have.'

Shamefaced, I mumbled an apology and handed her my coat. 'I was just . . . well, I was looking for somewhere to hang this.'

Another door swung open and I had a glimpse of the kitchen as a wiry, heavily rouged woman in a pink chenille dressing gown emerged with a tray bearing our afternoon tea.

'Let's go into the lounge room, shall we?' invited Edna in her posh voice. 'Mummy, you can put that down on the nest.'

There was, to be sure, a nest of tables to the right of the couch in the lounge room and the bedizened crone, who was presumably Edna's mother, thumped the heavy tray down on its surface with quite a loud crash. If I had expected an introduction to this lady I was to be disappointed.

'You can go off to your room now, Mummy, but don't forget to go to the toilet first.'

'I've been already, Lady Muck,' the elder snarled, 'and I was a *very good boy*.' Then she shuffled out, muttering.

Edna poured the tea and offered me a finger as she explained with some embarrassment, 'It's a little family joke we have, Barry. When we had a dog, Mummy used to take it for walks and when she came home she would always tell us if Topsy had been a good boy, or a *very* good boy.'

I pretended to understand. Edna seemed even more embarrassed. 'You must think I'm awful and uncalled for telling you that, especially when you're enjoying one of my fingers.'

From another part of the house I could hear a muffled chugging sound, difficult to identify. It could have been a washing machine, though I doubt Edna's household had progressed beyond the old copper, trough and wringer. It was about two years too early for the Whirlpool. Edna appeared discomforted by this interruption and, leaping up from her seat, she insisted on slapping a record on the ripple-fronted blonde-wood 'Classic' radiogram.

'Time for a little Mantovani,' she exclaimed nervously as the strains of 'Charmaine' insinuated themselves into the room. But I could still hear that insistent mechanical rhythm outside, in spite of Edna's efforts to obliterate it.

'What's that noise?' I asked.

'Look, don't worry about that, Barry.' I could see she was deciding whether or not to tell me something.

'If you must know, it's Norm's machine. He has a plumbing problem and the doctors have hooked him up to some wonderful equipment which does the work of his poor old prostate. I'm afraid it's a bit like an iron lung, only further down. And it's having teething problems,' she added anxiously.

Prostate? Iron lung? Teething problems? I tried to look sympathetic. I *was* sympathetic.

'He's only on it a few hours a day,' Edna explained. 'That's how he managed to toddle along to the show, but in a funny way he misses his machine.' As I pondered the image Edna had

45

evoked, she continued, 'There's a lot of equipment. We're trying to buy the home next door to house it and then we'll only have to run a duct through the bedroom window. There have been a lot of complaints from the neighbours about the noise of Norm's prostate governor but I've told them that there isn't a volume control on it.

'There is a knob, but I'm not touching that,' she added emotionally.

I was wondering if, under these difficult circumstances, Edna and Norman were conjugally suited, when there was a merciful interruption and Madge Allsop, whom I had briefly met at the passion play, entered the room.

'You don't know me from a bar of soap,' she exclaimed, 'but we met at the church.'

'Of course, Mrs Allsop. Who could forget you?' I answered truthfully.

Edna was clearly displeased by the irruption of her moth-like myrmidon. 'I think you've got a lot more to do in the kitchen, Madge,' she said tartly. 'Barry and I are talking business. Why don't you get Norm some afternoon tea?'

But Madge wasn't taking the hint. 'He's not allowed afternoon tea, Edna. Don't you remember? Doctor Rentoul-Outhwaite has got our poor darling on that strict diet. He can't have nice things like we do.'

'He's not *our* poor darling, Madge. He's my husband, not yours,' Edna sharply interposed. 'And close the lounge room door after you when you leave, prithee.'

As our acquaintance grew I observed Edna only adopted

archaisms like 'prithee' in moments of displeasure.

When the old Kiwi had taken the hint and left the room, Edna sighed deeply and rolled her eyes heavenward. 'Norm used to love his food but his urologist is practically *starving* him, poor petal. As a special treat I go into his room and let him sniff my fingers so he knows what I've been up to in the kitchen.' I was clearly witnessing my new friend in her most caring and compassionate mode.

The house in Humoresque Street was, except for the persistent rhythm of Mr Everage's unimaginable equipment, curiously silent, which was odd considering it was a house full of people. I knew for a fact that Edna's mother – was it Gladys? – lived under the same roof, then there was Norm, presumably sequestered in a spare room, and three young offspring occupying rooms, or a room, elsewhere in the comparatively small dwelling. There was no sound of children so perhaps they were still at school, or were corralled by Madge or farmed out to neighbours while their mother had afternoon tea with me.

Edna was clearly a bit nervous, not a frailty I had expected of her. The bone china teacup – a wedding present? – rattled slightly in its saucer as she daintily nibbled one of her own sponge fingers with passionfruit icing.

'It's my career, Barry, that I want to talk about,' she began. 'I have a feeling I've been given a wonderful gift by Dame Nature and if I throw it away it would be like, like . . .' She searched for the word '. . . blasphemy!'

Speechless, I merely assumed a serious expression and took a sip of tea in which several tea leaves floated. I now wonder what a fortune teller might have discovered reading my tea-cup. Could subsequent events and the dramatic change in my life which this woman would bring about have possibly been prefigured by a few soggy brown flecks clinging to the bottom of a Royal Doulton 'Harlequin' teacup?

'Look, I've come to a decision,' Edna resumed, 'and it's probably the biggest decision I'll ever make in my life. I've decided to put my family last. It'll be best for them in the end. I've known young mothers like me, or women who have been young mothers when they were young, who have sacrificed themselves and worked their fingers to the bone for their kiddies and got no thanks for it.'

Reeling from this bombshell, I exclaimed, 'But Edna, the theatre, indeed showbusiness, is a very insecure profession! I don't even think it can be called a profession, and there are more disappointments than triumphs. Are you sure you can take such a big step? What about your children? What about Mr Everage?'

'I've thought about all of this,' said Edna topping up our tea and injecting another cast of characters into my cup. 'I won't be deserting the little darlings, I'll be doing something they'll be proud of one day, and Madge has said that she'll look after Norm – which doesn't involve much more than throwing a switch, supervising his sponge bath and maintaining his page-turning machine. Last week he was stuck halfway through *The Kon-Tiki Expedition*.'

My role as an amused and snobbish bystander was expanding disagreeably. By default I had become a participant in Edna's

life, and had been somehow manoeuvred into taking respons-
ibility for her so-called career. Now she was involving me in a
major decision concerning the welfare of her family. What was
she, after all, but a somewhat over-talkative housewife with
delusions of grandeur and a stage presence which commanded
less respect than laughter?

I felt trapped. I needed a moment to think. 'May I use your,
er . . .'

'Amenity?' Edna completed the sentence. 'Please be my
guest, Barry. You'll find some pretty towelettes embroidered
by my mother on the vanity.'

'Vanity units', formica or laminex surfaces beside the
wash basin, were then considered ultra-modern. Sure
enough, when I entered the bathroom it was clear that
renovations had recently taken place. The original colour
was off-white and mottled cream but the lavatory seat, basin
and shower curtain were new and fashionably aqua (soon to
be displaced by avocado). On the lavatory seat stood a large
white plastic doughnut, presumably for the convenience of
the household invalid. I was surprised that Edna had not
hidden it away in anticipation of my visit. The soap was
Protex, recommended in the advertisements for diffusing
'the fragrant smell of the bushland', and there was also a
much eroded sliver of that popular abrasive, Solvol, invented
in Melbourne and known as 'the soap for hardworking
hands'.

I stood for a while pondering my situation as unwilling
adviser to a woman of limited talent and unlimited ambition.

I counted the toothbrushes, a little family of Tek in a chipped mug commemorating the coronation of King George VI, a souvenir which, in better condition, now might attract a surprising valuation on *Antique Roadshow*. The toothpaste was Kolynos, the new green variety with chlorophyll. Chlorophyll was one of the great discoveries of the 1950s, as was BO, for which affliction Protex was always close at hand. 'Did you Protex yourself this morning?' persistently enquired the radio.

As I stared at myself in the Kolynos-flecked mirror (behind which, I had little doubt, stood shelves of rarely used unguents and intimate emollients), I decided that I would have to nip this friendship in the bud. Most people whose opinion I valued thought I had quite a future in the theatre or in painting or writing – accomplishments yet to be called the Arts – and Edna was a time waster; a red herring . . . or at least a mauve herring. Like many seemingly shy people she was rapaciously self-centred.

As I passed through the hallway on my way back to the lounge room, observing the dark wainscot with its curio ledge encumbered with toby jugs, I heard the murmur of a radio from behind a closed door and the sound of someone coughing. Then I noticed that, on the wall facing the front door, hung a grainy and enlarged photograph of a baby in a gold oval frame. If it was one of Edna's children she would surely have a better snap than that, I reflected. When I re-entered the lounge Edna regarded me oddly.

'You've been looking at that picture of Lois, haven't you,

Barry?' she said huskily and, as if in answer to my thoughts in the hallway, she added, 'It's the only one we had. Norm took it a week before the tragedy.'

The tragedy? Did I have a dim recollection of a news story of many years before? A story of a baby's disappearance in the bush? A suspected abduction by a marsupial?

'You must know the terrible story,' she continued with tears in her eyes, tears I have rarely seen since. 'There were headlines all over the world,' she continued, 'and there's even been talk of a film starring Ron Randell as Norm and Googie Withers as me. They haven't cast the koala.'[1]

Edna blew her nose with unlady-like vigour and picked up a framed photograph, which she immediately proffered. 'This is my son Kenny. If he hadn't come along when he did I don't think I would ever have got over the loss of little Lo.'

I decided it would be tactless to probe, but resolved instead to ring up Keith Dunstan, my friend at the Melbourne *Sun News-Pictorial*, and find out the details of this grotesque case. Meanwhile, I looked at Kenny's photograph, a tinted sepia image of a toddler proudly holding a golliwog which, today, for obscure reasons known only to the white and politically correct, is a proscribed toy.

'He looks as though butter wouldn't melt in his mouth,

---

1 This film (working title *The Empty Cot*) was never made but 'Dame' Edna's recent fame in the United States has revived Hollywood interest in the project. Wes Craven has been mentioned and Jennifer Anniston and Rose Byrne have both been tipped for the role of Edna.

doesn't he, Barry?' exclaimed Edna. Her grief seemed to have receded with astonishing speed. 'Can't you tell he's a real little Turk?'

'I'd like to meet this little Turk,' I said, realising too late that I was already committing myself to Edna and her family, which is exactly what I had decided I would never do.

'You will, Barry, you will,' Edna crowed and then, as if she divined my worst fears, she added, 'I have a spooky feeling that you're going to be one of the family.'

5

The Sinful City

Australian lips had yet to taste yoghurt, avocado pears, garlic, balsamic vinegar, brie, hummus, pesto sauce, crème brûlée, chardonnay and arugula. We would soon be in the decade of the prawn cocktail, chicken-in-a-basket and Black Forest gâteau with a Tia Maria digestif, but not yet. Gastronomically we were at the kindergarten stage, still with the same boring rudimentary diet that had sustained us through the Great Depression. It is true that some of us, a lucky few, had dined in continental restaurants generally run in Melbourne and Sydney by Greeks pretending to be Italians. The food there was, in my mother's view and that of most other Australians, 'a bit on the savoury side'.

Sydney seemed to have more continental restaurants than

Melbourne and that was just one of the many excitements awaiting me in that sinful city. It was so liberating not to be living at home, to be working in a small theatre company and being paid for it, to have escaped the mayhem of the Melbourne Olympics and, above all, to be free of Edna Everage. Like Captain Oates I had told her that I might be gone for some time and I savoured her dismay with satisfaction. But it was not to icy oblivion that I escaped but to a sultry city in the north, filled with exotic and erotic possibilities.

It was only when I farewelled Edna on her front porch at Number 36 Humoresque Street, Moonee Ponds, that I saw the faces pressed against the window: the wan pleading countenance of Madge Allsop, the grinning and rather dotty face of her mother, and even the cheeks of that chubby cherub, Kenny, who was insolently poking his tongue out at me.

As I turned and escaped to the tram stop, I said, 'Good luck.' And then, with words which I would forever regret, I added, 'Let me know if there's anything I can ever do for you.'

My fellow players at the Phillip Street Theatre seemed so much more sophisticated than I. Well, that is not strictly true: I was immensely sophisticated in many ways except those of the world, and my new Sydney friends would be better described as 'worldly', or so they seemed. They were also more theatrical and showbizzy. They all had LPs of *My Fair Lady*, *Noel Coward at Las Vegas* and *Salad Days*, the West End hit with its irritatingly innocent songs, which was soon coming to Australia. During rehearsal I had found lodgings in Kings Cross, a *louche* district a short tram ride from the theatre. Nearby was an all-night café called The Hasty Tasty which always seemed to be full of sailors and prostitutes and it had small jukeboxes at each greasy table. Every time the door swung open the effluvium of fried onions, cigarette smoke and a snatch of 'Bee-bop-a-lula' was debouched onto the street. Not far away was the notorious Arabian coffee lounge said to be frequented by Rosaleen Norton, 'the witch of the Cross', a colonial disciple of Aleister Crowley, and an artist of execrable pictures wherein sacrilege and eroticism were feebly juxtaposed.

I rather liked a new coffee lounge called The Jedda which I discovered in a narrow thoroughfare off Macleay Street. It was the first café in Australia with an Aboriginal theme and was named after Charles Chauvel's celebrated colour film. The Jedda was small and everything was orange or terracotta, as we imagined the Australian outback to be. There were images of goannas, snakes and boomerangs on the wall which we had learnt to call 'Aboriginal motifs'. We had just discovered the decorative possibilities of our Indigenous people whom we all supposed, with copious crocodile tears, to be dying out. However, on the meaner streets of Sydney, real Aborigines still proliferated, usually in a state of inebriation and destitution. It was a sight unfamiliar to Melbourne eyes, for we were pro-tected against the more unpleasant aspects of our geographical and ethnographical isolation. We pretended we were living in the Home Counties.

The Jedda, however, was in other respects a traditional Sydney coffee lounge offering coffee, toasted raisin bread, grilled sandwiches and cockroaches. These insects seemed to be everywhere, darting up walls and across my bedroom lino like scuttling shadows, and no doubt cobbling the floors of Kings Cross kitchenettes. Public drunkenness, too, seemed more apparent in Sydney, reminding priggish visitors from the south that this was a raffish convict town, and the pavement outside every pub exhibited a spreading Rorschach blot of buff vomit.

The show I was rehearsing was an intimate revue; a new genre for Australian audiences though long popular in London. Most of the songs and sketches were lifted from British shows with only a few words changed. A handful of talented Sydney writers, notably John McKellar, contributed satirical items with local references. These always went down the best, and fashionable Sydney audiences – if that is not an oxymoron – hooted with laughter when the name of a socialite or local figure was mentioned in song or sketch. It was the first artistic expression of Australian 'gay' humour hermetically nurtured in caravanserais like the Long Bar of Ushers Hotel, where window dressers, airline stewards, antique dealers and closeted businessmen exchanged jests and rubbed more than shoulders.

This was the dawn of 'send-up' comedy, and there was a clever song in the show called 'Who's Going Up Tonight?'

delivered by June Salter and Max Oldaker, my mother's favourite matinee idol dragged out of retirement, standing in the
basket of a balloon. The song was really just a list of local
celebrities (before that epithet was coined), and as each name
was dropped the performers would roll their eyes or give each
other knowing little *moues*, to the delight of the audience. It
was a new sub-genre: Sydney Camp, which was to find its
ultimate expression in the films of Stephan Elliott and Baz
Luhrmann.

It was during rehearsals that I did an unforgivable thing
which I will regret for the rest of my life: I offered to do an
Edna Everage impersonation. None of the cast had met or even
heard of my prototype who was safely six hundred miles away,
so my rather crude drag performance was thought to be pure
invention and not the seamlessly accurate impersonation of my
new Moonee Ponds friend that I believed it to be. I wrote
a little doggerel called 'Maroan'; an extended joke, withal
snobbish, about the universal Australian mispronunciation of
the word 'maroon'. I delivered this flimsy recitation on
opening night in an Edna-like outfit and in a piping falsetto. To
my surprise, and certainly that of the management, it was a
resounding success.

I felt a certain exhilaration that my career was launched in a
city far from my home town and without the inhibiting presence
of my family and old friends. I had also shaken off Edna, whose
demands had become oppressive. However, she bombarded me
with postcards giving me her 'news': the state of her husband's
health, the funny sayings of Kenny, and the offer she had made

to the Olympic Accommodation Bureau of a spare room in her house for a visiting athlete. I felt deeply grateful to have escaped Olympic fever. But when I thought about it for a moment, I wondered to what extent I had really been liberated from the terrible thrall of Mrs Everage. Wasn't the most successful thing I was then doing on stage a homage to her? Was I not actually pretending to be Edna on stage in order to get easy laughs? And how would I have managed out there in the spotlight being *myself?* They were disturbing reflections.

In spite of the fact that I never replied to any of Edna's postcards she still kept sending them. This is a typical communication spread over two postcards:

Dear Barry,

Life in Moonee Ponds is as exciting as ever and we are doing our bit by billeting an athlete from Lapland. His name is Mr Klammi and my Lapp is a bit rusty I'm afraid, so we don't know much about him, except that he's very strong and he throws things. He doesn't seem to like my meals but being a Lapp he probably prefers continental food, or blubber.

Our new TV set is wonderful and it's a godsend to Norm when he's off his machine. He loves Jeff Corke and young Bert Newton. We like Graham Kennedy as well but sometimes he's a bit uncalled for and unnecessary and spoils himself.

I hope your play in Sydney is going well. It didn't get a write-up here. It's funny to think that I have been to London when I won the 'Lovely Mother Quest' but I've never been to Sydney. Perhaps I'll pay you a surprise visit.

My garden is looking gorgeous and I'm very pleased with my
perennial pea. Madge sends her regards. You've made a hit there.
Your friend, Edna

The threat of a surprise visit made me nervous. What if she 'popped in' unexpectedly in the middle of 'Maroan'? The programme took her name in vain by stating in indelible print that the sketch was performed by Mrs Edna Everage. I began to imagine legal complications.

Meanwhile, I was enjoying the new city, though it seemed a little bleak and treeless compared to Melbourne. I did not know then that another sometime exponent of Sydney Camp but an exponent of genius, Patrick White, was writing some remarkable novels in Castle Hill in Sydney's north-western suburbs.

My few friends were really just fellow actors in the show, though I began to meet a handful of would-be bohemians in the Assembly Hotel who called themselves 'The Push'. It was a forlorn group of suburban anarchists who disdained artistic endeavour, mainly because it was beyond them. Amongst them there was only one strikingly beautiful girl, Meg, who seemed to be a glamorous mascot for a clique of what would today be unkindly described as 'losers'.

Through an agent I obtained a few radio jobs: small roles in soaps to which I knew my mother and Ada Scott sometimes listened and also, almost certainly, Edna. They were serials like *When A Girl Marries*, *Dr Paul*, *Blue Hills*, and *Portia Faces Life*. I was not a good radio actor, and since the parts I was offered were small, there were sometimes many pages of script before I said anything. Often I missed my cues and became dependent on a nudge from an older or more experienced radio actor. They all smoked and so did I. The brand of cigarette indicated the smoker's status, or even sexual inclination. Feminine actors and women favoured Du Maurier and the prosperous preferred Benson & Hedges in its red and gold tin box. The king size cigarette had yet to be introduced by Rothmans. Everyone else smoked Capstan Turf and Craven A. The arty rolled their own, and the cravats, blazers and suede shoes smoked pipes.

To make up for the lost time in my prim and studious youth I joined the smokers and drinkers and, as there were at least seven live theatres in Sydney at this time, there was a party every night.

However riotous these after-show bacchanals, or however freely I abandoned myself to the party mood, I knew I was more than a little homesick for Melbourne and my old friends who still lived there. Flying in the face of the most prudent advice and joining a theatre company had put me out on a limb, and no one I knew much approved of what I was doing. Not even I really approved of what I was doing: small parts on the radio, a subsidiary role in an intimate revue starring – in my view – lesser talents, and too many hours in fumid clubs and taverns postponing my return to dismal lodgings.

My parents had gone away for a six-month world cruise and I was impatient to get to London, the theatrical Mecca, and a city I felt I already knew so well from books and films. I even visited the offices of the Blue Star Line in Sydney to enquire about the cheapest possible passage on a steamer across the world.

Fortunately, Edna's unwelcome missives had dried up from lack of encouragement and I had found distraction in a steamy intrigue with Meg, the passionate 'Pushette', who was inconveniently affianced to a poet and libertarian whose endorsement of free love did not extend to his mistress.

One night after the show, Ted, the stage doorman, said I had a visitor. This was rare. The other cast members, June and Shirley, Wendy and Pat, Johnny and Michael, Max and Gordon all received flocks of friends every evening, but I would leave the theatre most nights and scurry up the narrow lane to Phillip Street without a single friend or fan plucking at my sleeve. There seemed to be quite a crowd at the stage door that night and as I came up the stairs I was startled by a familiar voice.

'Look,' it said, 'you don't know me from a bar of soap, Mr Oldaker, but you took your part wonderfully tonight.'

I heard the muffled tones of Max's false modesty.

'Oh yes, you were,' shrilled the dreaded voice. 'I'm an actress myself and I'm a close friend of Barry's. That's me he does in the show.'

There she stood, for of course it was Edna, in a turquoise A-line crimplene frock, remotely inspired by something Audrey Hepburn might have looked good in. She was wearing a hat, gloves, and new upswept diamanté spectacles, which were called at the time 'cat's-eye' glasses. They made her beady eyes seem even beadier and I saw, without surprise, that she had cyclamen lipstick on her teeth. As she was a tall woman, roughly my height, she seemed to dominate the group at the stage door. Max stood there in his blue striped towelling bathrobe, his face still orange with his 'youthful' make-up, and I saw the unmistakable imprint of Edna's lips on his right cheek. So much for my fears of a surprise visit. Edna was positively crowing with pleasure and basking in reflected glory.

'How do you think the audience liked me, Max?' she asked, slipping effortlessly into familiarity. 'I thought I did rather well, but a prettier frock would have brought the house down.'

I realised that my performance, my send-up of this totally insensitive woman, and the response of the audience towards it, had been misconstrued as praise. Moreover, praise for *her*. I didn't get a look in. I was merely a cipher, a channel.

On seeing me, Edna beamed. 'I didn't tell you I was coming or you would have tensed up,' she said. Then, leaning closer to whisper in my ear so that I got a commingled blast of Kool Mints and Evening in Paris cologne, she whispered, 'I made quite a lot of notes but I don't want to give them to you in front of the others.'

Fifteen minutes later, over coffee and toasted raisin bread at Repins, Edna leant across the table and placed her hand on mine. 'I didn't mean to frighten you by popping up here and seeing the show without telling you, but Madge offered to look after the little ones and Norm's organ is quiescent.'

'It was a shock,' I replied, raising a limp finger of raisin toast to my lips. To my horror I observed that I had not removed the red nail varnish I wore in my Edna impersonation.

She saw it too. 'You silly billy, Barry!' she exclaimed. 'You wouldn't make a very good girl. I think the other people in your show were relieved to see how attractive I really am. You're lucky I'm such a good sport, but then I have to be with the Olympic Games practically happening under our roof.'

I gulped my coffee, noticing an enormous cockroach slowly ascending the wall of the banquette just behind Edna's head. Edna produced a notebook with a spiral binding from her purse – an ideal weapon, I reflected, for slapping a cockroach to death. I decided to let the huge glossy insect continue its ascent without remark.

'I just made some notes during the show which might help you, Barry. There were a few moments when I actually thought your performance was *almost* there,' she said encouragingly. At least she didn't say what a fellow actor once archly said to me in the dressing-room after he had seen the show: 'How did *you* feel you were tonight?'

With clenched fists to hide the nail varnish, and wishing that all this was not happening, I asked Edna to elucidate.

'Well,' she said, peering at her notes which had been scrawled in the dark, 'your legs are not your best point, so you should always try to act behind furniture. They make the audience laugh.'

'But this show is a comedy,' I protested. 'People are meant to laugh.'

'Look, Barry, there is one thing you need to learn. People should be laughing *with* you, not *at* you. Look at me, for instance. When we did that show together in Melbourne I got a lot of laughs because they were sharing my funny thoughts.

It certainly had nothing to do with my appearance.'

I stared across the table at the rather dishevelled wisteria coif, the fleshy nose, the feathered lipstick, the incipient double chin pressed against a strand of cheap 'pop pearls', and the dusting of Cyclax face powder caught in a crimplene fold of her frock. Then I remembered the gale of laughter from the audience when they first set eyes on her, which was long before she had had a chance to 'share her funny thoughts'. To think that I was sitting in this pestiferous café receiving theatrical advice from this self-deluding harpy!

'And another thing, Barry,' Edna continued, 'you gave me an Australian accent when you read that poem tonight and I haven't got one. Most people think I'm English, from Oxford. You wouldn't catch me talking like those politicians on the wireless.'

The ABC had just started to broadcast parliamentary debates and middle-class Australians were horrified when they realised that the coarsely spoken rabble on the radio was in fact made up of their elected representatives.

'When I was overseas,' continued Edna on the same theme, 'people didn't even know I was Australian, particularly if they were French, Italian or American. I had to make them guess, and then I'd say "I'm an Australian and proud of it!" Their faces were a picture no artist could paint.'

Edna's rather gloating references to her 'overseas' trips riled me. She'd only been in London for about ten minutes after winning the Lovely Mother Quest, and seen little more than a production of *My Fair Lady*, the Trooping the Colour and

Piccadilly Circus. She had, however, talked about it incessantly, notably on the Norman Banks programme on 3KZ, 'The Voice of The Voyager', where Australians who had been on trips droned on about their experiences, while their Melbourne listeners travelled vicariously. I never heard Edna on the show but it must exist somewhere in the National Sound Archives, and it would be instructive to hear how she strung out and inflated this fleeting visit to the Old Country.

I offered to walk her home to the Metropole, the brown Victorian hotel on Bridge Street where she was staying. The streets were crowded but I had become used to the higher level of rowdiness in Sydney's public places, probably due to the fact that the pubs were open later than in Melbourne. There seemed to be fresh Rorschach blots on the pavement to be avoided, and Edna nervously took my arm.

'I think I could quite like it here in the daytime, Barry,' she said, 'but at night there seem to be a lot of Sydney types around.'

My mother could have said that, I thought with a shudder of shame. For her, 'Sydney types' were a universal problem: they were not necessarily people from Sydney, just people who were common, or worse, on the ordinary side.

When we arrived at the hotel, Edna announced that she was leaving the next day. 'It's a flying visit, Barry. I'm going to Manly tomorrow for lunch with Norm's sister and then back to Melbourne on the *Spirit of Progress*. I saw the Bridge this afternoon and I don't know what all of the fuss is about.'

I shook her hand, standing well back from what looked like an ominous cyclamen pucker.

'I'm glad I saw your show, Barry,' she said, 'and even though it was only you trying your best, you poor chook, it was nice to see that they love me in Sydney. Imagine if it had been me up there on stage.'

'My contract here is over soon,' I told her. 'It won't be long before I'm back in Melbourne, and then I'm hoping to get overseas.'

Edna looked crestfallen. 'What would you do there?' she asked. 'Not act, I hope.'

'Well, that's what I plan to do when I find an agent.'

'That's what I need, Barry!' she exclaimed excitedly. 'An agent. Norm won't be here forever, bless his heart, and the kiddies are independent little things. If I had an agent I could be up there in lights.' Her eyes were shining. I realised this woman actually believed that she had a theatrical future and, moreover, a spectacular one. It was laughable and a little sad.

'Couldn't you be my agent, Barry?' Edna asked. 'Watching you on stage I get the feeling that you might be more comfortable doing something helpful behind the scenes. If you looked after me I could always give you a piece of the action.'

I had never heard this phrase before. In fact, it was a phrase newly minted and Edna had probably heard it in the movies. If I was forced to endure another minute of listening to this woman's vainglorious ambitions I might have contributed my own Rorschach blot to the landscape.

'Hope to see you in Melbourne when I'm back,' was all I could manage.

'Think about what I've just said, Barry,' Edna said in reply, ascending the steps of the hotel. 'You wouldn't have to dress up or learn lines or look as awkward as you did on stage tonight.'

Then she gave a sweet smile, fluttered her hankie, and was gone.

6

Humoresque Street

Tincture of Cubeb. 'What on earth was it?' I wondered, as I read the list of ingredients on my tin of Hudson's Eumenthol Jujubes. There was Tincture of Capsicum as well, and menthol and eucalyptus of course, and a mysterious constituent called squill. Or was squill in my cough mixture, Wycough (Why Cough, Take Wycough)?

I became addicted to the sugar-coated jujubes quite early in my life. My father, who suffered from a ticklish throat, always carried a Hudson's tin with him. They came as a shock to the palate at first, but once the sprinkled sugar had dissolved and you got down to the cubeb and all the other tinctures, the intense burning sensation had to be good for you, and subsequently I never went on stage without sucking on one. Later in life I had a similar experience adjusting myself to the medicinal jolt of Fernet Branca.

Sometime in the early 1960s they stopped making Hudson's Eumenthol Jujubes in Australia but I discovered that they were somehow available in Singapore, probably made under licence. Slowly the more exotic ingredients were omitted and the Jujubes lost their kick, as did Coca-Cola when its manufacturer started skimping on the cocaine.

I was back in Melbourne and rehearsing for another show, produced by an actor friend. It was a revue and one I had helped to write, but people kept asking me the same annoying question: 'Will Edna be in it?'

It seemed that she was getting to be quite notorious since my absence in Sydney. She had been a guest on *In Melbourne Tonight* with Graham Kennedy and had made rather a hit, I learnt. I suppose her naïve views, stridently expressed, struck the television audience as a novelty. Television itself was quite a novelty, though the Olympic Games had increased its popularity and there were already a few police dramas locally produced and, novelty of novelties, performed by Australian actors wearing suits and trilbies, getting in and out of cars.

It couldn't do any harm, I thought, to invite Edna to do a spot after intermission. It amazed me to think she could possibly be what in theatrical parlance is described as a 'draw', but I needed the show to be a success for I had already booked my ticket for that distant arcadia, 'overseas', and I needed every shilling I could scrape together. If a cameo performance by this deluded and publicity-crazed housewife could attract the morbidly curious I would be foolish to object.

Every life is full of paths not taken and ways not adopted. Being by nature avoidant, I've always sought distractions and detours, which have sometimes led me on exciting adventures that might never have occurred had I pursued a direct and purposeful course. Even at this time in my youth, with a career barely begun, I was aware that Edna, this silly suburban chatterbox, was a distraction; a detour which could only lead to a cul-de-sac. I had better things to do and yet I found myself once more approaching the house in Moonee Ponds.

As I neared Number 36 Humoresque Street, did I imagine it, or were there more Aborigines on the front lawn? And had the curtains in the front room, visible from the street, been replaced by Austrian blinds, then called 'festoon'? A television aerial sprouted from the roof and a new-looking Holden stood in the driveway. The doorbell, when I depressed it, chimed melodiously within. On my first visit I remembered that I had had to tweak the small brass butterfly in the middle of the front door to produce a metallic *brriing*.

This time the door was opened by a surly and rather over-weight child. She wore plaits and a blue gingham dress and was eating a very sticky coffee scroll, some of which adhered to her left cheek. She looked at me with dull, yet hostile eyes, one of which was in amiable disagreement with its neighbour, and called out 'Muuum, it's him for you', before turning her back on me and slouching back to the kitchen.

Edna bustled into the hallway. 'Look, Barry,' she exclaimed, 'it's lovely to see you. Didn't Valmai make you comfortable in the lounge room? That girl didn't learn her manners from my side of the family.'

I closed the front door behind me and was dismayed to feel the stickiness of coffee scroll bonding my fingers.

As we went into the front room I observed a change in Edna. (I noticed that she was constantly, to use a modern term, upgrading herself.) Her hair seemed to be a more intense shade of violet than usual, surely an 'assisted' hue, and not the trichological anomaly she often boasted about and which she believed set her apart from lesser, more monochromatic women. She was wearing her usual cat's-eye glasses but were these now slightly more elaborate and encrusted with a few more artificial gems than before?

As we sat down she apologised for her attire. 'I'm sorry I'm just wearing this kimono,' she said, gesturing to the peacock green embroidered garment enshrouding her tall figure. 'I know it's Japanese but the war is ancient history and most of us have buried the hatchet, haven't we?'

I admired the garment.

'I never wear it when I see my Uncle Vic,' she admitted. 'They called him the Butcher of Borneo and he's got a thing about our little slant-eyed yellow friends. He might get cranky if he saw me in this.'

I noticed a huge 21-inch Astor television set in the corner of the room which had previously accommodated the smoker's companion and a copy of the *Listener In* on the armrest of a capacious chair in brown floral uncut moquette.

Edna was still obviously thinking about the war, for she said, 'My Norm did his bit, too, Barry, but it was mostly desk work. He was already having a few waterworks problems and didn't pass the medical.' She stopped and I sensed a change in her mood. Then she turned and faced me directly, her eyes glistening. Were they tears?

'I shouldn't tell you this, Barry, but I married an *invalid* and a man much older than he led us to believe.' The emotional intensity of this sudden confession discomforted me. 'I'm sorry if this embarrasses you, but now that you are my manager you need to know who I am.'

Thank God this conversation was not taking place in the 1990s or Edna would have said, 'I want you to know where I'm coming from'; or worse, 'I want us to be on the same page'. If only all conversations could take place in the past.

'I am your manager?' I exclaimed in astonishment. 'Since when?'

'Look, Barry, I can read you like a book,' replied the woman who had probably read very few books. 'I know that, since you got back from Sydney, you've been too shy to approach me but I think we can help each other.'

If she had said this in the 1980s she would have said, 'I think we could help each other in a *very real sense*.' Whatever she said, it was outrageous. I was being press-ganged into an association with someone I was beginning to actively dislike.

Reading my thoughts, as usual, Edna said, 'I know you're planning to go to the Old Country to try for a career there but you'll be back soon enough with your tail between your legs and you'll need me then, Barry, you'll need me then.'

We were interrupted by an eldritch cry from somewhere in the house. It was more like the cry of some raucous bird. Edna jumped to her feet. 'That's my mother, Barry,' she said. 'She probably wants to be a good boy or a *very* good boy and I'll have to unlock her door.'

'You lock her in?' I asked.

'We have to, Barry. She wanders a lot. Once she got out the front door and we lost her for hours. I had to put a picture of her on the tree outside, hoping someone had seen her. I've stopped cleaning her room because she's in there most of the time, especially when Mr Klammi from Lapland was staying here. She had taken rather a liking to him, I'm afraid, and the doctors gave us something to put in her tea to calm her down.'

Edna ran off to attend to her mother's needs, if they were not already past attending to, and I sat slumped in one of those huge chubby armchairs wondering whether or not I shouldn't make a bolt for it. Then the slatternly child Valmai entered the room with her little brother Kenneth, and they stood staring at me. Luckily I did not have to shake her viscid paw.

'Do you like our mummy?' asked the small boy, a lettuce-green bubble of mucus in his left nostril.

What is the part of 'no' that I don't understand? There have been many, many times in my life when I have said 'yes' when I should have said 'no', but this occasion was a moral turning point, and when I shirked it I somehow betrayed myself forever. With these two children staring balefully at me like demonically possessed kiddies in a horror movie, my lips formed the word 'no' and I heard myself say, 'Nyes. Yes, she's a very nice lady.'

To my astonishment Valmai said, 'No, she's not. We hate her, don't we, Kenny?'

'Don't you talk like that or I'll wash your mouths out with soap and water.' It was Mrs Allsop who spoke, having come silently in from the dining room through the sand-blasted doors. 'Take no notice of the wee things, Mr Humphrey. They're overtired and overexcited. It's not easy for them in this house. It's not easy for any of us.'

The frowsty New Zealander gave me a meaningful look and I was surprised to find myself taking Edna's side. 'It's not for me to say, Mrs Allsop,' I replied diplomatically, 'but there seem to be a lot of people living here, and Edna has to juggle an invalid husband and a career.'

'She calls it a career, does she?' snapped the Kiwi with unexpected force. 'There's poor Norman hooked up to all of that technology while she's out gallivanting. If you could only have seen him when they were first married. I was the brides-maid, you know.'

I looked nervously towards the door, apprehensive that Edna might enter suddenly and overhear this disloyal tirade.

'He was choice,' the bridesmaid continued, her dull eyes briefly lustrous. 'Norman was older than Edna, of course, quite a bit older than he ever let on, but I noticed the grey hairs in his nostrils. They made him look so distinguished.'

Kenny and Valmai started fighting. 'The wee things are never cranky like this,' Madge apologised. 'There'll be tears before bedtime.'

I doubted it. To me they were just two badly behaved and rather unappealing brats who today would be diagnosed as hyperactive and started on Ritalin.

As she bundled the children out the door, Mrs Allsop whispered over her shoulder, 'I shouldn't have told tales out of school, Mr Humphrey. Don't let on to madam or she'll have my guts for garters.'

Was there another Edna, I began to wonder? Or did this foolish old woman nurse a real grievance against her friend? Before I could pursue this intriguing train of thought, Edna re-entered the room with two cups of tea on a tray and a plate of Melting Moments.

'Norm's settled down a bit, thank goodness, and I've just given him a quick sponge and put *The Cruel Sea* on his page turner,' she explained.

'Mrs Allsop was in here and collected Kenny and Valmai,' I said, accepting a teacup. 'She seems a very nice, helpful woman,' I continued, fishing.

'Helpful!' exclaimed Edna, rising nicely to the bait. 'Helpful, my foot! She's a drone, a parasite. If I didn't look after her she'd be on the streets. When her parents died in New Zealand she was sent to Melbourne to stay with her aunty and she went to Moonee Ponds Grammar. That's where I met her. Being an orphan she was bullied a lot, but I took her under my wing and I hardly ever teased her about her appearance.'

'Didn't she marry? What about Mr Allsop?' I asked sympathetically.

'Her husband died on their honeymoon in New Zealand, you know – the thermal area, actually. He fell into a pool of boiling mud.'

I recoiled, not so much from the horror of Mr Allsop's bizarre accident as from Edna's detached and heartless account of it.

'He was *tandooried*,[2] Barry. Since then I've looked after her like a sister and all she has to do are a few little chores for her keep.'

I reached for a second Melting Moment. Dare I dunk it in my tea?

'You can imagine how many thanks I get for putting up with her, can't you? Not a peep, not a solitary peep of gratitude. I bet she was talking about me while I was in there with Norm.'

'Certainly not,' I lied, as half a Melting Moment dropped to the bottom of my teacup. 'She was very quiet and obviously loves the children.'

'She was making an effort for you, Barry,' said Edna. 'That quiet mousy act is just put on. You should hear her talking to herself in the middle of the night. Her language would make a sailor blush.'

I had a vision of Edna in her night attire crouched outside

2 Recent research reveals that ancient Australasians shared genetic traits with Indian tribes.

Madge's door, eavesdropping on the poor widow's nocturnal Molly Bloom-like monologues.

'It's not the children she loves, Barry, it's my husband. She's had her eye on him for years and I've caught her sneaking uncalled-for publications onto his page turner. *Man Junior* and *Love Me Sailor*[3] were just two of them, and when I found them they went straight into the bin.'

'What harm could the books have done?' I protested, recalling a silly obscenity trial.

'They would have got him excited,' said Edna, 'and Doctor Rentoul-Outhwaite said excitement is the worst possible thing for his rogue organ.'

'The old woman seems very devoted to your family,' I said, in defence of the absent bridesmaid. 'I doubt she would attempt anything inappropriate with Mr Everage.'

'Don't be so sure of that sly minx,' retorted Edna vehemently, with a hard edge to her voice I had not heard before. 'We are her meal ticket, and she knows it. She's as poor as a church mouse. One false move and Madge will have to fend for herself.'

Suddenly Edna laughed with real merriment. 'It's funny, Barry, to hear you calling her an old woman when she's not even forty-five. She let herself go when her husband Doug was gathered, and now she gets her clothes from the thrift shop.'

---

3 Novel by Robert Close. Originally published in Melbourne in 1945 by the small firm of Georgian House – and banned shortly afterwards.

'Life must be hard for her. Hard, and a bit lonely, too,' I offered.

'Lonely, my foot!' exclaimed Edna indignantly. 'She's on easy street here and very, very spoilt. The trouble is, if I give her any of my hand-me-downs to wear she looks even more of a frump. Mutton dressed up as lamb, and New Zealand lamb at that.'

I decided to drop the subject of Mrs Allsop, widow, waif, and unlikely sexual predator. Edna and Madge clearly had some kind of sadomasochistic arrangement. I had heard far more from these women than I wished to hear and I had spent far too long in this ugly house, bursting at the seams with unattractive and what would now be called 'dysfunctional' people. My parents' large serene house seemed another world away. What was I doing here?

I looked at my watch. 'I'll have to be going, Edna,' I said, rising from an uncomfortable posture on the over-soft moquette. 'I'm sailing to Italy and then on to England next week on the *Toscana* and it may be a long time before I'm back. I just want to make sure you can be in my farewell show on Friday night at the Assembly Hall.'

Edna looked shocked. 'It's as soon as that, is it? What about my career? Wouldn't it be more sensible for you to stay in Australia and devote yourself to that? It's bound to be a lot more lucrative than struggling away on your ownsome.'

It occurred to me that Edna didn't mean to be insulting, it was just her narcissistic way of looking at the world, as though the world could not be looked at from any other point of view.

Here I was talking 'theatre' with a creature who had not spent more than sixteen nights on a stage of any description.

As I stepped out onto the porch to freedom I was aware of a renewed activity in the house behind me. Edna's mother's radio resumed its chatter. A bell rang (Norm's?). The sound of children brawling was followed by an ugly crash and Mrs Allsop's sibilant remonstrations.

On the tram I experienced a sense of delayed shock, and the blurred face of little Lois swam up before my eyes. Lucky Lois, I thought, to have been spared a childhood in that family. The koalas would have been kinder.

7

Exodus

S tanding at the rail of the *Toscana* as it sailed out of Melbourne, and watching the pink, blue and yellow tangle of
streamers tauten and snap, I felt a confusion of emotions as my
family, indeed my entire past, diminished and disappeared just
as my mother's raised handkerchief became a white dot, and
then the ghost of a dot.

I felt fear of course; fear of the unknown and of what might
or might not await me in London where I, along with thousands
of others, was meant to be seeking theatrical employment.
There is a line in a play by Ionesco which stuck in my mind. A
character says rather plaintively to his wife, 'My career is
hurting me.' Mine certainly was. It was not like painting jolly
post-impressionist landscapes, or dadaist collages, which

I could do in private. My job could really only happen in public in front of an audience. It was easy in Melbourne where I could be a talented 'one-off' and where too-clever-by-half perpetual undergraduates like me were, in my mother's phrase, tuppence a dozen. When I came to think of it, that was Edna's phrase as well. She had actually said it, rather brutally, on the wharf just before embarkation.

I was amazed and unnerved by the apparition of Edna at my farewell gathering on the pier at Port Melbourne. She was conspicuous in her scarlet overcoat with a shawl collar and a hat which was just a dome of white elasticised daisies; the ensemble undoubtedly purchased from a Moonee Ponds thrift shop. With her was a gangly adolescent with acne and a blue serge suit.

'This is my son, Brucie,' she said loudly. 'He's growing very fast. We'll have to put a brick on his head.'

In this epoch, any Australian over 5'5" needed to have a brick put on his head, never firmly enough in some cases.

'Pleased to meetcha,' said Brucie. I noticed, by the flocculent white epaulettes which embellished the shoulders of his suit, that he was an apprentice dandruff farmer. My mother, who was talking to Pat and Rosemary Ryan and a couple of my other friends, shot me a quizzical look.

'Read this on the boat,' Edna had whispered as she handed me an envelope. 'I am sure that we'll see you back here very soon, Barry. You're a clever little person but you'll find that when you get to the Old Country clever little people are tuppence a dozen. I have travelled, so I know.'

This was yet another allusion to Edna's fleeting visit to England.

Edna had buttonholed my friend, the young Tasmanian television director David Baker, and was talking to him effusively as my mother appeared at my side.

'What the dickens is that woman doing here?' she murmured out of the corner of her mouth. 'She's certainly been stealing your limelight lately.' I could not help but agree, though I was riled by my mother's discouraging habit of being the first person to inform me of a negative mention in the press.

On the morning after my farewell show my mother was on the phone earlier than customary. '*The Argus quite* liked it but *The Sun* only talked about *her*. You better look to your laurels, Barry.'

It is true that the critic barely mentioned my contribution or that of my fellow actor and producer, Peter. The headline had read 'Moonee Mum Steals Show' and the *Herald* even printed an old and unflattering photograph of Edna applying her 'lippy' beneath the headline 'A Star is Born?'.

Considering that, having promised to contribute a cameo to the show, she had rambled on for twenty minutes about her 'lovely home' and 'gorgeous family' to a snobbish south-of-the-Yarra audience who had lapped it up, she was lucky to have elicited the laughs she did.

Was I jealous? I stared at the horizon where the city of Melbourne was already a grubby blur against the sky. I suppose I had invited this unlikely competitor into my life and had only myself to blame, but now I was off on a new adventure and I would never see her again, ever.

The National Bank of Australia had a branch in Mayfair with a golden kangaroo on its shingle in Albemarle Street. Downstairs were comfortable appointments for the convenience of tourists who had come to the bank to cash traveller's cheques and to collect their mail. This pastel-hued subterranean refuge, rather like a small airport lounge, was presided over by Mrs Geary, a helpful woman with a grey bun, rimless glasses and dimples. I never knew her first name, though she looked like a Joan. Awaiting me at her desk were a couple of postcards and several flimsy blue aerogrammes from my far-off family. These communications from home possessed a strong and unintentional poignancy and, from my mother, many a paragraph beginning with 'I thought you'd like to know . . .'

'. . . I thought you'd like to know that Bob and Barbara are thinking about an old house in Kingsley Street. The estate agent calls it Edwardian and your father calls it a mistake. He thinks they should build in Balwyn.'

'. . . I thought you'd like to know that Miss Throat at Number 38 has gone to live in Adelaide with her sister.'

'. . . I thought you'd like to know that thrip have got into my *weigela* and Mr Dunt is trying a new spray.'

'. . . I thought you'd like to know that the Nettleton kiddies

The frump from Moonee
Ponds

Mrs Everage – an early snap

Edna in the kitchen, in the 1950s

A spokesperson for the nation

Madge – the patient
bridesmaid

The look that later influenced
Margaret Thatcher

With the late Mary
Whitehouse and a late koala

At Royal Ascot

The birth of a friendship

Walking the wombat at Windsor

The author in the year of Edna's discovery

Dwarfing the manager

Anxious manager

have come back from their holiday in Rosebud as brown as berries.'

'. . . I thought you'd like to know that Ada Scott has bought one of the new Kelvinator refrigerators which looks a bit silly in her funny little kitchen. She said it would take her a week to read the literature.'

'. . . I thought you'd like to know that your friend Mrs Everage has got her own television show and *The Argus* says it's excellent and thoroughly enjoyable.'

Why was everything in Australia 'thoroughly' enjoyable? If something was enjoyable wasn't that enough? Must it be *thoroughly* so? I wasn't so much irritated by that mildly irritating locution as by the mention of Edna. Moreover, there was a hint of grudging approval in my mother's tone, no doubt intended as a dig at me.

For weeks I had forgotten about Edna Everage and now, improbably, she had her own television show. If a woman like that with such limited talents could be given more than five minutes on an Australian TV programme I had left the country in the nick of time. I learnt that Edna's show was a weekly lunchtime slot called *A Touch of Refinement* in which Edna interviewed other housewives and occasionally female 'identities'; the fifties equivalent of 'C-List' celebrities. It was a live programme like most other Australian shows of the time, filmed with one camera and a simple set which was meant to be a corner of Edna's home. Her guests would demonstrate aspects of Australian refinement: there would be chats about etiquette, flower arrangement, cooking, handicrafts and invalid care.

Here, I gathered, Edna usually spoke from her own experience as the wife of a seriously incapacitated husband.

Women would come on the show to demonstrate some of the new appliances: spaghetti-making machines, fondue sets and electric frypans. Apparently Gretta Myers, a former Melbourne mannequin and proprietrix of a charm school in the city, appeared regularly talking about 'poise', an elusive quality to which most Australian women vainly aspired. There was a small studio audience and Edna ran competitions with prizes like aprons, mulga wood serviette rings and lunch for two at the Hey Diddle Griddle. It did not surprise me to later learn that my friend David Baker, the man I had seen Edna schmoozing on the pier, was the producer of *A Touch of Refinement*. My other friends in Melbourne, who gleefully reported all of this, never failed to tell me how popular the show was, not always in the way Edna intended, though no one spoke of ratings in those far-off days.

Following my long and uneventful voyage I spent two months discovering Italy with the money I had saved to tide me over in London. The *Toscana* docked at Venice which I rapturously explored with Ruskin and Baron Corvo as my guides. I went everywhere from Vincenza to Lecce, from Sorrento to Rome, Florence and Verona. I traipsed through museums, palaces and churches, and stared at Tintorettos, Tiepolos and endless Bassanos, and I heard those inescapable songs of the period, 'Volare' and 'Ciao Ciao Bambino', blaring in one hundred *cafeterias* across Italy. They all smelled of new cement and espresso coffee. In one of them, sipping a Cynar and soda and smoking a prickly Exportatione cigarette, I at last opened the envelope that Edna had pressed upon me at Port Melbourne.

Dear Barry,

I hope you are well after your trip. When I went overseas the Quest put me on a plane so I didn't have to get out in any of the unhygienic countries that you probably like. When in London don't miss Trafalgar Circus, the Trooping of the Guard and the Changing of the Colour. At Australia House in Strand Street they get all the Melbourne papers and you can sit there for hours.

I have enclosed a contract which I had drawn up by Geoff Nippard, the solicitor at Nippard, Nippard and Pruitt in Puckle Street. All you have to do is sign it. It just confirms that you are my manager worldwide and if you get me engagements I will see that you receive a little something. Well, that's roughly it, but Mr Nippard has put it in proper legal language. You might remember him incidentally, he was King Herod in the play at the church that I starred in and he is a very nice type of person. Everyone thoroughly enjoyed his performance.

Kenny won a prize in kinder for his finger painting of me. He's a special little boy and I think he'll go far. Incidentally, my TV show is the talk of the town. People drop everything to watch it. I thought you'd like to know.

Kind regards, Edna

She may well have thought I'd like to know about her horrible little son's artistic achievements and the success of her kitschy television show, but she was wrong. It was infuriating, however, that she employed the same phrase my mother frequently used; she, a woman so different in every respect from my parent.

Enclosed in the envelope was a rather long document drawn up by a suburban law firm with obviously no experience in the entertainment field, or 'industry' as it now absurdly calls itself. 'It's not worth the paper it's typed on,' I reflected. Why not sign it and see what happens? There would be no skin off my nose. I would never have to find her employment, and certainly could not do so long distance from London. But as her appointed agent I might derive a few welcome shillings from her budding television career. Prompted by self-interest I scribbled my autograph at the foot of this laughable document.

Mrs Geary at the bank kindly posted Edna's contract back to Melbourne for me. We had become quite pally since I was always cashing cheques and collecting my mail. I could also sit down there in comfort and read the Australian papers and magazines like *Walkabout*, the *Australasian Post* and *The Bulletin* (now defunct).

'There's a friend of yours on the cover of *The Bully*, Barry,' said Mrs Geary one morning as I descended to what I now thought of, rather affectionately, as the Club. 'Joan' came from East Malvern in Melbourne and had that easygoing over-familiarity which turned all Australian women into aunties. She held up the periodical for my inspection and, sure enough, its cover exhibited the beaming countenance of my protégé, her glasses glinting malignantly from the page. A rubric on the cover read 'Barry Humphries' Discovery Talks to Ron Saw'.

'Do you really know her that well, Barry?' enquired Mrs Geary excitedly. 'My sister saw her show on Channel Seven and said it was thoroughly enjoyable.'

I remembered Ron Saw from my Sydney days: a drunken bully and hack who had a regular column which was meant to be humorous. There is a type of comedy, often popular, seldom remotely funny, which is still practised to this day. It is as if there were a special sort of music composed for the enjoyment of the tone-deaf. Ron Saw's humour was of this hermetic order. His interview with Edna was not unfriendly, for he would have liked her because she was no professional threat to him and he could patronise her with impunity. And so he did in his *Bulletin* article, to which I could only bring myself to steal a glance.

I realised that these frequent visits to Mrs Geary's little Australian grotto, with its magazines and travel posters of the Barrier Reef, the Harbour Bridge and the Healesville Sanctuary, was my means of escaping from the pressures and exigencies of London where I was meant to be carving out a career. How daunting was that terrible image of me, the sculptor, chipping away at a huge effigy of myself in triumphant and histrionic pose. The reality was far less artistic. It meant interviews with indifferent agents in Regent Street, and auditions in West End theatres when, having only delivered a few lines of a speech or a few bars of a song, a tired English voice would come from the darkened auditorium: 'Thank you, Mr Humphries. Next please?'

A huge volume lay on a table in the waiting room of Fraser and Dunlop, an agency to which I had an introduction. I had obtained an interview with one of their lesser agents, Myrette Morvan, who had once understudied Cicely Courtneidge and in whom I soon recognised an uncanny resemblance to the famous comedienne. I examined the glossy pages and realised that it was clearly one of several volumes. This one was *Leading Men and Character Actors*. There were hundreds of artfully lit photographs of men wearing ties and, not seldom, languorously smoking. The important ones had whole pages to themselves and some did not need illustration; there was just a name, 'Ralph Richardson' or 'Felix Aylmer', printed across the page with their agent's details discreetly appended. Towards the end of the book were the pleading portraits of the less famous, some of whom could only afford a quarter page. Their credits were humble, like Roger Curnock's recent work: Third Pirate, *Sinbad The Sailor* (Eastbourne), Tiger, *Sailor Beware* (Leeds), Murder Victim, *Maigret* (Rediffusion TV).

Amongst the most discouraging entries were those in which an actor tried to display his versatility in several separate photographs: sucking a pipe and wearing a sailor's cap in one; with a burnt cork moustache, a cravat and a monocle – presumably a toff – in another; with a shawl over his head clutching a baby ('Miner's Wife at Pithead'), all of which remind me of an infinitely sad photograph I saw once in *Spotlight* of some poor northern comic with his hair combed in a distinctive forelock, his upper lip etched with a small black moustache, and wearing a clumsily wrought swastika armband. I felt that this macabre publication had been placed in the anteroom of the theatrical agency as a warning to provincial aspirants like me. It was a mummer's *memento mori*: it said 'get out while you can'. I have never found many actors famed for their transformative powers terribly convincing. Even a great actor like Alec Guinness always looks the same to me, however heavy and varied his disguise.

The interview with Myrette Morvan seemed to go well. I had been brought up listening to British comedians on the radio, recordings invariably made as their stage careers waned. Even as a small boy I had become familiar with a number of famous British music hall acts: George Formby, Sid Fields, Horace Kenney, Stanley Holloway and Cyril Fletcher.

One of my favourite comic turns, broadcast in Australia with great regularity, was 'Laughing Gas'. The setting was a lawyer's chambers in which a rich man's will was being read to a gathering of his survivors. A child tampers with a cylinder of laughing gas – inexplicably residing in the legal office – and the escaping gas slowly convulses those assembled, who laugh uproariously as their expectations of riches are disappointed. By modern sophisticated standards it sounds an unpromising scenario and even, thus baldly related, less than hilarious. To my childish ears, however, it was the funniest thing I had ever heard, and the funniest actor on the record was Cicely Courtneidge who played the disinherited wife. Her laugh was the best and most infectious of all; it was a chuckle which became a chortle, turning into a guffaw and then, for want of a better English word, a *fou rire*.

Looking across the desk at Myrette, I saw her countenance dissolve and transform itself into that of my favourite comic actress. I had presented her with a copy of my scrapbook, painfully assembled with glue and scissors from a bag of cuttings I had taken on my voyage. It gave my brief and less than lustrous Australian career some kind of epic grandeur. To my irritation, Myrette seemed particularly interested in the press cuttings about Edna Everage and I explained who the woman was and how happy I was to be 13,000 miles away from her. She laughed, and it was a chuckle which became a chortle, turning into a guffaw. It was a very familiar laugh, and I felt that the ice was broken when she asked to borrow the scrapbook, promising to return it at our next meeting. Our next meeting! I was to be *recalled*, perhaps even offered work.

I lived in Notting Hill Gate long before it had been Hugh Grantified. Very recently there had been race riots in the vicinity, and a celebrated serial killer called Christie had immured his prostitute victims in a decaying house only a few streets from my insalubrious basement. Smog hung like a sulphurous miasma over the city and its sallow hue and whiff of brimstone were a part of London, sadly banished by the Clean Air Act. Despite the glimmer of hope from Myrette, the reality was that I had few possessions, few prospects and little money left. If things continued on as they had I might even have to crawl back to Melbourne 'with my tail between my legs', as Edna had unkindly prophesied.

Returning home one autumn evening when the smog was particularly dense and so acrid that it stung the nostrils, I reflected on a futile day. I had auditioned for yet another show, and this time the dry English voice from the dark auditorium had interrupted me before I had barely opened my mouth: 'Thank you, thank you, Mr mumble, we'll let you know.'

What else had I done? I had browsed in some of the book-shops in Charing Cross Road and Cecil Court and seen volumes I could never hope to possess. I had bought myself a half-pint of bitter at the Salisbury, the actor's pub in St Martin's Lane with its Edwardian appointments and engraved glass. Across the counter, in the side bar, I had glimpsed Kingsley Amis, an author I greatly admired. He was surrounded by laughing friends and now I can only guess who they might have been: Philip Larkin, John Wain, John Osborne, Stephen Potter? It occurs to me now that he was probably doing one of his famous impersonations. This was before he began, in real life, to impersonate a curmudgeon, a role which unfortunately stuck. As my mother would have observed, 'the wind changed'.

When I got home to my damp dungeon next to the tube station in one of the Pembridges, with my gallon of blue paraffin to feed the thirsty heater, there was a message that Miss Morvan had called. Until I could telephone her back the next morning, I struggled to suppress my optimism. I had been waiting long enough for a job – nearly three months – and I deserved one.

Across the desk in her little office in Regent Street Miss Morvan looked very pleased with herself. It was, mercifully, an era before agents and producers claimed to be 'excited' about things. Excitement came later, and in abundance. Today when an agent tells you that NBC or Fox are 'very excited' about you or your project, you know it's a dead duck and it will never happen.

'Rediffusion Television do this lunchtime show hosted by Godfrey Winn and they are very interested in having you on the show,' she said. 'Apparently there is a man called Porter who was high up with the ABC in Australia and saw you doing that Edna thing that you do.'

As I listened to this speech, hope and dismay struggled for supremacy in my breast. 'Oh,' I said hastily. 'He probably means he has seen Edna herself somewhere. There are a lot of other characters I could do on this TV show. When is it?'

'It's tomorrow, Barry, and of course it's live,' declared my agent. 'But it's Edna they want. I hope you have the costume with you.'

As it happened, I *had* packed Mrs Everage's dowdy apparel in my suitcase, but for no reason that I could recall. 'Please, Miss Morvan,' I protested. 'I think I'd rather do anything else but impersonate that woman. This is the land of Charley's Aunt[4] and my Edna act will look like a very poor relation.'

'You're wrong, Barry,' insisted Myrette. 'Edna is the best part in your scrapbook – what marvellous reviews in the Melbourne papers!'

---

4 First performed in February, 1892, *Charley's Aunt* was an enormously popular farce in which the leading male character impersonated his aunt from Brazil.

I wished I could have explained that a marvellous review in a Melbourne paper by a critic who is also the sports writer, was not necessarily a sign of international excellence. I really needed the £5 Rediffusion was offering for my television debut but I made one last effort to shake off the succubus of Moonee Ponds.

'Edna is a very Melbourne character,' I tried to explain. 'They've only just cottoned on to her in Sydney and besides . . .' I continued, fighting for my life and what would now be called my 'artistic integrity'. '. . . My impersonation is based on a real woman who is a great deal funnier than me.'

Myrette Morvan was not, as they say, 'buying' this. 'My recommendation is that you should give them what they want, or what they think they want. It's a very good showcase for you.'

Flying in the face of my new agent's sage advice, I decided that I would perform one of my Sandy Stone monologues on the looming show. Sandy was a character I had created in the mid-fifties, a boring old man of the suburbs who sat in an armchair in his pyjamas and dressing gown, clutching a hot-water bottle and rambling on about the trivial details of his life.

I have elsewhere given an account of this debacle. I was given a wind-up signal very soon after I had launched into Sandy's intentionally boring monologue as it was clear to the few people in the studio, including the very tight-lipped Godfrey Winn, that my performance was simply boring and devoid of the redeeming features of satire, pathos, and especially humour. It was a catastrophic, shameful television debut, particularly as it followed rather a big build-up when I was announced as a bright young star of Australian comedy.

'Some mistake surely!' the producer must have exclaimed as I shuffled off the set.

How could I face Myrette who had undoubtedly been watching? Inserting my pennies in a nearby phone box I called Fraser and Dunlop. She was pretty angry. 'They cut you off when you had barely opened your mouth,' she said, 'and I don't blame them. Didn't I tell you what they wanted?'

Still covered with shame, I stammered that I couldn't really remember.

'They wanted Edna, Barry. It's Edna they all want.'

As I took the tube home I imagined I could hear distant peals of derisory laughter from 13,000 miles away and Edna's fatalistic words, 'You'll be back soon enough with your tail between your legs.'

8

Home Leave

36 Humoresque Street

Moonee Ponds

Dear Barry,

Since I never hear from you I thought I would scribble you a note to see how you are and let you know my doings. There were quite a few write-ups in the papers about you getting that part in the new musical show Oliver Twist. I'm sorry it's such a small role and it must have disappointed you not to get one of the leads. Still, Rome wasn't built in a day as they say in the classics.

I hope you and your little wife are not living off the smell of an oily rag over there. I saw her in the distance at your send-off and I wish I had met her properly but you probably wouldn't have liked that, since I'm a very good judge of character.

One of the papers said you were on television dressed up as an old man and apparently you could have done a lot better for yourself. Perhaps it was nerves? Next time I see you I'll try to help you with your self-confidence. By the way, I've sent you a few cuttings. Look for the one with the headline 'Our Barry Bombs!'

My show on Channel Seven is a great success and David Baker, the director, has become a friend. The children adore him. Last week my guest on the show was the beautiful model Bambi Shmith who is going overseas herself soon. I told her you were doing a spit and a cough in the Oliver Twist show and she said she might get in touch with you.

I nearly gave Madge her marching orders yesterday because she put a very uncalled-for book on Norm's page turner. It's something from her own unsavoury collection called the Kinsey Report and as far as I can gather everything in it is totally unnecessary. Naturally I binned the book and gave Allsop the rough edge of my tongue. She could kill Norm with thoughtless little acts like that and send his equipment into overdrive.

I thought you'd like to know that one of the mothers at Kenny's school asked him if he was my son. I suppose I will have to get used to this kind of thing.

I hope you are well in yourself.

Kind regards, Edna Everage (Mrs)

As I read this curiously offensive letter downstairs at the National Bank, 'Joan' Geary regarded me sympathetically.

'It's another letter from Mrs Everage, isn't it?' she said. 'I couldn't help seeing the name on the back of the envelope.'

'Indeed it is,' I averred. 'I wish she wouldn't keep writing to me about her family and her career.'

'Now, Mr Humphries, don't be cranky,' replied this self-appointed aunt to so many Australian tourists. 'She's a very clever woman and my cousin in Sydney never misses her television show. It's gone national, by the way, and everyone . . .' Under my breath I joined in the inevitable refrain '. . . *thoroughly enjoys it.*'

It was especially irksome that she had enclosed those negative press cuttings from the Melbourne papers, particularly since I had received identical enclosures in my mother's last letter.

'I just thought you'd like to know, Barry,' my mother had written, 'that something you did on English TV didn't make you a lot of friends. It's a pity you have to go all that way overseas just to knock Australia.'

'Knocking Australia' is something I have been accused of doing since birth, or near enough to it. In order to display an edifying patriotism all Australians with any artistic gifts whatever were expected to tell lies about their homeland to avoid being branded as a traitor. The few minutes of Sandy that I had been allowed to perform on the Godfrey Winn show was, if anything, a rather affectionate vignette of Australian suburban life. It was hardly making fun of Australia since it did not elicit a single laugh. But why should I worry about such trivial matters? I was, after all, in a West End show; a fact of which Mrs Geary was quick to remind me.

'A few of us from the bank went along to see you, Barry, the other night. It was an excellent show, but who were you?'

I politely explained my essential role in this Dickensian operetta, but privately thought of shifting my money to the Commonwealth Bank, if I only had enough money to cover the costs of the transfer.

I had enlivened the cast of Lionel Bart's *Oliver!* for nearly a year and had moved from slummy Notting Hill Gate to more salubrious accommodations in Highgate Hill. Some of my artist friends from Australia had moved to London and we formed a jolly little expatriate community. Wisely, as I thought, I had abandoned any attempt to do my Australian 'act' in London, or indeed anywhere outside of Melbourne where the audience would be tuned in, or as they say now, 'on the same page'.

One night I got a message from the stage door that an Australian acquaintance was at the theatre to see me. Over a drink in the Lamb and Flag my visitor explained that he was now an impresario, and not as I had formerly known him as a knowledgeable assistant in a record shop. He quickly got around to his point. Would I be interested in returning to Australia to do a one-man show? It was a tempting invitation from a genuine fan, but I felt it was almost too soon to be going home, having achieved so little in London.

David, this being the name of my new champion, assured me that my popularity had expanded from its modest proportions when I left Melbourne, to a sizeable following, thanks to some recordings of my monologues widely circulated in my absence. That the most popular of these discs contained a performance by Edna Everage riled me a little, but since she was not credited on the liner notes most people thought that she was me, or more precisely, I was her.

I told him I would have to think about it. Peter Cook, a new friend, had talked to me about joining a new production of his hugely successful revue *Beyond the Fringe* when the original cast went to America. In any case, none of these opportunities could be seriously considered while I was contractually bound to my 'spit and a cough' in *Oliver!*.

'What dates had you in mind?' I asked David. He sipped his gin and tonic and took a thoughtful drag on a Temple Bar cigarette, an Australian fag of considerable potency in which saltpetre flared and sputtered.

'It would depend, I suppose, on when she was free.'

'She?' I exclaimed, amazingly missing the point. 'Who is she?'

'I mean, she's interested enough. I put out feelers at first and then took her to lunch at the Florentino when she actually got quite excited. But the invalid husband is a problem, and the kids.'

'Hold your horses,' I interrupted. 'Do you mean to say that you want Edna in this show? I thought it was going to be a one-man show? Why drag that woman into it?'

The impresario seemed a little taken aback by my reaction. Did he think he was paying me a compliment by inviting that awful woman back into my life?

David extinguished his cigarette and turned towards me with a conciliatory smile. 'Things don't just stand still in

Australia because a few chaps like you take off in search of greener pastures,' he said gently. 'Since you left Melbourne, Edna has become a bit of a star in Australia and she would be a big plus in the show we're talking about. We have to sell tickets.'

I felt myself overwhelmed with a great sadness for which there was no verbal expression.

David ordered another drink, kindled another Temple Bar and moved closer. 'Since her TV show, Barry,' he said conspiratorially, 'your little protégé Edna has become box office. Let me put it this way: she can be available in two months' time and I put a hold on the Comedy Theatre. It would be a terrible pity for the show to go ahead without you.'

'So you see me as a support act, is that it?' I exploded. 'Some poor idiot hired to warm up the audience for this silly over-rated housewife?'

Bernard the publican set our drinks on the bar and looked at me quizzically. I must have raised my voice more than I thought.

'It's only right for me to approach you about this, Barry, since you are Edna's agent, or so she tells me. Whatever she earns from this show, with you or without you, will put a few quid in your pocket.'

'I don't want the woman's money!' I almost yelled, and a couple in the bar gave me a look. I realised that I was actually close to tears. 'Do you or do you not want me to do a one-man show back in Australia? And if I refuse the great honour

of having Edna on stage with me is the offer still on the table?'
I asked hoarsely.

David, for the first time, looked a little ruffled. 'I think you
would be wonderful together and a lot of people agree,' he said,
patting my arm. 'Of course you could do a marvellous show on
your own, but we need a sure-fire guarantee of success, and Mrs
Everage is certainly that. If you could see her TV show I'd be
surprised if you didn't find it thoroughly enjoyable.'

Deeply chagrined, I had no wish to burst into tears in the
saloon bar of the Lamb and Flag and decided to nurse my
wounded pride until I got on the bus which would take me on
the long journey to Highgate Hill. I bade David a restrained
goodnight and told him I'd think it over.

'I knew you'd see it like that,' he said, with an irritating wink.

There was a big turnout at the press conference in Melbourne
and I suddenly felt rather important – important, perhaps, for
the first time in my life. Pride had so nearly prompted me to
refuse the offer, but then I reflected that whatever Edna might
do in her half of the show would be eclipsed by my performance. I had written a long monologue for Sandy Stone
which would be far more impressive than any of Edna's shrill
meanderings. I even had a new character, inspired by the
Adelaide critic, Max Harris, a pompous figure diffusing an
aura of failure, who had given one of my records a stinker of a
review in a now defunct periodical. This was *real* satire, and

the audience might flinch but they'd relish it all the same. Compared to me, I thought with the modesty of youth, Edna was an intellectual lightweight.

'What have you been doing overseas, Baz?' asked a journalist from the *Sun News-Pictorial*, striking a raw nerve at once.

'Well . . .' I stammered, thinking fast. 'I've been in a long run in the West End and there's been TV jobs, of course, and, er . . . radio . . . Flat out, really.' I thought it unlikely anyone there listened to British radio, and could challenge my fictitious claim.

Patrick Tennison, a showbusiness writer for the *Herald*, was my next inquisitor. 'Will you be staying in Australia long, Baz, or will the bright lights of London lure you back?'

I was falling into a trap without knowing it. 'I have to go back as soon as this show is over because there are a lot of offers waiting for me. There's a play and a BBC TV offer that are too good to miss,' I improvised wildly.

'I get the picture,' said Patrick. 'I suppose all of your old mates back in Melbourne seem a bit boring compared with the poms you are hobnobbing with now.' There was a gust of sardonic laughter in the room following this exchange.

I was determined not to fall into the same trap twice when a lady from the ABC, with short hair and wearing something like a man's suit, thrust a microphone at me. Her name, of course, was Carmel.

'Mr Humphries,' she said, and I at once detected hostility in the 'Mr', 'do you mean to say that if this show goes well, and the jury is out about that, you would really rush back overseas?'

'Well, no, Carmel,' I said, clumsily backtracking. 'I mean,

Australia is a wonderful country and our culture is second to none. I think I might even consider staying here for as long as possible.'

'Yeah, that figures,' said my beefy female interlocutor. 'The word's around you're not doing too well over there.'

At that, my first press conference broke up in gales of good-natured Australian laughter. However, David assured me that it had gone very well and it was quite a good turnout, considering it was to publicise an artistic event.

'Is Edna going to do a press conference?' I asked apprehensively. I had only been in Australia for twenty-four hours and so far had not plucked up the courage to call her – the courage or the inclination.

'Oh yes, she gave a big one two days ago and packed the place out. We got wonderful coverage. I'll show you the cuttings later.'

'I'm surprised none of the press mentioned her to me today if she was so bloody good on Tuesday, packing the place out,' I snapped.

David looked a bit shifty. 'To be perfectly honest with you,' he said, using a phrase which, on the lips of a theatrical promoter, usually means its opposite, 'I don't think they connect you both. That's to say they don't quite realise you're going to be in her show. It could even be my fault, but don't worry, the tickets are flying out.'

I stepped out into Collins Street, which was once, by any standards, a beautiful street, and saw that in the short time I had been away the City Fathers had absolutely destroyed it.

It looked like anywhere. The glass office blocks which had replaced those opulent Victorian buildings of my youth already looked dated. In trying desperately to be modern, Melbourne had managed to look merely provincial.

My mother's Austin A40 seemed still to be in working order and may not have been driven at all in the past two years. Huge clouds of fuscous smoke billowed from the exhaust, much to the embarrassment of my passengers, but they were few. I thought of motoring out to Moonee Ponds to see what Edna was up to, but decided to work on my own contribution to the show rather than torment myself with her unwelcome intrusion. But there was more to it than that. When David told me, in an unsuccessful attempt to be tactful, that she was doing the second half of the show, I realised with a bitter resentment that she had usurped the curtain call. By the time I walked on stage at the end to take a bow, the audience would have forgotten who I was.

As usual, my mother made her own opinion clear. 'You certainly made a rod for your own back there, Barry,' she observed tartly. 'She's been in all of the papers already and I must admit that she was thoroughly enjoyable last night on the Graham Kennedy show with Princess Panda.[5] She hasn't mentioned you, though. I'm surprised you came all the way back here to play second fiddle.'

---

5 Panda Lisner, the barrel girl on *In Melbourne Tonight*, and described in one academic study as being '. . . renowned for her glamorous appearance and breathtaking ordinariness, was the most famous of a series of barrel girls and her demise highlighted the effective power of the segment as well as its fascinatingly ambiguous status'.

I learnt that my father had been into the theatre, trying to buy a block of tickets for his friends at the golf club as a rather poignant gesture of paternal support, only to discover, to his surprise, that the first night was sold out. The woman at the box office told me this, not omitting to mention that quite a few patrons had asked what time the second act started so that they could take their time dining at the nearby restaurants, the Latin and the Florentino.

'If only you had got your law degree, Barry, instead of frittering away your time in those student shows. You would have had something to fall back on now,' my mother continued.

'He'll always learn the hard way, I'm afraid,' my father added dolefully.

Then the phone rang, with a peculiarly ominous timbre which made me snatch it from its black vulcanite cradle.

'You've been here one week and not a peep out of you, Barry.' It was the voice I dreaded: Edna's. 'I have to say a big thank you to you for getting me this wonderful job, and I'd love to cook you a roast before we open on Friday. If you're not busy tonight I have a loin in the oven.'

I declined this odious invitation as politely as possible and explained that I had lines to learn and a couple of costume fittings.

'Look, Barry,' Edna persisted with a terrible brightness, 'do you want me to hear you? You mustn't let stage fright get you. I want you to be good on Friday night, or as good as possible. It wouldn't be fair if you let me steal the show altogether.'

I was grateful that this well-intentioned advice was

transmitted on the telephone and I did not have to confront the harpy who bestowed it.

'Thank you, Edna,' I croaked. 'Will Norman be coming to the show?'

'My very word,' said Edna. 'Wild horses wouldn't keep him away, but he's only well enough to come to my half. I hope you don't mind. His prostate monitor makes a funny huffing and puffing noise which might distract you. It won't matter to me because it will be drowned out by laughter and applause. Madge is coming too, though I've made her buy her own ticket. She's too spoilt as it is. You'll see her quite easily from the stage because she'll be wearing her apricot bridesmaid dress. She hasn't got anything else and I'm certainly not squandering money on a new frock for a woman who never goes anywhere.'

I discerned that the gentling of Edna had not progressed at the pace of her success, or rather, her notoriety. With a promise to see her at the dress rehearsal, I hurried back to my own preparations. The show was called *A Nice Night's Entertainment* and I was determined to excel and give that parvenu a run for her money. More than anything I wanted to walk off the stage at intermission and be able to say, 'Follow that, Edna!'

9

A Woman With a Past

Well, she did. And I was good. If I say so myself, I was
brilliant. My nostalgic Sandy Stone monologue was
funny, touching and elegiac; a blend of Beckett and Betjeman,
with a pinch of Pinter, yet totally original, a quiet tour de
force. My other offerings, especially my adroit demolition of
the critic Max Harris, elicited the right gasps and guffaws
from the more sophisticated members of my audience, and as
I walked to my dressing-room I could still hear the applause.

Nothing, however, prepared me for the clamour in the
auditorium when Mrs Everage minced onto the stage in her
awful slingbacks and floral polyester frock. There was an
uproar at her first banal utterance and it grew from there.
Glumly I sat in my dressing-room sipping wine and wincing at

every burst of laughter and applause that reached me from the stage. It's the power of television, I thought. These people never go to the real theatre, they just sit glued to the box every night and anyone who appears on it, however talentless, is a star.

When I stepped on stage at the end for the curtain call, there was a warm response from the patrons, but it was polite rather than tumultuous. I gestured to the wings and Edna entered in a new evening dress by Delphine of Burke Road, Camberwell, and the audience went berserk. Two sensitive-looking young men in the front row stood up and cried, 'We love you, Edna!'

'I love you, too,' cooed Edna in words which Liza Minnelli would later emulate, 'I love you so-ooo much!' Then everyone stood. I looked down into the auditorium at those rapturous upturned faces, which were glowing with light refracted from the stage. No one seemed to be looking at me.

Later, as I entertained a few sympathetic friends with a drink in my dressing-room, Edna put her head around the corner.

'Wasn't it wonderful, Barry?' she exclaimed. 'They adore me, don't they?' And then, like an afterthought, she added, 'Your bit went well, too, didn't it? David said he was very pleasantly surprised, and so was I. You nearly had the audience in the palm of your hand.'

And with that she was gone, to an after-show supper at Florentino thrown by our promoter, from which I had begged to be excused.

'It's no good sulking,' said my mother. 'You've made your bed with that woman and you'll have to lie in it. The show got very good write-ups and you got a nice mention as well. I wish I had been well enough to come along.'

'I hope you'll manage it before the end of the season,' I snapped. 'Personally I think it was my best work. Frank Murphy in *The Advocate* gave me a wonderful notice.'

'*The Advocate?*' exclaimed my mother. 'Isn't that a Roman Catholic paper?'

'Well, yes,' I replied, 'but Murphy is one of the most serious critics in Melbourne.'

'And what is Mrs Everage, may I ask?' queried my mother. 'Her maiden name was Beazley, which is as Irish as they come. Get her to spell Humphries and you'll find out soon enough.'

'Why should I do that?' I asked, mystified. 'Are you suggesting she's illiterate?'

My mother gave a dry laugh. 'Of course not, Barry, but if she says "haitch" you'll know she's a Catholic – Catholic or common. It's a well-known fact.'

'I don't believe she has any religious views,' I replied, 'so she's probably Church of England.' But my satirical dig eluded my mother, or seemed to. One could never be too sure.

My mother's religious prejudices were considerable and ran deep. One of five sisters, her only brother had married a Roman Catholic girl called Dorothy, whereupon my mother's

sister Dorothy changed her name. My poor uncle was practically ostracised for his apostasy, but as children we all liked
him on the few occasions when, fortified by a few drinks, he
paid us a visit. His aura of disgrace seemed to make him
even more appealing. Sometimes my mother's bigotry was
stupefying; all the more so since she was an intelligent woman,
but she spoke for her class, and although she was not by nature
unkind, she was instinctual, sometimes brutally so, in her
appraisal, and not seldom in her dismissal, of others.

'Whether or not you approve of Edna Everage,' I adjured
my mother, 'she is a fact, and an inescapable one. I probably
dislike her more than you do, but she does have tremendous
energy and a primitive theatrical gift. She's also funny, mostly
without knowing it. Thanks to her, I am back in Australia
seeing you and the family.'

My mother thought about this. 'I suppose I'll have to have
her around for dinner, but Mrs Ferguson won't like her, I'm
telling you now, Barry. There have been some funny stories
about her, *very funny stories.*'

My mother would not be drawn further on this subject,
though she had certainly whetted my appetite for gossip. It is
likely of course that she made up those hints of scandal, though
she displayed as usual a remarkable prescience, for there *would*
be funny stories, *very funny stories* much later. Perhaps my
mother had gypsy blood, for her dark Romany looks and olive
skin suggested an exotic antecedence. One day I might have to
give the family tree a good shake to discover what mysterious
beings are up there, clinging to the branches.

We toured Australia, quite cheerfully in fact, though Edna expressed anxiety about her husband and children every now and then which made her seem almost human. I kept remembering her motto, uttered soon after we met: 'Put your family last'. Madge the bridesmaid was holding the fort in Moonee Ponds, presumably in exchange for her keep.

In Adelaide, where we had two performances at the Town Hall, we checked into the South Australian Hotel, since demolished and much lamented.

'Would your wife like a key as well, Mr Humphries?' asked the desk clerk, looking at Edna.

'Mrs Everage is certainly not my wife,' I said through gritted teeth. 'She is a happily married mother of three.'

The clerk apologised profusely, though he was clearly making an effort not to laugh.

Edna turned to me gravely, and said, '*Four* actually, Barry, counting little Lois.'

For a moment I didn't know what she was talking about, but then I remembered the missing daughter. It was a strange story, and a story I was soon to learn more about.

In the break between the Sydney and Brisbane leg of our tour, I accepted an invitation to visit a large sheep station in the area of Wagga Wagga, on the Murrumbidgee River. It was an aspect of traditional Australian life hitherto unfamiliar to me, and although I did not know the Beaufort family, they had been to the show and had generously extended an invitation to me, *without* Edna, to enjoy a few days of pastoral relaxation. I knew that Wagga was the town where Edna had spent her earlier years and it was somehow connected with the tragedy that befell her daughter Lois so, for the sake of delicacy, I did not mention my destination to her, saying merely that we would meet again in Brisbane.

I, who was by then familiar with the West End of London, the Welsh borders, Oxford and Cambridge, and even the left bank of Paris, had never seen an Australian sheep shorn or a billy boiled on a campfire. Indeed, the first kangaroo I ever saw was at Whipsnade Zoo in Bedfordshire. Sitting on the veranda at the old Beaufort homestead, looking out over the verdant pastures with my host, Jim Beaufort, topping up my whisky glass, I felt my first, not altogether disagreeable, twinge of patriotism.

'I know every thistle on this place,' said old Jim, blinking into the distance and sipping his Johnny Walker. It was probably his fifth for the morning and it was only 11 o'clock. A bottle of scotch on the breakfast table seemed unusual to one of my austere upbringing but then, like most men of the land, Jim had been up and working since four.

On the following morning I told my hosts that I wanted to visit the township for a couple of hours and have a look around. A station hand ran me down to Wagga in the ute and I made straight for the public library on Trails Street. Soon, with the help of a very nice archivist called Thelma Choate, I was trawling through old copies of the *Riverina Leader* and the *Daily Advertiser*. At length, I came upon the object of my search. It was on the front page of the *Leader* under a grainy photograph of the young Edna pointing to an empty baby's cot. The headline read: 'Hope Fades for Missing Baby'.

Miss Choate leant over my shoulder. 'Oh, it was awful, that story,' she said. 'My cousin Margaret knew the family and everyone said there was more to it than met the eye.'

'What else did they say?' I probed the helpful librarian.

'Well,' she continued, 'that Edna, the mother, is on TV these days and thinks she's Lady Muck, but I'd say she told a lot of fibs to the police.'

'What kind of fibs?' I asked disingenuously.

'Well, blaming a poor koala in the first place. Look at this crackpot story.' Thelma passed me another brittle, yellowing copy of the *Riverina Leader*, which not only bore the same blurry image of my 'client', but a large photograph of a koala bear nibbling a gum leaf and looking curiously malevolent. The headline screamed: 'A Koala Stole My Baby'.

As I recall this, I am reminded of the Lindy Chamberlain case when a dingo was blamed for the disappearance of her infant Azaria. Had it been a copycat crime? And could Azaria's mother have known that a rogue marsupial had been a suspect in the abduction of Lois Everage nearly thirty years before?

Thelma brought me cups of tea and Butternut Snaps to sustain me as I devoured the unfolding drama in those desiccated tabloids.

Edna had, it seemed, returned to Wagga Wagga on a visit to show off her new baby Lois to some old family friends. It was a hot night and she had left the infant in its cot on the veranda and had slept past the 2 a.m. feed time. Waking in the early hours, she had run out to see to Lois and found the cot empty. She claimed there were some large footprints on the veranda which, in her distress, she had erased with a mop before the arrival of the police.

It would have been typical of the woman I knew to exhibit a spotless home, whatever the circumstances, much in the same way as a doctor's visit prompts many women to indulge in an orgy of house cleaning.

The neighbours had been alerted in the small hours by Edna's keening cry for assistance, but when help arrived she was hysterical and the local doctor administered a powerful sedative. A search was immediately ordered and continued over two days, but the surrounding bush was dense and not a single clue was found, except a small pink bootee made from Fleischer's 'Baby Zephyr' 2-ply wool on size 1 needles, with a crocheted pearl edge.

The mystery was never solved and the case was ultimately closed but it seemed that Edna's koala story had been given some credence by the police, since a feral koala had recently been at large in the neighbourhood frightening locals. Koala bears often suffer from chlamydia and the related unpleasant condition called 'wet bottom' which radically affects their normally docile and somnolent state. After the tragedy, Edna was exonerated and returned to Melbourne where she subsequently bore three more children. However, serious doubts lingered amongst the locals.

'That koala story is a lot of old twaddle,' exclaimed Miss Choate. 'They never grow big enough to pick up a kid, and why would they?' I nodded in agreement. 'But you'd be amazed at how many people swallowed that yarn. Actually, I felt sorry for the koala community.'

'What was Mrs Everage's frame of mind, do you think?'

'Look, they said that after Lois was born she went a bit dippy for a while; some women do. She got very moody and medical men have probably got a fancy name for it.'

'But what do you think happened, Thelma?' I asked, pushing the pile of old newspapers across the mahogany table.

'I'd say she had a funny turn in the middle of the night and went out on the veranda, picked up the bubba, took off into the bush and dropped her down one of those old disused shafts they have out that way. She was probably asleep and didn't even know what she was doing.'

It seemed too horrible. It was hard to imagine my Edna, for all her faults, committing infanticide.

But Thelma Choate was not so sure. 'If you ever meet her, have a good look at her,' she said. 'That woman is hiding a secret, and probably more than one . . .'

For the remainder of the tour, I saw my companion and co-star in a new light. No longer was she the vapid housewife and accidental comedienne I had known before. I was shaken more deeply than I thought possible by the revelations from the Wagga Wagga public library, which were so much at variance with the woman I thought I knew. Thereafter she became, if not nicer, at least more three dimensional: a woman with a past. A past is something we all lack in Australia. We have, of course, a geological past, for we inhabit one of the oldest landscapes in the world; 'The last of lands' in A. D. Hope's great phrase. This is why we have always flown to Europe to baptise ourselves in antiquity: to soil ourselves with it.

Ever and anon, the story of Lois crept back into my mind and I recognised some very loose ends. Where was Norm during all of this? Was he back at home too ill to travel? And Mrs Allsop, where was she? Clearly the story did not make a big impact in the Melbourne press since Edna went on to win the 'Lovely Mother Quest' a few years later, an honour which would not have been bestowed on the Medea of Moonee Ponds.

Because the story of Lois was so improbable and none of the explanations reflected favourably on Edna, it was not, strange to say, revulsion that I felt towards this silly woman, but a grudging admiration. She had fluttered out of the pigeon-hole I had assigned to her, and she might yet surprise me again with some future audacity, one which preferably would not involve the disappearance of a child.

At the end of the tour, and before my journey back to London, Edna and I had lunch again at Russell Collins, the Melbourne restaurant where we had first met. The atmosphere would strike a modern reader as eerie, since the only sounds were the clink of crockery and cutlery, the hushed voices of the diners, and the scurrying footsteps of the waitresses. In that halcyon age, no one thought that a meal would taste better if accompanied by piped music. The sound of bleating cornets, squealing trumpets and electronic twanging would become an appetite-suppressant and conversation blocker when later introduced at great expense by restaurateurs all over the world.

The Iceland poppies on their hairy stems which formerly glowed on every table had been replaced by Chianti bottles with candle wax dribbling down their necks, and the doilies of yesteryear replaced by red-checked tablecloths, but otherwise things were much as they were. The cream of tomato soup and the creamed sweet corn on toast were as ambrosial as ever. But the chef was becoming more adventurous: floating in my soup were small cubes of fried bread, which we would have called sippets, but I couldn't be sure. I wondered at the time whether that old medieval word, so identifiable with pea soup, was still in use.

'What are these?' I asked the waitress.

'Look, they're new,' she replied. 'We've got a fancy new chef. They're called cretins.'

Enlightened, I sipped my soup and crunched on a cretin.

Later, as we nibbled our steamed Golden Syrup pudding, Edna, who was actually looking quite pretty, leant across the table and pressed a small package into my hand. 'It's a book,' she said, 'and you might like to peruse it.'

With her permission I opened it then and there. The gift turned out to be a copy of *The Prophet* by Kahlil Gibran, in which she had inscribed a presentation in green ink: 'For my friend and mentor, Barry Humphrey, who helped me get where I am today. From his grateful client, Edna May Everage.'

She still couldn't spell my name, but it was a touching

offering. I had studiously avoided it, but since I had begun to see Edna as a person, I thanked her, and privately decided that I might actually dip into the Prophet's pool of wisdom.

'What are you going to do when I go back to London, Edna?' I enquired over the coffee and chicory.

'David is arranging quite a few lucrative speaking engagements for me and my *Refinement* contract has been renewed.'

'Refinement?'

'My *Touch of Refinement* show. I've lined up some wonderful guests for the next season like Mrs Jenny Hoad, the tennis player's wife, Zara Holt, Dame Pattie Menzies, Evie Hayes, and Jeanette Dallas Brooks talking about her fairytale marriage.'

I wondered why every wedding reported in the women's magazines was always described as 'fairytale'. Since most fairy-tales in my memory were extremely scary, it was probably not such a bad description of marriage after all.

'You never asked me to be on your show, Edna, and I'd be very happy to find the time.'

Edna looked embarrassed, for her a rare emotion. 'Look, Barry, I'd love to, but I'm sticking to well-known people for the time being, and although you are a clever boy, most people don't know you from a bar of soap, and I mean that in the nicest possible way.'

As we ascended to Collins Street I remained speechless after Edna's parting salvo. Perhaps it was a relief that she had reverted so magnificently to form, but would Kahlil Gibran have approved?

10

Established

I had me a piece of Edna, as I think they would have expressed it in Hollywood. It was only a small piece, but it was extraordinary how conscientious she was in sending me, care of the London bank, small percentages of her earnings. Incrementally it added up to a useful sum. The role of agent had really been thrust upon me and I was not, as they say today, very comfortable with it. However, I was back in London, out of work, and every little bit helped.

David, in faraway Melbourne, was already talking excitedly about another tour in a couple of years' time in major theatres, and was asking me to make sure Edna would be available. I couldn't help wondering if he would be equally enthusiastic if she wasn't, if it was just me doing a show of my own. Once again, I seemed to be a conduit to this woman. There is a theatrical term for what had happened to me and how I felt about it: Upstaged.

But none of these emotions – well, resentments really – detracted from my growing admiration for Mrs Norman Everage. In Australia, at any rate, she had become quite a star, especially in highbrow circles where she was described by some as a satirist. Of course she was not, since to call Edna a satirist would imply some form of conscious artistry; a keen, pitiless perception of modern Australian life and mores, which Edna could never have possessed. Her trick, her *donné*, was that she embodied the taste and manners of her age, and expressed them loudly, clearly, and with the precise attention to detail of a primitive artist. I had also begun to find her surprisingly likeable, despite the fact that her personality and her very appearance combined so many deeply unattractive elements.

I was not out of work for long. I found myself doing the *Oliver!* show in New York, living in Greenwich Village, and meeting such mythical figures as Marcel Duchamp, Salvador Dali and Jack Kerouac. I also spent a lot of time with Peter Cook and Dudley Moore who were doing their show, *Beyond the Fringe*, on Broadway at a theatre near mine. Peter, an attractive, undulating figure with a compulsion to perpetual jocosity had become, by my standards, extraordinarily rich. I must confess I was envious. Why not me too? I muttered to myself in ignominious moments of self-pity.

In London Peter had launched his famous 'satiric' nightclub, The Establishment, in Greek Street, Soho, and asked me if

I would do a cabaret season there when I got back to Britain.
To my amazement he didn't enquire about Edna's availability.
He hoped I didn't mind, he said, but he wasn't her greatest
fan; it was Sandy Stone he liked, my old man in the dressing
gown, who rambled on about his boring life in the suburbs of
Melbourne. Peter had good taste, I reflected. When I returned
to London after my New York adventure I discovered that the
Soho district had been transformed – it was somehow gaudier
and more scrofulous than before and hence, more attractive.
Psychedelia had not yet enveloped it with its multicoloured
tendrils, nor had Union Jacks yet sprouted in Carnaby Street,
but the Age of Aquarius was definitely dawning and The Establishment was the place to be. It was trendy, it was groovy, it
was s-o-o-o-ooper.

I sat for a photographic portrait with Lewis Morley who
had taken, or was about to take, his celebrated snap of the
notorious call-girl and waif Christine Keeler – nude, and strad-
dling a faux Arne Jacobsen chair.

I was very nervous about presenting any of my Australian
characters in England. 'The poms will never get it' advised a
couple of my Australian friends, adroitly implying two things:
that English audiences were not as smart as Australian ones
and that my failure was a foregone conclusion.

Trying to avoid such gloomy predictions, and buoyed by
Peter Cook's enthusiasm from afar – he was still on Broadway –
I decided I would do a monologue, about an Australian jour-
nalist complaining about England and a brief tirade from Mrs
Everage. In the past I had been rather proud of my Edna

impersonation and it was, after all, in the English pantomime dame tradition. Safely 13,000 miles away in Melbourne, Edna would never know that I was plagiarising her material in a London nightclub, and like all plagiarists past and present I could always call it *an homage*, if I was ever found out.

On opening night there was quite a large gathering in the long, narrow club and unfortunately, such was the lighting, I could see the faces of several well-known critics as they sat at tables near the stage and scribbled in their notebooks. The bar was not far off and it had attracted a noisy crowd of groovy people, who disdained to shut up once I had launched into my act. They seemed, indeed, to be talking and laughing even more loudly as I sat on the tiny stage in a threadbare armchair and intoned my long and, by satirical standards, over-subtle monologue. There was a vociferous Australian contingent at the back of the room; a claque led by Betty Best, the London representative of the Australian *Women's Weekly* and a well-known 'sipper'. Her raucous, over-the-top barracking alienated the rest of the audience and killed any laughs I might have otherwise obtained.

I was only about ten minutes into the show when I noticed a couple of people get up and wander over to the bar. As the sweat crept down my back, it suddenly occurred to me that I was failing and failing fast. 'Edna' will pick them up, I thought. If I couldn't give them political satire, which was the fashion of the day, at least I could give them a vaudeville turn without a hint of nuance.

In the small room at the back of the stage, I performed a

quick change into the motley outfit of Mrs Everage. 'They're loving it,' lied my dresser. 'It's just they don't know how to react.'

Deeply unconvinced, I jabbed my mouth with a bright cyclamen lipstick, plonked on Edna's yellow conical hat, and stepped once more onto the stage. This time, in the few minutes I had been backstage, I saw that several tables had emptied and the hubbub from the bar had grown louder.

I had hired a pianist to accompany me in a song called 'Australian Vitality', which I had heard Edna sing with great success in Melbourne and Sydney. It was a song about our superiority to the rest of the world and she always delivered it with an almost frenzied energy. Unfortunately the pianist, a Melbourne girl called Pat who had been recommended to me, suffered from stage fright. She had been fine in rehearsals but in the presence of an audience, even a rapidly diminishing audience, and with Betty Best stridently cheering her on, Pat went to pieces. What I sang and what she played were seriously divergent and I began to feel not merely a kind of cosmic dismay but also that I was actually physically disintegrating. The few people I could clearly observe at a table near the stage were not even looking at me, but were sitting with their heads bowed in embarrassment. Thank God Peter Cook isn't here, was all I could think.

No one came to see me after the show but before I skulked home, my dresser said, 'Don't worry, they're the toughest audience in London.' It was a cold consolation and my shame was even deeper when I thought that if bloody Edna herself had been there we could have had a minor triumph; we might even have snatched victory from the jaws of failure.

There were reviews, of course, which I didn't read, but now, after so many years – so many decades – I will dig them out. I was told they were bad, but like every bad review I have ever received, and there have not been too many, they hurt at the time, but when read in retrospect, when the pain has subsided, they turn out to be spot on, even those written by stupid bastards.

Never, ever again, I decided, would I do my act or anyone else's act outside Australia.

I remembered this vow fourteen years later on the first night of *Housewife! Superstar!!* at the Apollo Theatre in 1976. The audience was cheering; I could still hear it in my dressing-room. The assistant stage manager had run after me and said, 'They're still standing there, you'll have to give them another curtain call. You can't let her take all the applause.' But I knew that she could and she would, and it was not for me that the London audience was out there stomping and cheering, much as it seemed to have enjoyed my offerings that evening.

Edna had flown from Australia as the eponymous star of *Housewife! Superstar!!* and after a couple of television appearances, notably on the Russell Harty show, she had been a hit. No one had so far connected her with the debacle at The Establishment over a decade before. She was a refreshing novelty. If The Establishment had still existed, she would have been triumphant and the passé Harold Macmillan impersonators would have died a death. Admittedly, my Sandy Stone monologue (I wrote a new one every year) had really gone well in the first half so perhaps we had been ahead of our time. This night it was impossible to get into her dressing-room for the floral tributes, but Edna was typically generous about my contribution to the success of the show.

'I watched your effort from the wings,' she said at the after-show party as she introduced me to Princess Margaret, David Hockney, Mick Jagger and the young John Waters as though she had known them all her life. 'You were thoroughly enjoyable.'

We knew we were a West End hit when there was another television interview with a man called Michael Parkinson, a sports journalist turned perceptive TV interlocutor. It was actually Edna who was requested for the programme and I gallantly stepped down. Also being interviewed were Olivia Newton-John, whom I had known since she was a child, and the legendary actress and star of *Sunset Boulevard*, Gloria Swanson.

Gloria looked at Edna, who was wearing a leopard print dress, with an amused curiosity.

'Ocelot,' Edna explained. 'A lot of ocelot.'

The actress was speaking at some length about her career when Edna interrupted, 'We thought you were a *silent* star, Miss Swanson. It's lovely to hear you're far from it.'

Parkinson, always charming, then asked Edna if she was pleased that her present West End appearance had been so much more successful than the debacle at The Establishment.

It was a moment I had dreaded and it was happening on live television.

'I've never done a show here before, Michael,' she said. 'You must have imagined it.'

Parkinson then quoted from the review by Bamber Gascoigne who, in *The Spectator*, had described The Establishment show as 'distinctly soporific'.

It was clear to me, or as clear as it could be between the fingers I had pressed to my eyes, that Edna had no idea what the word soporific meant, but that it didn't sound like a compliment. 'I don't think it was me in that show,' she said after a long and thoughtful pause, 'perhaps someone pretending to be me. But as my mother used to say, imitation is the sincerest form of flattery. It was an expression of hers that has since caught on.'

I could see, sitting at home, that when the camera held her in close-up, her eyes had narrowed; she knew the identity of her impersonator, and there would be hell to pay. In contemplating revenge, I knew that Edna favoured the 'cold dish' theory. Unsurprisingly, the phone beside my bed rang sharply at midnight.

'You're a clever person, Barry,' said the dreaded voice. 'What does soporific mean?'

'Look, I'm sorry, Edna,' I expostulated, slipping into Edna's dreadful ocular-locutory habit of inserting 'Look' at the beginning of every sentence. 'It was a horrible place in a horrible neighbourhood and there wouldn't have been enough money in the budget to drag you across the world and expose you to such an unappreciative mob.' There was silence on the other end of the telephone so I gabbled on. 'You could say that I took the rap for you, really, and I didn't actually imitate you, it was more of a . . . well, a tribute. I suppose I should have asked you, I'm sorry.'

'It's water under the bridge now, Barry, as my mother would say,' replied Edna in a more friendly tone, 'but if I had been there, in the flesh, the show would probably have been a good deal less syphilitic.'

It was the wrong moment to correct her unfortunate malapropism.

She continued. 'The trouble is, you're putting the wrong idea in people's heads. There could be some silly folk out there who might think we are one and the same person, and that would be very bad for my image.'

The word 'image' was being bandied about a lot in those days. It came from the world of advertising and in Australia there was a great deal of talk in the press about 'Australia's overseas image' and people like me who did it irreparable damage by making unpatriotic jokes.

'You were very good on Parkinson,' said I in a placatory tone, 'and so was Olivia Newton-John.'

'She's a sweetie,' exclaimed Edna, 'and she's asked me for a few acting lessons. I've started a little acting school back in Moonee Ponds, you know, and I've got a few young pupils already. I was working with a little boy called Mel before I came away. Mr and Mrs Gibson drop him off on Thursdays.'

'How old is he?' I asked, glad we had changed the subject.

'Oh, did I say little?' Edna replied laughing. 'He's actually nineteen, but very small for his age — and adorable!'

Was Edna getting a little homesick? I wondered. Somehow, homesickness was one of the more tender emotions that was difficult to attribute to my co-star of the Apollo Theatre.

'Let's meet and have a little dinner at the Terrazza tomorrow night, Barry,' were her last words on the phone. 'There is something I have to tell you.'

La Terrazza was a very smart restaurant in Dean Street, Soho, run by Mario and Franco. Unlike Italian restaurants in Melbourne, the waiters were Italian and not Greek. Edna was already there in the corner, sipping a San Pellegrino as I entered. She was wearing her denim outfit with a lot of gold chains and a white silk scarf. Did I imagine it or were her eyelashes a little dewy behind her blue butterfly spectacles? The minute I took my seat she reached out across the pink tablecloth and put her hand over mine.

'Norm has taken a turn for the worse,' she said. 'Madge called me last night after we spoke and Doctor Rentoul-Outhwaite is suggesting a prostate transplant.'

I adopted an all-purpose expression of concern.

'They can do that op now,' continued Edna, 'or someone in South Africa can.'

'But isn't there a danger that his organ might be rejected?'

'Yes,' replied Edna thoughtfully, 'but he should be pretty used to that by now.'

'Will you have to hurry back to Melbourne to look after him? What about our show?' I exclaimed.

'Oh no, I won't be deserting you, Barry,' said Edna, crunching on a grissini. 'Norm's organ is out of my hands, and Madge will keep me posted. My career comes first, I'm afraid, Barry. Does that sound awful?'

The minestrone arrived and I noticed two tiny wisps of smoke escaping the waiter's nostrils. He had clearly had a quick drag on his cigarette in the kitchen.

Edna looked pensive. 'Funnily enough,' she said indicating to the waiter that she desired an additional parmesan sprinkle, 'I'm not really worried about Norm. He's as strong as an ox and could easily bury us all.'

I wasn't so sure. The man I had glimpsed on a couple of occasions was certainly not in 'showroom condition', as a car salesman friend of mine would have picturesquely expressed it. For all Edna's chattiness and insistence on niceness, was there something disturbingly unfeeling about this woman? She was certainly a complicated creature, but I had to remember the small and unexpected acts of kindness in the past, when I had been in hospital . . .

11

De Profundis

The sixties had ended and the seventies had dawned without me really noticing the transition. I had woken up in a small nursing home in a Melbourne suburb and discovered that I was not allowed out of bed.

'Where am I?' I had asked Genevieve, an attractive Irish nurse with a lewd smile.

'Get back to bed, you naughty boy,' she had replied. 'You're in a special hospital – a hospital for *thirsty people*.'

In the preceding decade I had, from time to time, spent weekends and even the odd week in discreet establishments like this in England and Australia, usually owned and run by psychiatrists hoping to win the Nobel Prize for teaching drunks to enjoy only the odd cocktail. Their patients usually died halfway through the experiment.

During these years of intemperance I had even managed to work, despite regular episodes of drunkenness, or at least I had given the appearance of working. Fortunately it was a decade in which most people I knew lived in a perpetual state of chemical exaltation. Somehow I succeeded in doing two Australian tours with Edna Everage in tow, then there was a television series for the BBC, a stint as Long John Silver in *Treasure Island*, a long-running play with Spike Milligan in the West End, and another Lionel Bart musical. To a few of these performances I look back with fatuous self-satisfaction; as to the rest, it is better to avert the memory. Conveniently, my recollection of this whole period is lacunary; full of gaps that will never, mercifully, be filled. Alcoholism is, amongst other things, a disorder of the memory: you wake up groaning 'never again' and before lunch you have had your second whisky and soda, not seldom without the soda.

One morning, as I lay in what proved to be my last nursing home, filled with rage, shame, resentment and, it must be admitted, fear, Nurse Genevieve brought in a huge and hideous bunch of gladioli for which the hospital had no sufficiently capacious vase.

'She's outside waiting to see you, Barry,' Genevieve announced excitedly. 'You didn't tell me you knew *her*! She's gorgeous.'

'How long has she been out there?' I groaned, feeling the imminent relapse of an ancient hangover.

'Mrs Everage has been waiting for three hours and she said

not to disturb you until you woke up. That woman is a saint.'

Before I could pretend to fall asleep again, a coruscating figure burst into my room. She was wearing a tie-dyed kaftan and a beaded headband of some nondescript ethnic pattern, Indian sandals and a generous squirt of patchouli, a scent popular with the demi-monde of the 1890s and revived by the hippy generation with whose number, Edna, it seemed, now sought to identify herself.

At the sight of my pale, bed-ridden form she threw up her arms in histrionic horror, so that the billowing sleeves of her kaftan fell back, revealing a tuft of hair nestled in her armpit like a small damp spider. The age of total depilation had yet to come.

'So this is where you are hiding, Barry!' she exclaimed, finding an aluminium chair and reaching for one of my chocolate digestives. 'On our last tour, when you started blotting your copy book, I began to think I would have to do the show on my own.'

'Blotting my copy book' struck me then as a genial euphemism for a life-threatening illness, but I welcomed it. I realised that I had actually *missed* this woman, and that I was not merely pleased to see her now, but – and I squirm a little in recalling it – was even *enraptured* by her sudden irruption.

'They were calling you some rather horrible names in the paper when you said those things to the policeman, Barry. He was only trying to get the keys off you and stop you driving.'

Edna was no doubt describing a real event and I had to pretend that I had been present when it happened.

'I stuck up for you, Barry, thousands wouldn't. I told that man who wrote for the *Kings Cross Whisper* that you were over-tired and over-emotional and that the doctor who gave you the tablets hadn't told you they didn't mix with crème de menthe.'

As I lay there in hospital I hoped that my demeanour looked suitably grateful. I wasn't sure what messages my expression conveyed, or how I felt or even, most of the time, who I was. It was to be a long convalescence.

'Thank you, Edna,' I managed to croak, wondering if the odour of patchouli, in sufficient concentration, could cause fits of asphyxia.

There was a long silence, which was unusual in her presence. I felt I had to add something. 'It was very nice of you to come and see me. No one else has.'

Edna took another biscuit. 'You probably scared a lot of people off, Barry, with your naughty ways, but you are my manager and in the theatre you are more than that — you are my warm-up act.'

Just when one was beginning to actually like Edna, she could be relied upon to say something devastating, but in the sweetest possible way.

'I hope I am more than that, Edna,' I said, though it is difficult to defend oneself convincingly and with dignity from a supine position in a drying-out clinic.

'Look, let me put it this way, Barry,' said Edna, standing and brushing away a few biscuit crumbs which were clinging to the CND[6] symbol suspended around her neck on a beaded thong. 'If the doctor says you are ever capable of working again, I would love to have you do a cameo in one of my shows.' Then she stooped, gave me a peck on the cheek and was gone.

Genevieve was immediately back in the room, starstruck and bearing a yellow plastic bucket. 'She's made my day, that lady, and she's so classy!' she enthused. 'I asked her if she had met The Seekers and she *had*! She knew them all . . . and Helen Reddy!'

'What's the bucket for, Nurse? Do you think that perfume might make me throw up?'

'It's for the glads, you silly arse,' she replied. 'Aren't they beautiful? They must have cost a packet. I'll put them in the window so you can look at them and think of her.'

I lit another Dunhill King Size and puffed at it peevishly. I was smoking about forty a day and my fingers were lacquered with nicotine. I might even have been a bit whiffy. The whole scene reminded me of an old man who regularly shuffled past my room on his way from the ward to the loo. He wore a faded fawn plaid dressing gown and looked remarkably like my Sandy Stone character, though he was probably no more than fifty years of age. He spent the day watching television and the elaborate cigarette commercials that regularly interrupted the programmes.

One morning he accosted me and, in a sibilant voice,

6 Otherwise known as the peace symbol, developed by the Campaign for Nuclear Disarmament.

(probably caused by a loose denture) and uncannily like the scratchy voice I used for Sandy Stone, he enquired, 'Excuse I, but have you been overseas recently?'

His last two words elicited a double whistle.

'Yes,' I confessed, 'in another life, I have.'

The old wreck became even more confidential. 'Have you ever been to the House of Dunhill?'

The word 'house' produced another piercing sibilation. I remembered the Dunhill commercial on the telly: a Rolls-Royce pulling up in Jermyn Street, a liveried doorman springing to attention, and an attractive aristocratic couple alighting on the pavement and glancing up at the name of the building in deco relief on its facia: 'The House of Dunhill'. Laughing, the woman accepted a cigarette from her companion and the camera zoomed in on the packet. The doorman flicked a Dunhill lighter and in a cloud of healing smoke they entered the building, presumably to buy more cigarettes. The old alky in the rehab corridor assumed a faraway look.

'When I get out of here,' he said, 'I am going overseas to see the House of Dunhill. It must be marvellous.'

On the word 'marvellous' he uttered a sound so shrill I assumed it was only audible to dogs and dolphins.

Edna popped in a few more times during my slow convalescence. Indeed, she was one of my few visitors other than the total stranger who appeared at the foot of my bed one morning, asked me my name, and promptly served me with divorce papers.

By the time I could totter out into the sunshine and resume my career – not exactly where it had left off – Edna's star had risen even further and her family saw less of her than ever. There were lecture tours, TV commercials and a new and surprising social life. During my absences in London and La La Land, Edna had forged links with a number of artists and authors and had even had her portrait painted by an artist I knew called John Brack. It was a frightening image. For the sitting, Edna had chosen to wear her peacock and cyclamen Thai silk outfit with its flyaway panel, the sheen of which Brack had miraculously captured. She wore long gloves which, in the portrait, looked as though they might conceal the claws of a harpy, and there was a predatory glint in her upturned turquoise spectacles. The painting now hangs in the Art Gallery of New South Wales on permanent exhibition and is one of its most popular pictures, but I cannot walk past it without a shudder. It is probably the depiction of her smile that I find is the most terrifying aspect of this portrait, and the teeth in particular. They remind me of a passage in the tale of 'Berenice' by Edgar Allan Poe:

. . . the white and ghastly spectrum of the teeth. Not a speck on their surface – not a shade on their enamel – not an indenture in their edges . . . I saw them now even more unequivocally than I beheld them then. The teeth! – the teeth! – they were here, and there, and everywhere, and visibly and palpably before me;

*long, narrow, and excessively white, with the pale lips writing
about them . . .*

Edna's immarcescible smile was never really pallid, and has most recently been incarnadined by MAC Cosmetics with a lipstick of her own invention – 'Kangarouge', which is popular with the young.

At this time, Edna had somehow managed to ingratiate herself with the curmudgeonly author, Patrick White, who adored his small circle of female friends, which then included Cynthia Nolan, the saturnine wife of a famous Australian painter, and the authoress Christina Stead. The thought of Mrs Everage as a member of Patrick's *salon* seemed to me ludicrous, and I felt, rather in Edna's defence, that she had been cynically adopted as a kind of camp mascot. Poor, silly Edna, I reflected.

However, the fact remained she was earning a great deal more money than I was as I scrambled to get my life back on track. Gone were the romantic pleasures of youth: the amorous dusks, the unreluctant lips. I did, during a brief interlude of bachelorhood, have a girlfriend called Lucretia, raven-haired and voluptuous, who, unlike her staid classical namesake, would not have found the approaches of Sextus Tarquinius faintly repugnant.

But now, no more – for the time being at least. Austerity, hard work and a new beginning awaited me . . .

We were eating our fruit salads, and even at La Terrazza they were English fruit salads consisting of a few slices of apple and a couple of grapes over which syrup had been drizzled. I realised Edna was still talking. I must have switched off a long time before, remembering that most painful phase in my life when the garrulous creature across the chequered tablecloth had been my sole hospital visitor. Now, five years later, we were in unlikely tandem and stars in the West End of London.

'Are you all right, Barry?' she asked, signalling for *il conto*, with a scribbling gesture in the air. 'A penny for them?'

I presumed she meant my thoughts. 'It would take too long, Edna,' I truthfully replied, reaching for the bill. But she had got there first.

'I'll pick up the docket, Barry,' she said, producing, to my amazement, a Diners Club card. 'My new accountant, Mr Oldman, tells me that I can deduct you.'

It was wonderful how Edna's every act of generosity had a little sting in its tail. So now I was deductible and simultaneously demeaned. I was maliciously pleased she still called the bill a 'docket'; an echo of the old Russell Collins days when the legend, 'thank you', in diagonal script, was inscribed on the folded paper on a saucer.

As we left to go to the show at the Apollo, I asked, 'Was there something else you wanted to tell me?'

Edna dropped her bombshell. 'I hope I'm not telling tales out of school, Barry,' she announced, 'but Mr White, our producer, wants me to take my show to Broadway and I'm going to tell him that I insist that you come too . . . in some capacity.'

As a matter of fact our producer, Michael White, a man of finely tuned theatrical instincts who intuitively knew which unremarkable girl one passed in the street would be the 'in thing' *next* year, had hinted to me that New York had shown interest in what Edna insisted on calling 'her' show.

'That's very nice of you to put in a word for me, Edna,' I said with wasted sarcasm as we strolled down towards Shaftesbury Avenue, 'but I wonder if the Americans will get it?'

I remembered Peter Cook's Establishment club and the shame of failure. I could see those New Yorkers sitting in uncomprehending silence as Mrs Everage let fly with one of her shrill but essentially regional tirades about suburban life. Did America have suburbs, I wondered? Would duck-egg blue venetian blinds be particularly risible to sophisticated New York theatre-goers? Would jokes about gladioli be especially hilarious, particularly when these rather dangerous flowers were flung at them from the stage with the force which Edna usually expended in her finale act? There had already been cases of dislodged contact lenses, and one man had asserted through his lawyers that a severe blow inflicted to the side of his head by a glad travelling at 20 miles per hour had impaired his sexual function. So much for the aphrodisiacal properties of the *gladiolus*, as claimed by the pygmies of Paraguay.

Our London season ended its successful run and soon after we were on a flight to New York. I am sure that Edna was already rehearsing her acceptance speech for every major theatrical award in the United States and it was a relief, in the light of my own misgivings, to have such an optimistic companion, for Mr White had appointed an American producer, Mr Cantor, whose demeanour gave melancholy a bad name. He was obviously happy to accept the money, which the London producer had invested in the New York show, but he had never seen it and did not appear to have the faintest idea what it was all about, nor did he seem to care. We were put up at the Salisbury Hotel opposite Carnegie Hall and the next day Mr Cantor took us down to see our theatre. It was about as far away from the bright lights of Broadway as it was possible for a theatre to be and was, at that time, 'dark' with a few human bundles sprawled on the steps, trickling urine. There seemed to be no restaurants or even bars in the vicinity, so with a sinking heart I realised that our modest offering would be unlikely to attract passing trade.

Housewife! Superstar!! opened and closed, but a lot of smart people came, including Stephen Sondheim with his friends, and Edna performed valiantly in spite of lukewarm reviews and one downright stinker in the *New York Times*. As the business trailed off to nothing, Edna, ever optimistic, would duck out of the stage door just before the performance and peer up and down the street to see if any tardy customers were approaching who might well boost audience numbers up to as many as twenty. If the cast at any time should outnumber the audience it was not, traditionally, necessary to proceed with the performance, but since there were only two of us, the show invariably went on.

I'm wrong to say there were two of us when, in fact, on the first night there were three. We were introduced on stage by an Australian diplomat called Les Patterson, a man I had unfortunately met before, who was on some sort of retainer from the Australian Tourist Board to promote our cultural achievements. He had interrupted the London show more than once, usually in a state of extreme inebriation, and been encouraged to excesses of lewdness and expectoration by the laughter of an audience which could not believe that this man was an accredited representative of the Australian government. His reappearance in New York, especially on our first night, probably alienated the reviewers more than the show itself, and he was scourged by the critics.

It was impossible to explain to incredulous friends and journalists that this shambling, belching figure in a stained powder-blue suit, whose substantial member seemed to struggle impatiently against the fabric of his left trouser leg, was tame when compared with most other Australian politicians at home. He suffered, it later emerged, from a condition called RPS (restless penis syndrome). Edna loathed Les Patterson, and she admitted to me later that she had met him in Melbourne many years before her marriage when she had, to use an expression she never used, once 'dated' him. Patterson, as far as I could gather, had made some inappropriate suggestion accompanied by an unacceptable gesture, and Edna confessed that it had almost put her off Sydney for life.

'Why Sydney?' I asked.

'He is so horribly Sydney, don't you think, Barry? No one from Melbourne would behave like him. I doubt if any of his ancestors came to Australia of their own accord.'

This is the only reference I've ever heard her make to our convict past.

However, Mrs Everage was strangely unperturbed by our off-Broadway debacle. 'I'm not going to let that horrible man spoil my trip,' she declared as I sat gloomily with her one morning in the Russian Tea Room, nibbling on blinis. 'I'm not going to let Les Patterson live rent free in my head, Barry.'

I noticed she was beginning to adopt certain catchphrases of popular psychology. Moreover, she had moved into another hotel. It was the raffish Chelsea Hotel on West 23rd Street, which had considerably declined since Mark Twain stayed there and was now a haven for *louche* would-be artists and Andy Warhol hangers-on. I had heard of Edna pointedly referring to a friend of hers called Andy, but I did not realise who he was until she introduced me to a deathly pale, albino-like personage with bleached spiky hair and a languid manner.

'He's doing my portrait,' she told me excitedly. 'He just takes a few snaps and fiddles with them. He wants me to be in one of his films too, and his friend John Waters is writing something called *Hairspray* and calling one of the characters after me.'

I found it hard to envisage Edna, or the Edna I knew, the Moonee Ponds mum, in this aberrant milieu. Would she be smoking dope next?

'You probably want to go back to Australia soon, to lick your wounds, Barry,' she said to me impertinently one day, about three weeks after our show had folded. 'But I like it here, and so might you if you came with me and Liza to Studio 54 one night. I want you to meet my new girlfriends Divine and Brigid Polk.'

I found Edna's most recent excursions into the demi-monde rather disturbing but I did accompany her one night to Studio 54 where she seemed to be on very friendly terms with the boy drink waiters who, like lissom ganymedes, danced, rather than walked, amongst the thronged patrons, wearing hotpants and little else.

'Hi, Edna!' they cried.

'Hi, darlings!' she replied gaily, snatching a Harvey Wall-banger from a proffered tray.

She had begun, regrettably, to address total strangers as 'darling', a theatricalism like 'boobs', which was subsequently appropriated by ordinary, and sometimes *very* ordinary, people. The drinking too, though moderate, was out of character, but I thought she deserved a fling of some kind before returning to Moonee Ponds; moreover to a urologically challenged husband, a resentful New Zealand bridesmaid and three poten-tially delinquent children.

I decided that whatever she wanted to do, and I dreaded what that might be, I would return to Australia. As unobtrusively as possible, too, for I could already see the faces of those grinning journalists.

'Show didn't go down too well in the States, did it, Baz?'

'Reckon your mate Edna will have to hang up her glads and go back to Moonee.'

I shuddered to imagine the full extent of my countrymen's *Schadenfreude*.

'I'm staying on a while,' Edna announced just before I left. 'I'm going back via Las Vegas. Lee would never forgive me if he knew I'd been in America without seeing him.'

'Lee?' I enquired.

'Liberace, you silly billy,' said Edna. 'I met him on his last tour in Australia and we clicked.' She gave me a meaningful look and the teeth of Berenice flashed.

'I think we might click again.'

12

Home Truths

'You see, Barry, not everyone likes you,' said my mother with a hint of triumph.

She had just been listening to a popular phone-in radio programme on which an elderly ignoramus and harridan housewife had been sounding off about me and the gross disservice I continued to do to Australia's overseas image. Apparently there had been others on the programme as well, none of whom had ever seen me in the theatre, but whose splenetic outpourings – so worthy and so patriotic – the disc jockey had fomented with considerable relish. My mother could not help but agree with it all. It was, after all, officially sanctioned: it was on the air.

To have left America, smarting from critical rejection, and

abandoned by my feather-brained protégé, only to fly 10,000 miles back to Melbourne to rent a car and be greeted by my own mother as if I had committed some act of treason, was a dispiriting homecoming.

She was sitting in her favourite chair with its tasteful mushroom upholstery, the chair she had occupied almost without interruption since the death of my father on the fourteenth hole of the Riversdale Golf Club. She looked thin and sallow, but strangely robust in the blue peignoir I had bought her from Georges. Behind her, through the French windows, a huge camellia flashed its glossy leaves and displayed like big pink brooches the enormous blooms my mother so loved.

Not everyone likes you. It was a disappointing salutation as I stooped over her chair to kiss her cheek, though a painful arthritis of the neck prohibited her from making more than the slightest responsive twitch. Every now and then my mother could sound just like Edna. It was a chilling thought which, if further provoked, I might one day share with her. She would be horrified.

Melbourne enfolded me like a favourite frayed sports coat. In my hired car I drove down the familiar streets in the suburbs that never seemed to change, though the city centre, in its quest for up-to-dateness, was more or less a write-off, but old friends still lived there, prosperous and cocooned in family. Actors I had known and worked with in my youth were now doctors and detectives on television and the beautiful young actresses who had stayed safely in Australia had grown older, had married, and would soon be playing lesbian convicts in

Prisoner: Cell Block H, a riveting 'soap' about caged women. It was the end of the road, and few of its stars went on to a post-vincular career.

Then, artists who had resisted the siren call of 'overseas' sanctimoniously boasted that they did so out of loyalty to the local industry; that they could easily have become Hollywood stars but they chose to give their talents to Australia and to that 'cultural renaissance' that was always thought to be happening, or about to happen. Patriotism was an alibi for cold feet. Well, for better or worse, I had at least taken the plunge, and in the nick of time before I could be recruited into a fictitious hospital or police force.

I had been back in Australia nearly two weeks, more or less skulking. I supposed that only a few friends and family members knew I was there. There were still a couple of hacks I might bump into, who regularly wrote nasty articles in the *Australian* and the *Sydney Morning Herald* exposing me variously as a fraud, a middle-class snob, a fascist, out of touch and not faintly funny. Indeed, to this day, there is a pompous old bore and ex-Xavierian[7] who writes a political column in the *Herald* and who periodically feels the need to squeeze his pustules in public on the subject of me and my undeserved popularity.

Before leaving Melbourne, I thought I should take the long drive over to Moonee Ponds and see how Edna's forsaken family were managing without their gallivanting matriarch.

7 Xavier College, a prominent Roman Catholic school and acne centre of Melbourne.

I suppose I should have telephoned first but I thought it might be more amusing and instructive to catch them unawares. Night was falling as I stood once more on the familiar porch with my finger on the bell. There were signs of neglect. The hydrangeas had dried up and the small front garden seemed woefully derelict. In the fading light I saw that the bank of gladioli against the fence, which had been Edna's pride, had clearly not seen a drop of water for weeks, and the flowers stood sere and shrivelled like bundles of papyrus. The gusting north wind carried to my nostrils a peculiarly acrid stench. Someone must be burning rubbish nearby, I surmised.

At length, Kenneth Everage opened the front door and stared at me through the flyscreen. He had grown a lot since I saw him last and he was wearing flared jeans and clogs, his skinny torso enclosed in a pink T-shirt advertising a popular dance orchestra called The Sex Pistols. His mouth was full of dressmaking pins and he held a length of fabric in his hand.

'My mother's out the back,' he managed to mumble through the pins. With the raised pinkie of his free hand, he smoothed the hairs on his left eyebrow.

'Who's that, Kenny?' came a shrill cry from within.

Without admitting me to the house, Kenny retreated into the shadowy hallway.

Then a woman's voice with a distinctly Kiwi twang said, 'Show him into the lounge room, Kenny, and get him a wee cup of tea. Barry is practically family.'

Looking rather the worse for wear in a fawn dress I had seen before which exactly matched her skin in colour and texture,

Mrs Allsop appeared in the doorway and ushered me in.

'Listen,' she said, 'you must think we're awful, but Kenny is so busy with his fashion design course his manners have flown out the window.'

'Is Edna home then?' I asked in astonishment as I seated myself in a Genoa velvet armchair.

'Only just,' said Madge, her eyes rolling upwards. It was only the second moderately disloyal gesture I had ever seen her make.

'She's in a filthy wee mood, too. I was so busy with Norm I'd let the garden die and old Mrs Beazley is a handful at the best of times. Edna is out the back at the incinerator, having a clear-out. She won't be best pleased seeing you without her lippy and a nice dress, and I think she's caught something called jet lag, but don't worry, I don't think it's infectious.'

As I passed through the house towards the back veranda a humming noise came from Norm's room and I noticed the whole house vibrated imperceptibly, teacups chattering on the dresser. Reading my thoughts, Madge explained, 'That's his prostate machine. His wee organ was rejected after the op. I always turn it to low when the doorbell rings but normally it's deafening, especially if he has a power surge in the middle of the night.'

It was almost dark when I stepped into the back garden. At its shadowy extremity behind a trellis I saw a black metal drum with a great plume of sparks rising heavenward.

'Edna!' I called. 'I thought you were still in the States.'

'Just as well I came back when I did,' said a soot-smudged,

dungareed figure hurling enormous bundles of heterogeneous objects and textiles into the inferno. 'Madge has let this place turn into a pigsty and I'm amazed Norm is still alive. As for my poor mother, she's been left to rot in the front room. We had to get the fire brigade to dig her out. This is what happens when you trust people.' Edna's sigh was almost a groan of despair. 'They always let you down. Promise me you'll never trust a poverty-stricken New Zealand widow,' she concluded bitterly.

Not being, for the moment, able to envisage such a situation, though glancing over my shoulder to see that Madge was not in earshot, I politely gave Edna my word.

Dropping her pitchfork and a bucket of rubbish, Edna suddenly lunged forward to give me a hug and a peck on the left earlobe. It was a display of intimacy as surprising as it was anomalous. She had never kissed me before and it was impossible to imagine her kissing anyone, let alone passionately, as she may have once done, long ago, with the father of her children. Many years were to pass before she adopted the modish, and rather un-Australian habit of presenting both cheeks on greeting.

'What are you doing down here in the dark, Edna?' I asked, clamping a handkerchief to my nose and mouth. The stench from the incinerator was becoming unbearable, perhaps even toxic.

'I'm burning my mother's things,' she said simply.

The firelight reflected in her eyes like red-eye in an amateur snapshot.

'It's not altogether Madge's fault,' she added generously. 'This was once my mother's house, so Norm and I let her live on here, but she's a terrible hoarder. She's never thrown anything out. She's got copies of the Melbourne telephone directory going back to 1942. When the fire brigade broke into her room one of them had to run out into the street and have a bilious attack.'

'But,' I protested, 'doesn't she mind you clearing out all her belongings? That bed jacket, for instance?' A garment which Edna had just held over the flames on the prongs of her garden fork sent up a gorgeous fountain of sparks. 'Surely those books and photo albums might have sentimental value.'

I had no sooner referred to them than Edna swiftly consigned them to the bibliocaust with the rest of her mother's magazines and knitting patterns.

'Mummy won't miss them,' said her daughter with something like merriment. 'Besides, she's asleep. We gave her one of Norm's knock-out drops. She'll wake up sometime tomorrow and wonder why her bedroom is ten times bigger than it used to be.'

We were interrupted by Madge's cry from the back door, telling us there was a cup of tea and a pikelet waiting for us on the kitchen table. As we walked back to the house, Edna muttered, 'Don't touch her pikelets. It's about all they eat in New Zealand apart from pumpkin soup. But if you look at her fingernails you won't need my advice.'

Seated at the laminex kitchen table in that relentlessly aqua and buttercup yellow kitchen, Edna rather crossly slammed down her Melbourne Olympics souvenir mug. 'What happened to the Earl Grey?' she snapped at Madge who was busy buttering pikelets with her fingers, which confirmed Edna's minatory words in the garden. 'I'm sure Mr Humphries would prefer Earl Grey.'

Whenever Edna referred to me in Madge's presence, she always did so with a formality usually reserved for servants. If Madge had ever called me Barry in her presence she would have had a fit.

Earl Grey tea was a recent discovery in Australia and came into vogue at about the same time as Scrabble and homosexuality. I've never particularly cared for warm beverages that taste of bath salts but this was one of Edna's first forays into Sophistication. It was odd to be with her again in such a humble setting when I had last seen her chatting to Leonard Cohen in a dimly lit bar in Greenwich Village.

With her undeniable ESP, Edna suddenly declared, 'Guess who I had a letter from this morning?'

I shrugged and gave my brow an interrogative corrugation.

'Leonard Cohen! My Lenny! You might have heard that we saw quite a bit of each other when I was at the Chelsea Hotel in New York,' she added coyly and with (did I imagine it?) a faint blush. 'He said he'd wished he'd written his Chelsea Hotel ditty about me. But I think it's about that Janis Joplin minx.'

Edna, sitting there at her own kitchen table in her sooty overalls and sfumato make-up, leant towards me and looked searchingly into my eyes. 'That Janis Joplin was a bit of a sipper wasn't she, Barry?'

I said I thought she was, but wasn't everyone?

'You and Janis had a little thing once, didn't you, Barry, when you had that terrible flop at The Establishment?'

Sometimes I wish I remembered more about the sixties, or less.

Suddenly, with a slight pang, I did recall an erotic interlude after a liquid lunch at Hennesseys on the Portobello Road: Janis's bourbon breath, her lewd smile and slattern's hair. 'I suppose we did,' was all I could say, a bit embarrassed.

'Len and I had a bit of a thing as well,' she continued to my astonishment. 'He wanted to do naughty things until I explained I was an unhappily married woman. That always puts them off I believe,' she added sagely.

'*Unhappily* married!' I exclaimed. 'But what about Norm? I thought you were a devoted couple.'

'If only that were true, Barry,' she said, her eyes filling with tears. 'Of course we were, many moons ago, but things have not been easy lately, as you can imagine.'

As if to reinforce her words there was a sudden mechanical roar from somewhere within the house, like a generator starting up.

'One day,' Edna sniffed, 'I'll tell you about something I did; something wild and passionate and uninhibited.'

'Can't you tell me now, Edna?' I asked her.

'No, Barry, I can't, because I haven't done it yet,' she said. 'But when I have, I'll let you know. Call me old-fashioned but it won't be until Norm has been gathered.'

For a moment I wondered if I was hearing the whole truth.

Changing a delicate subject, I asked. 'So Leonard Cohen stays in touch?'

'Oh, yes. I never thought I'd like a Canadian, but Canada is exactly the same as Australia when you think about it, except for the pine trees, the Mounties, the beavers and Celine Dion. On top of that Leonard said that I could possibly be Jewish.'

'Jewish!' I exclaimed with an involuntary hint of anti-Semitism.

'Well, to start with I'm clever,' said Edna, 'actually more clever than most people, and from a certain angle . . .' Edna tilted her head, displaying a profile that was certainly non-Aryan or at least un-Nordic. 'Also, when I was very young, I could play mah-jong and canasta without anyone teaching me. That has to prove something!' Then, triumphantly, she added, 'And at the age of ten I could over-cook chicken.'

Throughout this extraordinary conversation I had been uncomfortably aware of Madge Allsop's presence in the kitchen as she slowly, perhaps too slowly, prepared more inedible and dangerous pikelets. Suddenly, in imperious tones, Edna addressed her bridesmaid.

'You're taking a dickens of a long time over those pikelets, Madge, and probably listening to every word we're saying, too.'

The New Zealand crone turned towards us a face of blank innocence.

'Don't give me that look, as though New Zealand butter wouldn't melt in your mouth,' Edna snapped. 'I happen to know you've been writing a diary about everything that happens under this roof and that you probably expect to sell it for a lot of money one day.'

Madge looked horrified at this suggestion and I could not help but reflect that her story might be very saleable indeed in some quarters.

'Well, Madge,' Edna continued with a note of malice in her voice that I had never heard before, 'if you look under your mattress where you keep your evil jottings, you'll find nothing but fluff. It's not just Mummy's things I've been dropping in that incinerator, but some of your rubbish as well. I doubt Rupert Murdoch will give you a penny for a pile of ash.'

Madge fled from the kitchen and after a few moments we could hear the poor woman keening in the distance as she realised the fate of her memoirs.

Edna gave me one of her broadest smiles as she rose from the table and flicked Madge's pile of pikelets into the pedal bin.

'Don't worry, Barry, she won't give me any trouble. I'm her bread and butter, and the roof over her head. If she didn't have me, she'd have to go back to Palmerston North[8] and she's certainly not wanted there.'

There was a voice at the kitchen door. 'I'm up, Mother.'

It was Norm in pyjamas and dressing gown, his sparse hair dishevelled, his face waxen. Trailing behind him were tubes and ducting which, if followed like Ariadne's thread, would probably lead to his prostate monitor which continued to

8 The eleventh-largest city in New Zealand.

thunder away. Possibly Norman Everage had antecedents in the north of England where, to this day, a husband might sometimes call his wife 'muther', though it was a particularly unsexy form of address with a hint of the incestuous. Did that famous northerner D. H. Lawrence ever call Frieda 'muther', I wondered?

'What are you doing up, Norm?' cried Edna in alarm. 'Did Madge disturb you with her whimpering?'

'No, Mother, it wasn't her,' replied her urologically challenged husband. 'Doctor Rentoul-Outhwaite says I need to get on my feet every now and then, and I was having a bit of a scout around my room looking for some of my books.'

'What books, Norman?'

Her ghostlike husband was stretching a bony hand towards me in greeting.

'For heaven's sake, Norm,' said Edna, 'you're straining your ducting. If you're looking for those war diaries of yours and those dusty old photo albums of you and your mates, you won't find them in your room any more. Since I've been away, this place has become a dust bowl and a paradise for silverfish.'

Norm looked devastated. 'But Mother, those war diaries they . . . they were interesting, weren't they?'

Edna laughed. 'You silly billy, Norm, you haven't looked at them for years and you never really served in the war like my brave Uncle Victor. You weren't fit enough, and who'd want to read a diary about you doing office work?'

'Well, I would, Ed. I would.'

'Well,' said Edna, 'it's a fine time to want to read your old diaries now because they're in the incinerator along with all those photos and the silverfish, but if you really want to read something decent I'll put another publication on your page-turning machine. How would you like *The Devil's Alternative?*'

For a second Edna's husband looked at his wife as though she was the Devil's Alternative, and with a tragic nod in my direction he shuffled back to his room. I never saw him again.

'Thanks for popping in, Barry,' said Edna, 'but I'd better go back and give that incinerator a poke. Have you ever noticed how hard it is to burn books?'

13

Back With a Vengeance

As we were about to open the biggest show of our joint careers, Norm died. Death chose, as is His custom, an inconvenient moment, and I feared that Edna would be too distraught, or would wish to appear too distraught, to make opening night. Some weeks before, Qantas had brought Norman Everage to London along with Mrs Allsop and what would now be called a 'carer' by the name of Sister Thelma Younghusband, a battleaxe of whom Edna was ridiculously jealous. Sister Younghusband had spent some time in the Far East in her early years of nursing, and Edna was concerned that she employed oriental techniques when she administered the more intimate phase of Norm's sponge bath. I had ridiculed this suspicion several times but for

Edna, the Younghusband threat was an *idée fixe*.

'That's how Mrs Simpson got the Duke of Windsor,' she proclaimed. 'A lot of women used to go to Singapore and learn horrible, heathen practices to use on defenceless invalids.'

'I don't think the Duke of Windsor was an invalid,' I protested, 'and I don't think Wallis Simpson ever went to Singapore.'

'Well, you *would* think that wouldn't you, Barry? You're such a male chauvinist!'

It was the catchphrase of the period, and I had forgotten that Edna was acquainted with Dr Germaine Greer, the eminent Australian thinker and feminist. She had often claimed that Germaine, a frequent visitor to the house in Moonee Ponds, had picked up a few valuable tips in male management from the Everage household. Throughout the seventies Edna maintained, no doubt to Dr Greer's intense annoyance, that she had single-handedly dictated *The Female Eunuch* with a minimal contribution from Germaine.

However, we had a major production to mount and little time to do it. *Back With a Vengeance* at the Strand Theatre in the Aldwych was probably the most important show of my career, and it was enough for me to try and get it on the road without having to find accommodation for Norm and his equipment.

'Lord Norm must be comfortable, Barry,' said Edna loftily, and I realised that she really believed that if she were indeed a Dame of the Realm, her spouse would automatically be a Lord. Edna had taken to calling herself 'Dame Edna' ever since a socialist Prime Minister of Australia, Gough Whitlam, had in

Hats off

Edna hears an unpalatable truth

Introducing Charlton
Heston

Singing with Jerry Hall

Sharing a joke backstage

Edna the spectacle

OPPOSITE: A radiant Edna

Transported by Sir Richard Branson

opposite: Edna posing

The Kiwi help

jest addressed her as 'Dame Edna' during the filming of a documentary. Edna had leapt at the title, insisting that the Queen had ratified the honorific, and this indeed may have been true since by now Edna had forged strong links with Buckingham Palace. Perhaps she deserved a Damehood, for Australia was very short on Dames due to a creeping republicanism, and we only had Dame Joan Sutherland. These were the days before Nicole Kidman or Cate Blanchett or even Elle Macpherson.

Edna Everage had become, without question, the most famous Australian woman in the world, though I found it hard to put my finger on the reason why. I suppose she was a woman people wanted to believe in, yet the rumour persisted that she and I were the same person and that I, by some terrible mental aberration, had chosen to dress up in her gaudy habiliments and parade myself on the stage, soliloquising in a falsetto and chucking gladioli. It was preposterous of course, but it must be an attractive myth for it found its way into several books and biographies and may even be perpetuated on Wikipedia. Not owning a computer, I wouldn't know.

Norm had barely been installed in a mansion flat in Westminster when his condition, always perilous, worsened. As Edna was busy rehearsing with me at the Strand she was temporarily residing at the Savoy for its convenience to the theatre. She kept saying that she must visit her husband to ensure 'that Younghusband woman wasn't "tampering with his equipment"', to use her distasteful phrase, but she rarely got around to it. Compassion was not Edna's strong point, although, paradoxically, she often said, 'Barry, my problem is I care *too much*'.

Certainly, it was a problem she successfully overcame.

Just before our gala opening night, with Princess Diana in attendance, the event I dreaded occurred: Norm flatlined. Edna, always an instinctive publicist, and seeking to put a positive spin on her bereavement, proudly announced at a press conference that she was donating her husband to medical research and that he would soon be globally recycled. She even arranged to show a short film tribute to her late husband at the beginning of the show, working in the cutting room overnight while Madge and I were left to arrange the funeral.

The media were unanimous in their praise for *Vengeance*. There were headlines which Edna might have written herself, such as 'Brave Edna Triumphs', 'Grieving Widow Smiles Through Her Pain', 'Dame Edna Wows Di'. Most of the newspapers carried photographs of Edna and Princess Diana; Edna in a magnificent, if slightly provocative, black taffeta dress. I appeared in most of the photographs, but was usually cut off, or was in blurred focus, and I was never mentioned in the caption.

Two weeks into the run, I called a business meeting. I had important matters to discuss with 'Dame' Edna, much of it to do with taxation since the show seemed destined for a huge financial success, but she constantly avoided me.

'*Can't you see I'm grief stricken?*' she always cried. 'That murderess has a lot to answer for!'

She was, of course, referring to Sister Younghusband, who had been quite genuinely distraught at the passing of her patient.

One morning the nurse came to see me at my home in Hampstead without an appointment. I opened the front door, not at first recognising the middle-aged woman who flung herself into my arms, sobbing uncontrollably. I led her into my den and brought her a cup of tea.

'That Edna,' she at last managed to say between bitter sobs. 'She didn't care for him at all, and as for that bridesmaid of hers, that Madge . . . Goodness knows what kind of relationship *that* is. I've lived in nursing homes long enough to have a pretty shrewd idea.'

I looked at the woman on my sofa. She no longer resembled the battleaxe that I had first supposed her to be, in her neat tweed suit with a cameo brooch pinned to her blouse and with her plain, but not unappealing tear-stained face beneath an iron-grey bob. Now she struck me as a deeply hurt and well-intentioned woman.

'He was the sweetest, gentlest man I have ever tried to nurse back to normalcy,' she said. This was the age of Normalcy. We had not yet reached the epoch of Wellness.

'You mentioned Edna and Madge?' I said, choosing my words carefully. 'Are you implying, Sister, that there was something, well, improper in their friendship?'

'I don't know what's improper any more in this day and age,' said the nurse, snatching a rosette of Kleenex from the box I proffered, and dabbing her eyes. I noticed she was looking around my study which was lined with indelicate engravings by Franz von Bayros and Felecien Rops.

'Perhaps there is something the matter with me. Perhaps there is something wrong with being normal,' she declared, inspecting a particularly licentious image in which three *fin-de-siècle* Viennese ladies cavorted with gross impropriety in a boudoir. Her lips tightened into a thin disapproving line.

'I have never suspected anything of the kind, Sister Younghusband,' I said, 'and I think you should realise that anything improper is impossible. Mrs Allsop comes from New Zealand.'

The nurse stood up, sensing perhaps that a longer sojourn in my den might well place her in moral danger. 'Edna didn't care for him one little bit, Mr Humphries,' she said, her voice wavering. 'In she'd come with that bridesmaid of hers, eat the grapes and be off to her posh new friends. It broke my heart to see it, but Norman didn't seem to mind so long as I was there.'

Her self-control collapsed and Thelma Younghusband, in floods of tears, fled towards the front door. As I ran to open it, she turned, and with a visage smudged by grief and in a muculent voice, she said, 'Yes, Mr Humphries, I'm crying, and I will cry for the rest of my life! I loved that little man. I bet *she's* never cried. Look at her eyes next time; they are eyes that have *never shed a tear.*'

With a muffled howl she stumbled down my front steps and was gone.

I thought about the nurse's words which had been uttered with such savagery. It was true that I had never seen Edna give a real demonstration of emotion. She did not seem to feel things in the same way others did.

That evening I tapped on her dressing-room door. I had arrived at the theatre very early to rehearse a song and had not expected to find Edna there. Quite often she would turn up fully dressed, minutes before the curtain rose, much to the consternation of the stage manager. Katie, her maid and dresser, admitted me and I found Edna sitting at her dressing table, peering into the mirror.

'That Nicholas de Something in the *Evening Standard* was right when he called me an "attractive Barbra Streisand",' she exclaimed. 'Aren't I lucky, Barry, to have such wonderful skin? I hardly need any make-up at all. Did you know the skin is the largest organ of the body?'

'I suppose I might have,' I replied.

'Would you like to touch my largest organ? Most people want to but they're too shy to ask.'

I seated myself down on a chintz sofa, uncertain how to begin. Flattery was the best way to start, I decided. 'You're wonderful in the show, Edna, amazing really considering the bereavement. It must be hard for you.' I was watching her eyes in the mirror; they did seem remarkably dry. Perhaps she was born without tear ducts.

'I believe in professionalism, Barry,' she said, applying a little rouge with a sable brush. 'Call me old-fashioned, but I do. I have been saying goodbye to Norm in my heart for quite a few years now. I will always miss him but he told me a big fib before we were married and I never got over it.'

Katie became extremely busy, primping a costume and bustling about, so I knew she was listening.

'A fib?' was all I could say.

'He told me he was ten years younger than he really was and I only found out when we were signing the register and he had to put down his date of birth. I married a senior citizen!'

'But he did give you three children, Edna,' I said, not merely in defence of Norm, but also perhaps in defence of all older men who dissemble about their age in pursuit of sexual gratification.

'There were four, Barry. Don't forget Lois.'

It occurred to me that Edna loved Lois the most of all her children, possibly because she was dead.

'Katie!' Edna cried, addressing her maid. 'I think I'll wear the apricot chiffon tonight. Could you pop downstairs to wardrobe and give it a steam?'

The girl did as she was bidden and when we were alone in the dressing-room, Edna turned towards me wearing an expression on her countenance I had not seen before.

'I was a very wicked woman once, Barry, and I've never told a living soul. I want to make a little confession to you.'

I decided this might be the best opportunity to employ 'uh-huh therapy'. 'Uh-huh,' I said.

'Many moons ago, when I was up in Sydney giving a talk to the Sydney Institute on "Whither Australia", someone took me along to a concert at White City.'

'Uh-huh.'

'Do you know who I mean by Frank Sinatra?'

'Uh-huh.'

'Well, Barry, it was Frank and I was in the front row and I'm sure he could see me from the stage and when he sang "Strangers in the Night", he seemed to be singing it just for me.'

The mention of 'Strangers in the Night' very nearly caused me to say 'uh-ugh' but I restrained myself, already aghast at what might be forthcoming.

'After the concert I had a note from one of his minders, that Frank would like to meet me. I already knew I was his type since he'd been married to Mia Farrow and we have the same bone structure.'

'Uh-huh.'

'I expected his dressing-room to be packed with groupies,' Edna continued, moving her chair closer to mine, 'but we were alone, just me and Frank Sinatra. "Edna, you're a classy broad", I remember him saying, offering me a cigarette. I didn't want to seem prim so I tried to smoke, and had a coughing fit. Then Frank asked me out.

'"How about you and me hitting the town, babe," he said grabbing me roughly by the shoulders. "But I'm an unhappily married woman," I said, hoping that wouldn't put him off. "Just the kind I like, kiddo," he said. "Let's go back and have a drink in my suite at the Boulevard."'

I tried to say 'uh-huh' but it emerged as an incredulous

croak. Edna shifted her chair even closer to mine and resumed her remarkable narrative.

'I was carried away, Barry. It was as though I had taken a drug and all I'd had was a little cocktail Frank had spent a long time fixing up for me in his kitchenette. Things went woozy and I woke up fully undressed in a strange room. Where was I? I wondered, and I could hear someone in the bathroom, singing "My Way" very badly and slightly off key. It *had* to be Frank Sinatra, and the woman in the bed had to be me – an unhappily married woman, far from home.

'Suddenly a burly man appeared beside the bed, holding a walkie-talkie. "Get your clothes, lady," he said roughly in an American accent, "Frank's busy but there's an envelope on the hall table. Pick it up on your way out." When his back was turned I clutched at my frock which was in a heap on the floor and retrieved my undergarments which seemed to have found their way to the bottom of the bed. I felt soiled, I felt used.

'Oh, Barry, the shame of it, the shame! And I could still hear Frank crooning away under the shower as though he hadn't a care in the world.

'Somehow I got out of that room and into the lift. I didn't dare look at the faces of the hotel staff and I was praying the *Kings Cross Whisper* would never get hold of the story. I've been so anxious about what you'd say if you ever found out . . . What a fool I made of myself–'

I interrupted. 'I never heard a hint of this, Edna, though it's amazing the Sydney press didn't pick it up. Frank wasn't their favourite boy in those days.'

'Look at my eyes, Barry,' said Edna suddenly. 'What colour are they?'

I peered through the gem-encrusted apertures of her spectacles. 'A sort of greenish-grey, with a bit of hazel,' I said.

'And do you remember Kenny, my son, who designed this frock? Do you remember the colour of his eyes?'

I didn't, and I said so.

'They're blue, Barry, they're blue! My son is Kenneth Sinatra.'

14

Success

W e transferred from the Strand to the historic Theatre Royal in Drury Lane and the audience expanded to fill the new venue. We had a hot ticket. Edna always seemed to have the audience in the palm of her hand; she could do no wrong and I travelled comfortably in the slipstream of her success. She rarely invited me to her little after-show celebrations in the dressing-room or at The Ivy restaurant, but I glimpsed quite a few of her famous visitors including Michael Caine, Charlotte Rampling, Stephen Sondheim, Judi Dench, Sting and Princess Michael of Kent. Not a sign of Frank Sinatra, however.

Edna never returned to the conversation we had shared in her dressing-room and I wondered if she regretted telling me, fearing perhaps that I might one day betray her confidence and publish her confessions in a book, but I believe she thought me incapable of such a treacherous act. What a foolish woman she was.

Edna was beginning to show a great deal of interest in material things. She started to buy art, mostly by female artists like Tamara de Lempicka and Frida Kahlo. Some years later film producers begged her to play the role of both these women in feature-length movies, but she was always too busy, and generously recommended that they cast Salma Hayek instead, a little known Lebanese actress whom Edna pitied.

'Tell me when my eyebrows start growing together in the middle, Barry,' she often said.

The revelations about her son Kenny's possible parentage had set me wondering about the welfare of her children. Madge had gone back to Moonee Ponds after our opening night, charged with looking after them, but I was beginning to receive alarming reports. Brucie seemed to have his head screwed on and was studying accountancy. Young Kenneth had become Australia's youngest dress designer and his mother was enthusiastically promoting him by wearing the creations of this juvenile prodigy on stage. It was Valmai who was the loose cannon.

One afternoon I received a phone call from the Australian High Commissioner and I feared it might be yet another official complaint about Les Patterson who, when drunk, periodically interrupted our show. I think he was in love with Edna but regarded her as inaccessible. If only he knew how available she could be, I thought, remembering that the Boulevard Hotel in Sydney was not only Frank Sinatra's preferred Australian abode, but also the sometime accommodation of Bob Hawke, our rough-hewn Prime Minister and, had he but known it, a popular location for the sexual intrigues of many politicians.

But it was not Les Patterson he wanted to talk about.

'Look, Baz,' began the High Commissioner, 'Dame Edna's daughter has got herself into a fair bit of strife back in Melbourne. Her and another sheila were picked up in Myers pinching some panties and a whole swag of other stuff. When the store detective accosted them they let fly with some pretty nasty verbals that I can't repeat.'

'Who was the other woman, Geoff?' I asked. 'She must have been leading Val astray.'

'No way, Baz,' said the dignitary. 'Valmai was the ringleader all right, and she's as tough as old boots. Between you, me and the gatepost, I'd say they were a couple of deadset rug munchers.'

'What's that?'

'You know, Baz, fur traders, bush bandits . . . *Lezzos*!'

'Has this hit the press?' I asked, fairly horrified.

'Not yet, Baz, but it's something they'll really lap up, if you'll excuse the expression.'

I had to break news of the incident involving her daughter to Edna as gently as I could, but it was a matter of some urgency and I could not mince my words. Surprisingly, she took it quite calmly, if a little cold-heartedly.

'That girl has been asking for trouble for a long time and

she has certainly been mixing with some weird Sydney types who have put silly ideas into her head. This is what comes of leaving hopeless old Madge in charge of my children. I'll call a friend of mine who is high up in the Melbourne Police. A little cheque from me will do the trick and, being a senior policeman, I'm sure that he will accept it without embarrassment, though they generally prefer air tickets and holidays in Thailand.'

And so it was. A week later I put another call in to Australia House.

'It's all gone quiet, Baz,' said Geoff. 'She got off without a charge and an apology from Myers because she reckoned she was just going out into the street to check the colour of her panties in daylight. Smells fishy, I reckon, if you'll forgive the expression.'

The uproarious laughter of the Australian High Commissioner echoed through the phone as I replaced the receiver.

Back With a Vengeance had been running for several months at the Theatre Royal before I finally got Edna to sit down for a proper business discussion. I was earning quite good money from my role as producer and the commission on Edna's share of the take, but all the money passed through the hands of her accountant before anything filtered through to me. Edna had engaged the services of Ian Smee B.Sc. ACA who had been highly recommended to her by a singer called Gary Glitter whom Edna had met in the first-class lounge of Bangkok airport.

'He's saved me a bundle,' Edna told me, 'and he's set me up with a very sexy little scheme in the Cayman Islands. I'd swear by him on my mother's grave, if she was dead.'

'I think my accountant might like to get a few up-to-date figures from him, Edna,' I said gently. 'The show has been running to full houses for a few months now and, apart from the odd cheque, I haven't seen any numbers.'

Edna laughed. 'You won't either, Barry. Ian says it's best if we keep it all verbal, so as not to alert *you know who*.' She winked and tapped the side of her nose with an index finger.

It all felt far from satisfactory and I thought I should probably meet this Ian Smee to see if my observations tallied with those of Gary Glitter.

The accountant insisted on buying me lunch at Scott's on Mount Street, and I had a good opportunity to study him across the Dover sole meunière. The first thing that struck me were his cufflinks, which were very large, gold, and appeared to have come from a Harrods cracker. He wore a shirt in a style much favoured by accountants: a blue striped front with a contrasting white collar. His tie . . . Well, he wore no tie. He wore his shirt open at the neck to suggest casualness and that he was a man in a hurry. It was a fashion which would later catch on big time: men who wished to advertise their success would also soon neglect to shave and refrain from tucking in their shirts.

Ian had an infuriating habit of saying 'to be perfectly honest with you'. Between the dressed crab and the crème brûlée he must have said it at least twenty times. He also seemed slightly ill at ease in a grand restaurant where I was known and he was not.

'To be perfectly honest with you, Barry, Edna is very special to us at Goldblatt, Williamson and Smee and we have her specific instructions to look after you, to be honest.'

'I'm glad to hear that,' I replied a bit pompously.

'Oh, yes,' continued Smee, hooking food particles from the interstices of his badly capped incisors with a toothpick. 'The dosh goes straight from the theatre to the Netherlands and after a ridiculously small withholding tax we bung it across to Hong Kong where it travels on via San Francisco to the Isle of Man.'

'But the cheques I've had seem to come from Luxembourg,' I said. 'Is that OK?'

'To be perfectly honest with you,' said Ian Smee, skolling his espresso and frowning at his enormous gold, faux Rolex watch, 'it's best you don't ask too many questions. Just thank Christ Edna's looking after you.'

And with that he seized my hand in a knuckle cruncher and was off into Mount Street, leaving behind a strong and pungent whiff of Kouros for Men.

I was far from comforted by my meeting with Edna's financial adviser, but my own lawyer, a fellow Australian, seemed to think everything was, in his own words, 'kosher'. He liked saying 'kosher' and he liked saying 'at the end of the day', and he particularly liked saying 'I have to say'. When I expressed my financial anxieties to him directly, and gave a sketchy description of the profoundly sleazy man who had bought me that expensive lunch, all he said was, 'I have to say, at the end of the day, everything's kosher.'

I received an approach from David Bell at London Weekend Television proposing a series for Dame Edna. These were the days when people in executive positions in television companies actually went to the theatre and liked showbusiness. It was a long time ago. I negotiated what I thought to be a good deal, though I was chagrined to note my services as a performer were not required. Edna was the star, and I was merely a go-between; a conduit, a cipher. I suggested, however, that she do a talk show, a genre then hugely popular, where the public felt they were on intimate terms with famous people seated on couches talking about themselves and their latest film/book/football match/TV series/album/wife/catamite.

The accountants to whom David Bell was ultimately responsible weren't too certain that this was a good idea, and one of them may have picked up the scurrilous rumour that Edna was not what she seemed. The fact that I would be in the control room while Edna was in the studio went some way towards reassuring them.

Thus it was, when our triumphant season at Drury Lane ended, that we found ourselves in rehearsal for what would be a groundbreaking, cutting-edge, seminal, pivotal and much imitated television format. It was to be called *The Dame Edna Experience* and it became a cult series, internationally acclaimed. I feel justified in employing this absurd hyperbole since I had little or nothing to do with the show, but it marked the apotheosis of Dame Edna.

As if following some kind of grim cycle, my own domestic life had once again hit the skids as it had a decade before. So, when we had finished filming the first series, Edna decided she had to get back to Australia to take over the reins of parenthood. I wondered if her children would now recognise her. All seemed quiet on the Valmai front, though my spies informed me that she no longer lived in Moonee Ponds and was 'sharing' with a metalworker called Trish in the nearby suburb of Northcote. Brucie had branched out from accountancy and was developing various enterprises like macadamia furniture, bankrolled, as I later learnt, by Edna.

I had lingered in London for a few days after Edna's departure in the hope of a welcome cheque from Luxembourg with Smee's compliments, but nothing came. I had other legal concerns of a matrimonial kind so, avoidant by nature, I jumped on the next plane to Sydney trusting that everything would sort itself out in the end. If Ian Smee was not returning my calls, he was probably, like most business people in England, at lunch or on holidays or had 'just stepped away from his desk'.

Again, with a dream-like sense of déjà vu, I found myself behind the steering wheel of an Avis rental on a Melbourne street visiting my mother who was, by this time, seriously failing in health. The camellias no longer adorned the tree but were a brown mulch at its foot, but my mother, desiccated though she was, still remained as shrewd as ever.

'I hope you're making plenty of the wherewithal, Barry,' she said. 'You were never good with money, were you?'

'I never had any to speak of,' I said.

'Watch that woman, Barry, and you know who I mean by *that woman*,' cautioned my mother. 'She's a user, and she'll bleed you dry if she gets half a chance.'

'Edna is a complicated woman,' I explained, 'but she's not a thief, to be perfectly honest with you.' I stopped short as I heard myself employing Ian Smee's favourite phrase. Edna might be honest, I thought, but what about her 'people'?

'There was a man here the other day from the tax department and he wanted to know where you were. I hope you're not in some kind of trouble, Barry. Your father always used to say, "Barry will learn the hard way".'

The mention of my mother's visitor was like a cold hand entering my breast and closing its icy fingers around my heart.

'Don't worry, Mummy,' I said, arranging the carnations and daphne I had brought her in a Gouda vase, 'I've dotted all the "t"s and crossed all the "i"s. Everything is kosher.' Where had I heard that phrase before, I asked myself. And why was it not reassuring?

'I want you to come out to the cemetery this afternoon, Barry.'

It was Edna's voice on the phone. 'We're all going to have a look at Norm's obelisk.'

Sure enough, an impressive black limousine picked me up

from the Windsor Hotel at 2 p.m. It was full of people. Edna sat in the front seat next to the driver wearing a black outfit, as if she had slipped back into mourning as a sort of afterthought. In the back with me was Bruce Everage, a serious young man with damp hands, dandruff and a very worried expression. Perhaps the bottom had fallen out of macadamia furniture, I thought. Kenny, who seemed almost too young to shave, gave me a whimsical look and pursed his lips in greeting me. He seemed comfortably in touch with his feminine side, though he wore some kind of leather outfit with a lot of chains and a little leather cap with a chain over the top, serving no purpose that I could divine. On his left cheek he bore the crimson imprint of his mother's kiss.

'Where's Valmai?' I asked cautiously as we took off for the cemetery.

'She and Trish are coming in Trish's truck,' said Edna in an offhand way, as though there was nothing at all peculiar about two young women adopting this form of transport.

Was she in denial about Valmai's gender choice, I wondered? Or was she a better actress than I thought?

At the Carlton Cemetery we turned a few corners, passing neglected tombs and several new mausoleums in sparkling granite with oval photographs of Sicilian peasants embedded in their architraves, and names like Rizzoli and Martucci engraved on their stone lintels. Norm's obelisk was unmissable.

'I never told you this, Barry, and I suppose you would have thought I was hard-hearted when Norm found the road too weary and the hill too steep to climb, but I commissioned a famous Australian sculptor to design this.'

It was indeed impressive, and yet ambiguous. A huge sphere of red-veined marble rested on a white plinth which bore the legend 'Here lies some of Norman Everage, beloved husband of DAME EDNA EVERAGE'.

Edna looked at it for a while and rummaged in a Fendi purse for her handkerchief. Was this the moment, I wondered, when she would at last shed a tear for her departed husband? Instead she deposited a generous dollop of spit on the lace hanky and gave Norm's obelisk a vigorous buff.

'Those horrible birds,' she said, as if she was making an important ornithological discovery. 'They go to the toilet wherever they like.'

No one, I noticed, asked what had inspired this inflated marmoreal gland. The physiological object, or its maquette, lay below, or elsewhere.

15

Born Again

Back at the Windsor Hotel on Spring Street, Melbourne, late on a winter afternoon, I felt more intensely than I had ever felt before the mood of melancholy that hangs over the city at this time of year. It always seemed different in the summer, with trips to the beach or 'spins' into the country, when the city parks and gardens, filled with English trees, bloomed and blossomed, and we could almost believe we were in the Old Country, or at least in some kind of geographical comfort zone. But Melbourne on a winter evening always felt to me like the uttermost part of the earth with its alien skies, gamboge with archipelagos of tattered indigo clouds, and Antarctica just over the horizon.

It was strange being a Melbourne person and yet living in

an hotel like a tourist, though admittedly it was a Grand Hotel. The Windsor was one of the few important buildings from the Opulent Era that the wreckers of the fifties and sixties had left standing, and presumably this was an oversight. I occupied a suite of rooms on the second floor which was more like an old-fashioned suburban vicarage embedded in an hotel. There was even a fire in the grate, always well stoked by a porter, and I could stand at one of my tall windows and gaze at William Wardell's neo-gothic masterpiece, the triumphant cathedral of St Patrick, completed at the turn of the nineteenth century, with its spires conceived by Wardell and added, like an after-thought, in 1938.[9]

Edna, somehow gentler after her bereavement, seemed fully occupied with her family, devoting much time to her favourite son, Kenny, who seemed to have many talents. In spite of his gifts as a *wunderkind* of the fashion world, he had expressed a keen interest in working for the Qantas airline as a steward, or as what would now be pretentiously called an 'inflight service director' so as to avoid being stigmatised as a mere servant. Kenny, his mother told me proudly, liked the coral pink blazers he had seen the airline stewards wearing when they had taken a trip to Singapore together. He had also worked in a record shop, and an antique shop, specialising in Lalique glass, whimsically called Dead People's wedding presents.

9 William Wilkinson Wardell, 1823–1897, was a London-born ecclesiastical architect of St Patrick's, Melbourne; St Mary's, Sydney; and the gothic ES&A Bank in Melbourne which has accidentally survived.

Edna's relationship with Valmai seemed more fraught with difficulties, and it was during this time that she embarked on a disastrous course of protecting Valmai from the consequences of her many delinquencies. Many years and heartaches later, at a closed meeting of Megastars Anonymous, Edna learnt that she had 'enabled' her daughter by constantly bailing her out and failing to let her reach her 'rock bottom'. For Valmai, 'tough love' came too late.

I had my own anxieties, however, as the money I was owed in London never materialised, and Ian Smee seemed to have disappeared off the face of the earth. But wasn't embezzlement something that befell other people? I asked myself. Was it conceivable that, thanks to Edna and her venal adviser, I had been working these last few years for nothing? On top of that, the rumblings from the Taxation Office grew more audible. Had I dotted the wrong 't's? I wondered. Perhaps that honest-faced, smiling Australian lawyer with his white collar and contrasting shirt had not been kosher at all, at the end of the day.

Weeks of inertia and, I now realise, depression, dragged on, although I somehow managed to write a book and spend time with my family and friends. There could be a very big tax bill in the pipeline so I decided that a new show was the obvious money-earner if I could cobble one together.

Spring finally came and at our old family beach house at Mornington, amongst the sweet-scented tea-trees, I began my labours, rethinking a theatre show that would present some new characters of mine, like Lance Boyle, the corrupt but loveable trade union troubleshooter. Edna would take a back seat in this production as I conceived it, and I would restrict her appearances and take upon myself the financial and artistic burden of the show. That way, I reasoned, the Ian Smees of this world would not have their hands in my pocket.

I had reached a stage in the script when I thought I might need to have a chat with Edna about her new, 'less arduous' role in the forthcoming production, but when I telephoned Moonee Ponds, Kenny told me she was 'having a break' some- where and he didn't have a contact number. He sounded shifty but he did let slip that the old house was for sale and they were moving to a modern apartment in St Kilda Road. Australians were just beginning to call flats 'apartments', which made them sound more impressive, and possibly more saleable. People overseas had apartments, though not the sensible English, who still had no objections to living in a flat. The idea of moving to St Kilda puzzled me since I always thought Edna considered it to be a Roman Catholic enclave, though the Jews, with more justification, might have claimed it as theirs.

Thereafter, every time I telephoned Edna she was never there and neither was Madge. I could find no one to tell me where she might have gone or for how long, so, in desperation, I called Goldblatt, Williamson and Smee to see if they had any information or even a telephone number. The person who answered in London imparted the chilling news that GWS no longer existed and was, moreover, in receivership. All their files had been seized by the Department of Customs and Excise and the company was under investigation by the Inland

Revenue office. Mr Smee's whereabouts were unknown, Mr Goldblatt was on the Costa del Sol and Mr Williamson had committed suicide. Feebly, I asked if they had heard of Dame Edna, or knew where she was, and the girl on the other end of the line got quite excited and said that she didn't know, but there had been a lot of calls and she had referred them all to Edna's agent.

'Dame Edna's agent?' I exclaimed, not yet recovered from the demise of Smee's office and the consequent disappearance of all my money. After a brief delay, Meredith, who had insisted on telling me her name (though why I would want to know that only God knows), came back on the line.

'All enquiries for Dame Edna have been referred to the Talent Factory, Shepherd's Bush, attention Wanda Smellie.' Meredith laughed as she told me this, though I saw little to laugh at.

There had to be a mistake. Was it possible that Edna had appointed another agent without telling me and without officially terminating our contract? Did our friendship and long association mean nothing? I called Ms Smellie and was put in a queue. I listened to what I presumed to be heavy metal for at least seven minutes before the operator came back on the line to ask me, for the second time, whom I wanted and why. When I told Mahbuba – she thought I'd like to know her name – she asked me if my call to Wanda Smellie was in connection with Rod Stewart, George Michael or a group called Camel Toe.

'None of them,' I snapped, close to tears. 'I want to talk to her about her client Dame Edna, and I'm ringing from Australia, for Christ's sake!'

'Don't use dat tone with me, sir,' said Mahbuba in a manner which suggested that if I raised my voice again I could be up before the Race Relations Board. 'Lady Edna,' she continued, 'she new client, she been on our books only few months now and we no give away personal details. Better you write letter.'

My patience was at an end and I was devastated by what I had just been told, and its implications. 'Just give me Ms Smellie, please Bubbagumba, and I'll discuss it with her.'

'Dat's not my name you silly sir, and Mrs Smellie, she step away from her desk – she off-site!'

'What else is new?!' I yelled, slamming down the phone.

If Edna had walked into my room then, I would probably have thrown the instrument at her.

Edna, it seemed, was also 'off-site'. She had vanished and I was not at the moment inclined to raise the hue and cry. I knew that if she were ill or had even died, Kenny would have been the first to know, and his tone of voice on the telephone, though guarded, was not grief-stricken. To mention her disappearance to the press would have been a very bad idea since the taxation authorities, who may have been quietly pursuing her, might think she was on the run and the whole thing would rebound on me.

In the light of what I had recently learnt about her emotional constitution, my instincts told me that she was lying low some-where and, moreover, not lying alone. Sexual passion was never something I could easily attribute to that woman, so the revelation about Frank Sinatra was a shock from which I never quite recovered, but she had talked quite a lot lately about her new gynaecologist, Dr Julio Iglesias, the father of the famous Iberian singer. Dr Iglesias had assured her that she still had her 'drives and juices', to use Edna's unappetising phrase. Suitably aroused, these may well have impelled her to some act of romantic folly which might one day be revealed, but until then I would keep on writing the new show.

Oddly enough, I felt a burden had been lifted from my shoulders. I no longer had to be responsible for this woman's career.

'She's held you back, Barry, can't you see that?' said my mother, who had just had her hair done, as she always did in anticipation of my visit. 'If it hadn't been for meeting her, you might have had a nice profession and not a hand-to-mouth ragtime job like the one you've got now.'

My mother's generation still employed the name of the dance-craze of 1911 as an epithet denoting chaos or just fre-netic muddle. However, my career *was* pretty ragtime. I needed to get it back under my control and, if possible, as I approached middle age, pick up a few profits for myself.

'I hope Edna will be in the new show,' said an excited journalist over the phone after I had announced my new theatrical offering. 'We all love her.'

'Of course she will,' I heard myself saying, 'but she's

changed quite a bit since her last tour and she's even more glamorous.' Then I added, 'You mightn't recognise her.'

I had made a bold decision. Since Edna had defected, perhaps forever, I would impersonate her myself! It was something I had done in the past with great success. Well, at least once, anyway. We were almost exactly the same height and if I rehearsed my falsetto voice there was no reason why the 'new Edna' would not deceive even the most observant *aficionado*, though it might be best to avoid the ministrations of Dr Iglesias and his rather alarming new invention – the heat-seeking speculum.

It is not the purpose of this biography to explore my own sentimental history, or to cause embarrassment to the women I have known in my life, or to whom I might have been married; however, at this rather lonely period in my career, I embarked upon an *affaire* with a BBC make-up artist called Vanessa who was on vacation in Australia. She had long legs which attractively converged and, oddly enough, no navel. Her doctor father, the obstetrician who delivered her, had by some surgical sleight of hand erased, what was to him, an offending belly button. As she reclined immodestly on her back in my suite at the Windsor, the absence of such a significant anatomical punctuation mark gave her torso a curiously uninterrupted look.

Vanessa was an amusing and somewhat saucy blonde, or partial blonde, whose favourite phrase was 'be my guest', an invitation hoarsely uttered before striking a concupiscent pose. Sometimes I thought she may have been a contortionist, or at least an aspiring one. I'm reminded of James Mason, that wonderful actor, introducing me to his wife, Clarissa, and proudly murmuring when she was out of earshot, '... and she's a *contortionist!*' Pillow talk with Vanessa was often difficult as the soles of her feet were not infrequently pressed to her ears.

It looked as though she might have moved in, and I didn't, as they now say, have a problem with that. On the contrary, she was bright and good company and I told her of my secret plan to become Edna myself.

'I could help you with that, baby,' she said gleefully. I had never been called 'baby' before and it was not exactly descriptive but nice all the same. 'I'll get Richard at Wig Specialities in London to send out a couple of mauve wigs. They must have your fitting on record, but I won't say they're for you. This is a secret, right?'

She did have a habit of saying 'right'[10] a bit too often, but beggars can't be choosers.

We did a few trial make-up sessions and, as a matter of fact, in an outsize frock, I actually looked better than Edna; I looked something that she had never been – pretty. Vanessa hooted with laughter.

'You look quite sexy in that outfit, baby, rather a turn-on,' she said, and I hastily changed back into myself before the perverse creature had a chance to invite me to be her guest.

There was still no word from Edna. Like Agatha Christie,

10 In contemporary usage 'right' is now referred to as 'OK'.

she had vanished, but for much longer. Kenny told me on the telephone that the old house at Moonee Ponds had been acquired by the National Trust and was to become a Dame Edna museum and tourist attraction. I viewed this idea with deep scepticism but refrained from comment.

'Will your mother be coming back to open it?' I probed.

'No way, José,' he said absurdly, and once more I heard the defensive tone in his voice. 'If you really must know, Mum's gone to meet the Dalai Lama and hang out in an ashram. She told me not to tell you, but she wants to be born again!'

She will be, I thought, she will be.

16

The Talent Factory

I was naïve to suppose that Edna would be out of my life forever. Like Henry Higgins, I had grown accustomed to her face, and even at her worst, as she had been on that night beside the incinerator assisting in the combustion of her family's memorabilia, there was a kind of brutal panache about her which disarmed total condemnation. I could never in my most extravagant imaginings picture her in spiritual colloquy with the Dalai Lama, sitting crossed-legged in a saffron peignoir on a Tibetan hillside, but since that far-off evening at the Holy Trinity, Moonee Ponds, when I had first seen her, mauve hair clotted with Vick's VapoRub and stooped over her Saviour's feet, she had had many unforeseeable adventures.

My friend Vanessa had postponed her return to London and

was eager to assist in my transformation. Together we visited department stores in search of large flamboyant dresses, something I could not have done on my own without embarrassment. At one particularly expensive shop in Melbourne called Delphine, which specialised in pricey Paris modes, I pretended I was looking for a dress for a very tall female friend, larger than Vanessa – my size, actually. As I slipped into a changing room with an armful of silk and chiffon, the sales girl smirked knowingly. 'You don't have to pretend that you're buying these for a friend, Mr Humphries,' she whispered. 'All the boys get their frocks here.'

To my irritation, Vanessa enjoyed this humiliating episode, but she was a useful collaborator – conspirator, really – and especially helpful in her own field of expertise: make-up.

There was a television appearance coming up in Sydney with Mike Walsh, a popular midday TV host, whose audience consisted almost entirely of women and Edna lookalikes. I had promised them my client Dame Edna, and they were not to be disappointed. I would deliver her all right. I just hoped they wouldn't spot the deception. I felt a surge of power and excitement. I had been marginalised too long.

On the morning of the show we spent several hours at the Gazebo Hotel in elaborate preparation for 'Edna's' interview. I had shaved up as well as down in order to present Vanessa with a smooth and flawless canvas on which to create her masterpiece. The wisteria-tinted wig from London, inspired by the coiffure of the young Margaret Thatcher, fitted perfectly and the fake jewellery looked better than the real thing. Unfortunately the rings that we had bought, encrusted with paste diamonds like chunks of broken milk bottles, didn't fit, but Vanessa said I could probably have them resized for Edna's next appearance. She had done that with her mother's wedding ring, she explained, kicking off a sandal and displaying a gold band encircling the first metatarsal of her exceedingly long Morton's toe,[11] a propitious deformity of which she was hugely proud.

I began to feel uncomfortably nervous as we put the finishing touches on my disguise. Vanessa produced her new Minolta camera bought duty-free in Singapore for only a fraction more than what it would have cost on the Tottenham Court Road. Suddenly I was beset with anxiety as to what I would say once I was on the set and face to face with Mike Walsh. I had impersonated Edna before, but long ago in Sydney when the real Edna was unknown. I could have been fat with frizzy red hair for all the audience of those days would have known, but today I was appearing on national television in the guise of an already recognised star. My mimicry had to be flawless. The real Edna could chatter away about anything but I was naturally more circumspect — even, I reluctantly admitted to myself, ponderous at times. The main thing was to maintain the vocal impersonation, the uniquely Australian rising inflection at the end of each sentence and Edna's habit of saying 'Look' before practically every sentence.

11 First identified by orthopaedic surgeon Dudley Joy Morton. A common term describing the condition where the second toe is longer than the big toe. In ancient Greece a Morton's toe was considered a sign of royal descent.

Vanessa, posing as my assistant, personal photographer and make-up artist – which she was – said she would try and sit in the front row of the studio audience and if my voice threatened to drop into a more masculine timbre she would do a little 'voice up' gesture with her fingers. Through my sparkling harlequin glasses I looked at her with gratitude and incipient ardour. What other girl did I know who would devote herself to such a bizarre task? She was really quite a perfect young woman, notwithstanding her Morton's toe and her omphalectomy. If I ever fell in love I hoped it would be with someone like her.

As I stepped out into the street to the waiting taxi in uncomfortably high heels, I was greatly reassured when a couple of women passing by called out 'Hello, Possum!' I cooed back, 'How very sweet of you! Don't miss me on Mike Walsh today, will you, Possums?' Vanessa gave me a broad wink and a little thumbs-up sign as we climbed into the cab.

'I'm buggered if I know what I'm going to say on this show,' I said anxiously. 'What if he asks me about the Dalai Lama?'

Vanessa shot me a panic-stricken look, jabbed her finger in the direction of the driver and gave me the 'voice up' signal. Thereafter, I remained exhaustingly falsetto and in character for the long drive out to Channel Nine on the North Shore. I wondered what I would do if I needed to pee. It would have to be the Ladies room. They were always cleaner anyway.

I had been to Channel Nine many years before in the very first weeks of Australian television and now, all these years later, the building was substantially the same. There had been a rough attempt at landscaping around the entrance but otherwise the studios looked rather like a run-down factory. As we swung into the driveway I noticed an enormous white Rolls-Royce, of the kind favoured at Greek weddings, standing at the studio entrance. Could this be Kerry Packer's vehicle, I wondered, thinking of the formidable but ill-favoured tycoon who ran the network and much else.

As we tottered towards the reception area, I narrowly missed spraining an ankle in my high heels in the gravel outside. The girl behind the desk looked startled, almost as if she'd seen a ghost.

'Excuse I,' I shrilled, 'I think Mike is expecting me on his lovely show.'

The receptionist, whose name-plate proclaimed that she was called Fellatio, or something like that, seemed transfixed, and appeared to be dialling a number on her avocado telephone. Behind her were blown-up photographs of Mike with some of his other guests: Tom Jones, Spike Milligan, Diana Ross, but mostly people I didn't recognise. Somehow I felt I was not getting the VIP treatment I had expected.

'I'm Sue Farrelly,' said a young woman at my elbow. 'I'm Mike's producer. Can I help you?' She seemed to be laughing. There were even tears in her eyes.

'Look,' I replied magnificently in character, 'I don't think I need an introduction, Possum. Please just show me my dressing room so that Miss Peddlingham can touch me up.'

At this, Ms Farrelly was unable to contain her laughter, which emerged as a painful snort. 'I'll take care of this, Felicia,' she said. Giving the receptionist a rather rude conspiratorial glance, she ushered us through a doorway and down a series of shabby corridors.

Absolutely nothing had changed since 1956, I reflected. There was still the same smell of tomato soup (or was it baked beans?), the effluvium from an adjacent canteen.

'There is someone here you just have to meet in our green room,' Sue said, flinging open a door. 'It's our other celebrity guest.'

I saw a nuggety little woman in a black leather pantsuit seated on a couch and leafing through a copy of *Variety*. She had an unnatural tan, cropped grey hair and narrow black-rimmed glasses, and she was smoking.

Beside her stood another woman, tall and thin, in a fuchsia cocktail dress that was heavily beaded. There was also an encrustation of rhinestones on her extravagant glasses which glinted beneath a lilac coif. The eyes behind the glasses widened in astonishment.

'What the dickens do you think you're doing, Barry, dressed up like Lady Muck?!' exclaimed Edna, for it was she.

Lady Muck was a personage also frequently evoked by my mother during my childhood to describe pretentious women. She was the antithesis of another mythical figure, the Wild Man from Borneo, with whom anyone who was deranged or just mildly untidy was inevitably compared. 'You can't go to school like that, Barry. You look like the Wild Man from Borneo.' Perhaps long ago, at the Royal Exhibition in Melbourne in 1888, these two great anthropological archetypes had been displayed and had thereafter entered the racial memory.

'Have you gone completely dippy?' continued Edna heatedly. 'Who are you supposed to be in that silly get-up? I think I moved my affairs to Wanda Smellie in the nick of time.'

The other woman ground her cigarette into an ashtray and glared at me. I felt shamed, busted, overwhelmed by emotions I had not felt since I was a schoolboy dragged to the headmaster's study by Peter Beer, the head prefect, for dodging compulsory football. It was ignominious thus to be found out and at a loss for a plausible explanation.

I was not the clever actor and writer I had thought I was but simply a man approaching middle age, wearing a wig and a frock in a room full of scornful and reproachful women. Why wasn't Edna in Tibet for Christ's sake? I wondered. Why had I not been suspicious, or at least sceptical when Kenny had deliberately leaked that misinformation?

'But Edna . . . I thought . . . Well, aren't you supposed to be in Tibet?'

'Does this look like Tibet?' exclaimed my former client, surveying what I assumed to be the green room which was adorned with more photographs of Mike, arm in arm with Jerry Lewis, Des O'Connor and Lauren Bacall.

'You're on in a couple of minutes, Dame Edna!' Sue Farrelly had reappeared. 'Do you want me to get rid of these people?'

Edna gave Sue her sweetest smile. 'I'm sure they'll leave of their own accord, Ms Farrelly,' she said. 'To think that I told Wanda such nice things about you, Barry, and now she sees you like this. She's come all the way from London to hook up with me and lock in a few deals. Nothing could have prepared her for this.'

I noticed Edna was beginning to use showbiz speak. Vanessa looked ready to bolt.

'And who is this, prithee?' asked Edna, turning on the girl and slipping from the theatrical mode to the archaic.

'This is Vanessa Peddlingham, a friend of mine.'

Edna's gaze combed the young woman from head to foot. 'Are you a friend of Barry's lovely wife?' Edna enquired with more than a hint of malice. 'If she knew he was in the habit of dressing up in female apparel she would have divorced him long before she did. I always felt sorry for her, and seeing you now, Barry, makes me pity her even more.'

A young man in jeans and a Mike Walsh T-shirt appeared at the door. 'You're on straight after this commercial, Dame Edna,' he said, but he said it to me.

'Oh no, he's not,' snapped Edna. 'He's an imposter and he's leaving now.' Then she swept out of the room.

'I think we'd better fuck off as well,' said Vanessa with her usual bluntness.

'Yes, I think you should,' interrupted Ms Smellie, lighting another cigarette and struggling to her feet. For such a small person she had a disproportionately large gluteal development. 'Thanks to your mismanagement, Dame has been under a lot of strain. She's in emotional overload.'

It was the first time I had ever heard this phrase, though more recently it has been applied to the amateur Scottish singer

Susan Boyle, whose precipitous television success took a grave psychological toll.

'Dame's condition has deteriorated since the show in London and that Broadway fiasco,' continued the agent. 'Far from being in Tibet, Edna has been in a rehabilitation centre in the Queensland hinterland called the Golden Window under an assumed name, getting back her health and sanity. We leaked the Dalai Lama story as a smokescreen and in your case it seems to have worked.'

At that moment I decided Wanda Smellie was one of the most unpleasant women I had ever met in my life.

'Edna has always defended you,' she went on, 'but having seen you now with my own eyes, I can see what an unstable person you are. Unstable, and . . .' the agent cast a contemptuous eye on my finery, '. . . *deeply disturbed.*'

Attired as I was, and in that horrible little green room in Sydney, I would have been at a severe disadvantage in any business discussion, but I heard myself protest, 'Edna and I have a contract. I represent her and when her son told me she was visiting the Dalai Lama and might have to cancel this important television appearance, I thought the simplest thing would be to cover for her. I was doing her a favour.'

'That contract isn't worth the paper it's written on. Our legal team at the Talent Factory said it was a joke.' Wanda Smellie put her face so close to mine that I could inhale her breath, in which tobacco and gastritis commingled to produce a curiously nutty odour. 'We look after some of Elton John,' she continued, pausing to let the famous name sink in. 'Now, if Elton lost his voice or couldn't do a gig, do you think that I'd put on a pair of glasses and a red wig and go on stage and sing "Rocket Man"? Do me a favour, Mr Humphries, and do Dame a favour as well!'

Wanda Smellie, aptly named for a woman whose oesophagus seemed to be directly connected to her bile duct, was not an American but she had the American habit, born of colonial ignorance, of treating a title as though it were a Christian name.

Vanessa was tugging at my arm and I should have delivered a zinger in response to this hateful creature. If only I could have come up with a brilliant one-liner and demolished the harridan who had stolen my client and, I dare to admit, my friend. But no words came. I tried to imagine her enormous bum enveloping a piano stool and her nicotine voice croaking 'Daniel's Song'.

'We've ordered you a taxi,' coolly interposed Sue Farrelly. 'You might like to know that Edna is killing them out there.

'She's in top form,' Sue added. 'She's telling Mike all about life on an ashram with the Dalai Lama. It's absolutely fascinating!'

17

Smail's Place

Soon after, Vanessa returned to London and her job at the BBC. I said I hoped to see her when I got back to England and characteristically, she replied, 'Be my guest, baby,' but with a discouraging absence of sentiment. Did I imagine it or had I disappointed her in some obscure way? The confrontation with the real Edna and the insulting behaviour of Wanda Smellie was an embarrassment, certainly, and when we got back to the Gazebo Hotel it was salt in my wounds when Darryl, the gay doorman, greeted us with 'Loved you on Walshie, Edna!'

But I suppose I had lost a lot of points with Vanessa; I was suddenly a failure, and out of a job. Perhaps I only imagined a cooling of her previous ardour, but I had lost my self-assurance.

'You did make a fool of yourself.' It was Wanda Smellie's voice on the telephone and I was glad to be relieved of her physical presence. 'Dame was very upset when she left the studio, but she's too much of a professional to let it show.'

Professional, I thought. What total rubbish! She's never been more than an inspired amateur.

'I think she thought that you respected her,' continued the dwarfish Wanda. 'The way you've bungled her career makes me think otherwise.'

'Edna was nothing when I met her!' I exploded with a surprising savagery, looking across the hotel room at the tousled bed where Vanessa and I had slept before she left for the airport. Perhaps in its inner recesses it was still warm from her body. 'Edna was a silly suburban housewife who *begged* me to represent her. I pretty much gave up my own career to put her on the map, and now that she's a bit of a star, she's fallen for your sales pitch. She'll regret it one day, you bet your life.' I had to sit down. My heart was pounding as my old adrenalin addiction kicked in.

'Dame belongs at the Talent Factory,' barked Wanda. 'Right now we are crafting a whole new career strategy for her. There'll be books, films, merchandise, oven mitts, records, and even wigs and glasses.'

'Wigs and glasses?'

'You don't know how many people there are today who want to be Dame. Our team at the Talent Factory has done market research in Japan and that's just the tip of the iceberg.

Dame needs to be an international brand and we are in the business of seeing that she becomes one.'

This was a period in recent history when everyone was 'in the business' of doing things. They were even 'in the business' of doing business.

'I notice you call Edna "Dame",' I said with heavy sarcasm. 'Are you American, Ms Smellie?'

'I live in south London,' she said, 'but as a matter of fact, my room-mate Fran comes from Los Angeles. Why?'

'It explains something, that's all,' I replied. 'And don't think I am dependent on Dame Edna for a living. I have my own career, my own interests, which are quite separate from hers. In fact, I haven't held her back as you say, it is she who has held *me* back. You have done me a favour, Ms Smellie, a big favour.'

I replaced the receiver feeling the exquisite tendrils of adrenalin reaching out to every extremity of my being.

'Good riddance to bad rubbish,' said my mother. 'I wouldn't lose any sleep over that woman.' There was rather a large headline in the *Sun News-Pictorial* on her lap: 'Edna Signs With Top Agent' and then a photograph of my ex-client with a champagne flute and a triumphant-looking Wanda Smellie, looking surprisingly like Elton John on a bad day. 'We're proud to have her,' the agent was quoted as saying. 'She's a major talent and a very handsome woman.'

With Vanessa gone, I moped around Melbourne spending

time with my daughters, and returned to my old love of painting, mostly exuberant landscapes, which belied my mood of despondency. I saw some old friends, two of whom were from my university days, and it occurred to me that for the past few years I had spent most of my time with strangers and very little with the people I cared most about.

New restaurants were springing up in the city and I read in *Australian Gourmet* magazine that there was one highly recommended in unfashionable Moonee Ponds, of all places! That evening I suggested to my brother that we drive out there and sample the cuisine. It was called, rather unpromisingly, 'Smail's Place', and the chef was a fellow called Clifford Smail who had formerly worked at Glo Glo's.[12] It was a long, narrow establishment, formerly a Greek café, and there was a large, crudely painted panorama of an idealised Athens on the wall as a testimony to its previous incarnation. There was no menu but instead the bill of fare was written on a blackboard and carried from table to table by a young waiter whom I thought I recognised. Moreover he seemed to be looking at me intently.

I love soup. 'What is the soup?' I asked the youth. It was described on the blackboard merely as Soup of the Day.

'I know that waiter,' I said to my brother Michael. 'I've got a feeling that I even know him quite well.'

The young waiter returned to the table and proudly

---

12 Glo Glo's was a fashionable restaurant in Toorak owned by the *grande dame* of Australian restaurateurs two decades ago, Gloria Staley, whose grandchildren quaintly addressed her as 'Glo Glo'.

announced, 'I've asked Cliff and he said it's *soupe du jour*.'

'It's Kenny, isn't it?' I exclaimed. 'Edna's boy. You've grown such a lot that I didn't recognise you.'

Kenny pursed his lips and writhed slightly. 'Look,' he began, his mother's son, 'I'm sorry I told you Mum was in Tibet on the phone that time but we all had to say that. She's gone back overseas now with that new ball-breaker of an agent.'

'And how's Valmai?' I enquired. 'Behaving herself?'

'She's down in Daylesford with Trish, running a Battered Wives hostel. It's just me and Madge at home now. I'm working here for Cliff to make enough moolah to get through my fashion design course at the Royal Melbourne Institute of Technology.'

'But what about old Mrs Beazley?'

'Oh, Nanna's still there in the front room. She's collecting stuff again, mostly plastic bags. She's getting a bit more exercise lately since we found her that old shopping trolley.'

As we waded through the nauseating fare, a glutinous risotto of chard and yabbies followed by Phillip Island skate with an oxtail and apricot *ragu*, I thought what a nice young man Kenny seemed to be. His apparel could best be described as skimpy, tight white jeans and a sleeveless T-shirt and he had dyed the tips of his hair blond like Billy Idol and done something to his eyebrows, but I was ashamed not to have recognised him immediately. I suppose I had warmed to him a little because he seemed to be on my side rather than Wanda's.

'This is on the house,' said Kenny, placing the gooseberry and goat's cheese crumble before us.

'How is your mother, Kenny?' I ventured to ask.

'She's in LA doing a show for NBC, and I'll be doing the frocks!' he declared excitedly.

A very large bald man with a black beard and a blood-stained apron appeared at our table. In his left earlobe an earring glinted piratically.

'This is my boss, Clifford Smail,' said Kenny. There were too many 's'es in the sentence for Kenny to articulate without sibilance.

The restaurateur extended a beefy hand with the cracked and grubby fingernails common to all chefs, especially tele-vision chefs with their fingers in close-up. 'Beauty,' said Clifford. 'We're big fans aren't we, Ken?'

'Has Dame Edna ever eaten here?' my brother asked, trying to conceal with a napkin his barely devoured entrée.

Kenny suddenly looked anxious. 'Don't tell Mum I'm working here,' he said. 'She thinks our family is above this kind of thing now. And she's not that wrapped with Clifford, is she, Cliff?' The two men exchanged a rather meaningful glance.

'I'm afraid your mother has given me the sack, Kenny,' I said ruefully. 'But please let her know that I'll always be there if she needs me, *as she will*.'

To my surprise the entire meal was free, which is just as well since, on the return journey, my brother had to stop the car at the corner of Mount Alexander and Elizabeth streets so that I could be violently sick.

How time had flown, I thought. Kenny was just a child when I first met his mother and now he was growing up and forging a career of his own. Not without bitterness I wondered, how much progress had I made in all that time? I had been sidetracked by Edna; diverted from what might have been quite a spectacular career.

My flight back to London went via the United States and I yielded to the temptation to stop over in Los Angeles for a couple of days. I had a friend at NBC who might sneak me into the studio audience for Edna's first recording, which I hoped would be a great success – or did I? There had been a lot of publicity about *Dame Edna's Hollywood*, especially back in Australia.

When I visited my mother before the flight she told me that the papers were full of it and everyone was talking proudly and excitedly about Edna's US debut. My mother diffused ambiguous messages. On the one hand, she had appeared to despise Edna as a 'common upstart' and a waste of my time and energy but now, knowing I had been rejected, she almost seemed to be on Edna's side. 'Her show is going to be wonderful,' she said. 'I hope we get it in Australia.'

'Yes, Mummy,' I said. There were new buds on the camellia outside her window.

'It's a pity *you* don't get nice publicity like that, Barry. That Les Patterson has disappointed everyone I've spoken to and I'm sick of telling people how nice you were once.'

'But *Les isn't me*,' I besought her. 'He's a vulgar Australian politician who people find rather funny.'

'We are an Australian family, Barry, and if we are not proud of our politicians how can we expect foreigners to look up to us?' she said finally.

It was a losing battle; a defeat I must gracefully concede, and it was time to go. I felt a wave of compassion for her in her widowhood, alone with sorrow and regret.

'Lots of love,' my mother said as I rose to leave. She had only recently begun to employ this fashionable valediction. It was tastefully impersonal; a way of using the word 'love' without compromising herself.

I stooped over my mother's chair to kiss her cheek. It was the last time.

Sitting high up at the back of the bleachers in NBC's Studio 4 in Burbank for the taping of *Dame Edna's Hollywood*, I thought how strange it was to be a part of Edna's audience but to have no part in her show. There was great excitement in the studio and a large and expensive set had been constructed, which was Hollywood's idea of Edna's home. It was a vast Spanish-style interior with a sweeping wrought-iron staircase, reminiscent of Norma Desmond's mansion in *Sunset Boulevard*.

Down on the studio floor, amongst the cameras, I noticed Wanda Smellie and another woman in earnest conversation with the floor manager. A man in overalls was primping a huge urn of gladioli. A luxurious brocade sofa stood downstage and this, I presumed, would accommodate Edna's talk show guests.

A middle-aged comedian in a tuxedo called Hal something did the audience warm-up and he was actually quite funny, though I felt rather sorry for him; once a well-known face on TV, he was reduced to playing second fiddle to an Australian self-proclaimed superstar. As he rehearsed the audience in their applause and delivered his time-worn wisecracks, Hal reminded me of Pat Hobby, F. Scott Fitzgerald's Hollywood hack. Now came the countdown, a big announcement, and an explosion of applause.

'Hello, Possums!'

Edna stood at the top of the stairs in, it must be said, a spectacular gown of gold and crimson with a shoulder line reminiscent of a sequined Sydney Opera House. She had only recently started calling her audiences 'Possums' as a term of endearment, though it puzzled Americans, who thought of these marsupials as pests, not seldom rabid. They were certainly not cuddly objects of affection.

I watched the monitors suspended above the studio audience and as the camera came in for a close-up, I saw something in Edna's eyes that no other person would have recognised or even suspected. The smile was the same, the raised arm holding a salmon-pink gladiolus was as declamatory as ever, but all the same I *knew*: on this night, perhaps the most important moment in her career, Edna didn't feel funny.

The band in the studio played 'Niceness', her signature tune, as she descended the long flight of stairs to her position centre stage. The warm-up man was conducting the audience, waving his arms and urging them to bring their ovation to a crescendo, cutting them off when the star hit her mark.

After a nervous start the monologue seemed to go well, then Edna, unused to reading a teleprompt, faltered twice. I could detect her wavering confidence. Was there even the slightest hint of desperation in her delivery? She announced her first special guest as Cher, the popular singer and actress, who descended the staircase to a vociferous welcome which required no encouragement or flashing 'applause' sign. I wondered how much Cher had cost the programme. NBC probably had to pay her make-up girl the kind of fee Edna herself might have commanded in London or Sydney for an entire television appearance.

The two divas chattered away entertainingly and the show was gaining momentum until there was an unexpected inter-ruption. The studio lights flickered, faded, and went out. The floor manager, listening intently on his headphones, then turned to the audience and told us there had been a technical fault with the lighting and all would soon be well. It was then that the old Edna at last asserted herself.

Leaving Cher alone on the couch, she stepped forward and said to the audience, 'Sorry, Possums, it looks as though the Mexicans in the basement have stopped pedalling.'

There was a collective gasp, then a titter. No one in those days yet spoke of 'political correctness', though like a terrible fungus it was soon to envelop and distort every form of human communication. But Edna had committed the ultimate sol-ecism; she had facetiously referred to the American underclass, the disenfranchised Hispanic serfs who, for next to nothing, did all the dirty work that Americans refused to do. They blew the leaves, they cleaned the offices and hospitals, they collected the garbage, they toiled in the orchards and vineyards, and they populated the slums.

The technical hitch seemed interminable and, as the audience grew restless, Hal the warm-up man resumed his patter. I learnt much later that the camera crew, indeed every technician on the set, had nearly walked out as a protest against what might now be called Edna's 'racist slur'. But catastrophe was averted and they must have been persuaded to change their minds, for after a hiatus of thirty long minutes, the lights came on again and the show resumed. Perhaps the toilers in the cellar *had* renewed their labours. Edna and Cher launched into their duet, 'I Got You, Babe' and the audience applause was not so much in appreciation, but as an expression of relief that the sticky moment had passed and harmless merriment restored.

Edna introduced her next guest, the craggy-faced actor Jack Palance, and as soon as he appeared at the top of the stairs I feared the worst. He had obviously indulged liberally in the backstage hospitality. An audience is a sensitive animal and when it smells trouble, or alcohol, or both, it gets very worried. There was a hush in the studio as the actor clung to the banister and stumbled towards Cher, who had risen to welcome him. Somehow he collapsed onto the couch and I knew how Edna must have felt as she foresaw the looming disaster. On his pugilist's face he wore a smile of mischievous benignity and I dreaded to think how the girls would deal with him. At the best of times sober women are poor comforters and sorry companions for men crowned with vine leaves. To subject them to an interview, however informal, would be an insuperable task.

Jack's eye fell on a large bowl of fruit on the coffee table and he picked up an orange, then flung it into the audience. Plums and bananas followed as Cher and Edna cowered at the other end of the sofa. I saw Wanda Smellie running onto the set and talking in great agitation to the producer, who stopped the cameras, and bravely went over to intercept Palance, who seemed to be having a wonderful time. I tried to read the mood of the audience as I habitually did from the stage floor. Sitting way back where I was, I got the impression that the people around me were beginning to think that all of this mayhem was planned; part of a joke that was slightly beyond their reach. Suddenly, assisted by a couple of security men, Jack left the set waving and smiling, and I learnt later from my friend at NBC that the only way they were able to get rid of him was to offer him a drink, or a series of drinks, back in the hospitality room.

Thereafter things improved. There were flashes of the old Edna, cameos from Larry Hagman and Bea Arthur and a melange of other ingredients which, judiciously edited, could be boiled down to an appetising *bouillon*. I bravely decided to visit Edna in her dressing-room after the taping but there seemed to be such a large crowd of people milling around, including Cher's large Jewish family and a number of young men who might have been hairdressers or airline stewards, that I decided to give it up. I glimpsed Wanda in the distance looking proprietorial, but if she saw me she gave no sign of it.

I think Edna did a second, or even a third show for NBC, but *Dame Edna's Hollywood* was never picked up for a series and I am ashamed to confess that I took a dishonourable pleasure in hearing of her disappointment. Wanda was probably pushing her too hard, and Edna's humour, at its most spontaneous, did not spare the delicate sensibilities of American audiences at that time. I could see, even from my remote vantage point in the studio, a few very anxious executives. What would she say next? I imagined them thinking. They all hoped that if the show was a hit they would take the credit, but if it failed, what then? Who would take the blame and carry the can?

Thus, most of the networks concentrated on 'developing' shows that would never be made. It kept them busy and, though they might miss out on the glory of success, they avoided the sack. It was not a recipe for adventurous television.

18

Cold Print

No longer a participant in Edna's career but a mere spectator, I tried, once back in London, to pursue an independent life. There were film offers and an approach from an old-fashioned publisher who wanted me to write my autobiography. What would I write about, I wondered, what had I done? Looking back over my entire theatrical career I seemed to have played second fiddle to Mrs Norman Everage of Moonee Ponds, the self-styled Dame Edna.

I met Fanny, the encouraging young editor assigned to the project, but I was disconcerted to find that she had very confused ideas about my role in Edna's life. She actually believed, as some others did it seemed, that Dame Edna and I were one and the same person. Luckily her misapprehension was revealed in one of our first conversations about the book, when she said over lunch at Le Caprice, 'There will be a big readership for this, Barry. There's not much of a stigma attached to cross-dressing these days.'

'Cross-dressing' was a distasteful American term deeply imbued with puritanical anxiety. I think it originally described persons who obtained a sexual *frisson* by swapping clothes with members of the opposite sex, surely an innocent enough game, but it had acquired a pejorative meaning by the time Fanny dropped her bombshell over the fishcakes at lunch.

Rather angrily I tried to set her straight, but she only smiled indulgently. 'However you want to tell the story is fine by Macmillan,' she said. 'And I've already sold the serial rights. The *Sunday Times* might even pay us for a photograph of you in the dressing-room being transformed into the Dame.'

She scribbled something on the menu and passed it across to me. It was a figure; a big figure; a telephone number.

I'm not given to rages, not even stage rage, but very occasionally and under extraordinary circumstances I feel I could be on the verge of a cerebral haemorrhage. 'Fanny!' I exploded, so that a couple of people in the restaurant looked up. 'Fanny,' I resumed in a more subdued tone, 'they can pay what they like. They'll never get a picture of me dressing up as that woman and that's that.'

Fanny's indulgent smile broadened. Now it was as if she was soothing a naughty child having a tantrum. 'I can understand if you don't want to give away trade secrets, Barry, but readers will expect something new. My friend Vanessa Peddlingham told me she got a few good shots in Sydney a while ago. We could use them.'

'Vanessa is a friend of yours?' I was genuinely surprised. 'Well, ask her to tell you that she witnessed the real Dame Edna and me at one and the same time in Sydney. I just so happened to be dressed up as Edna on that particular morning when I bumped into Edna.'

'Of course you were,' said Fanny, looking slightly worried. She looked like a woman who was humouring a harmless lunatic. 'But if you were not the real Dame Edna and there was this other Edna, who was she? Or even *he*?'

I felt as though I was slipping into some kind of quicksand and to struggle or protest would only mean that I would sink even faster, and deeper. The young woman across the table reached out and placed her warm hand over mine.

'Just go home and write the book, Barry, and write it before Edna writes hers,' Fanny said. Then she gave me a broad wink and signalled for the bill.

Escaping from Edna was proving to be almost impossible. My accountant was also receiving enquiries from the Inland Revenue office concerning her tax affairs. It seemed that Ian Smee, who was responsible for Edna's tax returns, had been in grave dereliction and had not even paid her VAT. He had 'done a runner' after the dissolution of his company and he was probably being pursued by the authorities. He was the kind of sleaze who might even shop his client Edna to the Revenue to get himself out of trouble.

It was thought that I might be able to cast light on this murky affair but I was relieved to learn that I, at least, was not under investigation. I tried to refer the correspondence to Wanda Smellie at the Talent Factory but there was never any response from her and I decided to call in there myself and take a look at the set-up. Why not? My divorce from Edna had been sad but not acrimonious.

The Talent Factory was on a canal near Westbourne Park underground station. It was located in what had formerly been a factory making zip fasteners, but within everything had been modernised in a style influenced by Philipe Starck. The reception was vast with vermilion walls and grotesquely inflated furniture painted an electric blue. A girl with spiky pink hair and enough rings on her forelip to hang a curtain sullenly directed me to Wanda Smellie's office on the second floor. On the wall behind reception hung one of Andy Warhol's portraits of Edna, made presumably during her brief Studio 54 period. The girl saw me looking at it.

'That's Dame,' she said. 'We've just hung that. Neat isn't it?'

On my way up to Wanda's office I saw large photographs everywhere of vaguely recognisable rock stars and a few well-known faces like Rod Stewart and Eric Clapton. Wanda came out of her office to greet me and even seemed quite pleased to see me. She was wearing exactly the same black leather clothes she had been wearing in Sydney, though I noticed a very large gold Cartier watch, of the sort *nouveau riche* actors conspicuously display in their press photos.

'I was hoping you'd drop in, Barry, so you could see with your own eyes the kind of service we can offer Edna,' she said.

We entered her office, which was painted yellow with a large 'artwork' by Bruce Nauman on the wall, the glowing neon letters flashing on and off simply read 'EAT, SHIT, LOVE'.

'It's one of his best pieces,' said Wanda, proudly nodding in the direction of the offensive installation. 'They wanted it for Bruce's big retrospective at the Whitney, but we would miss it too much here. It needs to be cherished.'

There was no reply to this, I thought, turning my back on Mr Nauman's infantile exhortation, or mantra, or whatever it was, or tried to be. 'It's a wonderful building you have here, Wanda,' was all that I could boringly manage to say.

The little but chunky woman then led me down a corridor which was really a gantry in the former factory, now painted emerald green.

'You did your best, Barry,' she said, 'but we feel Dame deserves the special service we give all our stars. This is just part of our accounts department.' Wanda flung open a door and in an enormous room painted orange I saw what must have been twenty workstations with young men and women crouched at their bulky computer screens, jabbing away at calculators. Loud rock music blared.

It was only possible to converse without yelling when we were back outside in the corridor. 'I really wanted to ask you if any of your accountants were sorting out Edna's tax problems.' I ventured. 'I have forwarded all of the correspondence to you.'

Wanda simply laughed.

We were back in her office and her PA, a rather limp youth wearing sneakers and a mullet hairdo, brought me a decaf cappuccino – then a novelty.

'Financial enquiries don't come to my desk, Barry. I am strictly creative. Andrew or Sangita deal with all that shit and if there's a problem they can't solve they use Andersens or any top-of-the-range, blue-chip accountants.'

I looked impressed, a wonderful acting feat considering my view of accountants. 'I hope you manage to make a lot of money for Edna,' I said, 'and I'm sure you will invest it wisely.'

'Only the best for our Dame, Barry, believe you me.' Wanda lit a cigarette. 'I'm locking in a book deal as we speak. It's her autobiography and it's going to be hot. If I get the advance I want I'm sending it straight to Bernie.'

'Bernie?'

'Madoff,' supplied the agent. 'He's the new whiz-kid of Wall Street and we've offered him all of our big clients. He's pretty choosy about who he helps but the Talent Factory has influence and he's doing amazing things with our clients' money.'

This world into which I had intruded was too rarefied for me and the news of Edna's incipient memoirs had plunged me suddenly into a mood of apprehensiveness. As I left, in a voice which I hoped sounded casual, I asked Wanda if, by any chance, Edna had started writing.

'Oh, yes,' she enthused, 'it's great stuff and she's very nice about you, considering.'

'Considering? Considering *what?*' I snapped, taking the bait.

'To be perfectly honest with you, Barry,' said Wanda, using Ian Smee's ominous phrase which wafted an unpleasant little gust of déjà vu, 'you had a major international talent handed to you on a plate and you blew it. You blew it! But don't worry – in the draft of the manuscript I have seen Edna gives you a nice little mention, but so far you're only half a page.'

Of course, I should never have gone to that office and put my head in the lion's mouth. Her breath had not improved incidentally; it was like an open grave, even at several paces. I wondered how her girlfriends coped with it, or what measures they took to avoid it.

As the days and weeks passed, I constantly reproached myself for calling in at the Talent Factory. It seemed to be teeming with people pretending to be busy; feigning efficiency. They were all strutting around thinking they had the most glamorous jobs in the world, and because many of the clients were rock stars and record companies they were all on a raft floating on a sea of limitless money. I could imagine how efficient their accounts department would be, the department which was meant to defend Edna against the depredations of the Inland Revenue office or the embezzlements of Smee and others. If there were ever a real crisis they would drop her like a hot cake.

Wanda Smellie was just a senior agent in this company and there were others higher up that no one ever met. But why should I care? Edna Everage was no longer my concern and I hoped – I genuinely hoped – she would enjoy her new world of hype, limos, fancy friends, Tiffany, Cartier, and rock and roll while it lasted. I just hoped that the inevitable disillusionment would not descend too brutally.

Meanwhile, news of her book hung over my head like a sword of Damocles. Back in Melbourne, with her health rapidly failing, my mother had sent me a letter enclosing a clipping from *The Age*. The headline read:

Our Edna wins record book deal: five figure rumour!

Dame Edna Everage said yesterday she was 'over the moon' about the contract she has just signed with a major international publisher for the world rights to her eagerly awaited memoirs, provisionally titled *From Moonee to Millions*. Her agent and sole representative Wanda Smellie revealed that the book would contain some sensational revelations about the celebrities in Edna's life and her single-handed ascent from drab suburban house-wife to glamorous superstar. In a statement issued to the press, Dame Edna said: 'I feel my adoring public needs to know me better. There have been ugly rumours about who I am and what I am and horrible people have tried to jump on my bandwagon, some very sick people indeed who claim they invented me. My book will be a no holds barred, tell-all, and fearlessly frank story which will give hope to people all over the world. I feel that Dame Nature herself wants me to write this book. She is my ghostwriter. One day – who knows? – my book might be compulsory reading, and lovely people like the Gideons will place it in hotel rooms all over the planet. There might even be marvellous folk on bicycles called "Edna's Witnesses" who will knock on doors and read an inspir-ing paragraph from my wonderful publication.'

My mother had not appended a comment to this nauseating news item. In my despondent mood, however, I sensed an implicit taunt. She was on Edna's side, I reflected gloomily. So Edna had risen to her present elevation 'single-handedly', had she? I supposed it didn't really matter that she had airbrushed me out of her life and elided my influence. Other people, I was sure, would spring out of the woodwork claiming credit for her invention, and future biographers and theatre historians would be besieged by informers and amateur impresarios eager to spill the beans.

I telephoned Vanessa and a child answered the phone. It went away for a long time and I listened to a great deal of clattering, echoing footsteps, and the distant sound of a television. I was about to hang up when Vanessa picked up the receiver.

'How are you, baby?' she enquired when I announced myself.

'Who is the kiddie?' I asked.

'It's Caleb,' said Vanessa. 'I'm sorry I never told you I was a one-parent family, but it didn't seem sexy. My sister looked after him while I was in Australia, but I couldn't leave him in her hands forever. You were very sweet to me in Sydney though.'

'What about the BBC?' I asked.

'Redundant,' she replied glumly. 'I overstretched my leave, thanks to you.'

'Do you need some money, Vanessa? I feel I owe you something.'

There was a long pause during which little Caleb could be heard clashing toys and loudly seeking attention. 'I'm fine, baby,' said Vanessa at last. 'Thanks all the same. I've come into a bit of unexpected dosh and I suppose it's thanks to you.'

My heart sank. She had obviously sold the photos of me as Edna, and what else? I remembered that at the time of our affair she was a bit keen on photography, especially Polaroids of an intimate nature.

Guessing that I was a jump ahead of her Vanessa protested, 'I never said anything negative about you. How could I, baby? But some of the snaps I took when we were getting ready for the Mike Walsh show were worth a fair bit, you know, and I didn't think you'd mind. They show what a brilliant guy you are and what a whizz I am with the make-up.'

Caleb, it seemed, had won his mother's attention and our conversation ended abruptly with Vanessa's, 'Talk to you later.'

I felt betrayed on all quarters and a book was soon to appear depicting me as a deluded Dame Edna wannabe, probably embellished with Vanessa's unauthorised photography, and all masterminded by Wanda of the mephitic breath.

Under intense pressure from Fanny, my editor, I sent her three chapters of my autobiography which seemed duller each time I read them. They described my childhood and prosperous middle-class family life in a nice neighbourhood in the far-off forties. I wrote of my early ambition to become a magician, and my admiration for that forgotten Hollywood cowboy, Gene Autry, a miniature version of whose pearl-handled pistol, fringed leather bolero and chaps my mother had bought for me at the Myer Emporium. I dwelt amusingly on my adolescence and university days and had got as far into my story as the moment when I first glimpsed Edna Everage.

Fanny responded enthusiastically but she had major reservations. Over another lunch she told me, with a visible struggle to be tactful, that my book needed to 'take flight'. 'It's too bogged down in, well, the truth, for want of a better word,' she declared obscurely. Seeing my jaw drop, she hastily continued, 'It's great, it's evocative, but when we get to the Edna bit the readers won't buy it.'

'How do you mean they won't buy it?'

Fanny decided to come clean. 'To be perfectly honest with you, Barry,' she said, inducing a small vein to throb on my right temple, 'most people know, I mean *think*, that you are Edna, and it's a marvellous creation. Why not just relax and tell them how you invented her?'

'Are you serious?' I protested.

'Couldn't be more serious,' said my editor seriously. 'The publisher is adamant. We probably won't publish the book at all if you keep up this pretence – his words, not mine.'

I felt I was going slightly mad. 'What evidence have you got, Fanny? What hard evidence?'

'We have pictures, Barry, and we paid a young female photographer a lot of money for them. She also told us that she'd met another friend of yours in Sydney who liked to get into Edna drag. It sounds like all you Ednas belong to some sort of club. It could make for a juicy bestseller.'

So obviously Vanessa had shopped the photographs to at

least two publishers. Suddenly I thought, why not? I needed the money, rather badly as a matter of fact, and it might be fun describing my insidious slide into female impersonation. I imagined the real Edna toiling away at her book, undoubtedly prodded along by a ghostwriter. I only hoped I could get mine published before hers.

Out of the blue came a lucrative opportunity to leave town. I was offered a good role in a television film of Graham Greene's novella, *Dr Fischer of Geneva*. There was a marvellous cast: James Mason, Alan Bates and Greta Scacchi and we would film it in Switzerland. It was a heaven-sent excuse to quit London for a while and remove myself from publishers, agents and multiple Ednas.

One night after filming beside Lake Geneva in the freezing cold, Greta and I wandered into the opulent lounge of the Beau-Rivage Hotel and spotted Graham Greene himself at a corner table, scribbling in a small notebook. Seeing us, he rose and apologetically indicated the little leather-bound volume.

'It's my address book,' he said. 'I'm just crossing out the dead.' I never thought, then, that one day my own address book would contain more exits than entries.

I enjoyed being with this small company of British actors. It was a novel experience for someone like me who customarily worked alone. I only met other actors at benefits and memorial services, and it was while working on this television film that I got to know Alan Bates, who was exactly my age – born on the same day, as was also Yasser Arafat.

In the hours between filming I worked on my book[13] and it was liberating to pretend that Dame Edna was a colourful figment of my imagination. Fanny was right: cold facts make dull reading.

Back in London I discovered there were a lot of messages on my answering machine, which was still a novel device. Vanessa had called quite regularly proposing lunch, dinner and much more. Then there was an almost incoherent message from Edna saying she was desperate to see me and she couldn't explain why on the phone. I ignored Vanessa's messages, knowing that I would ultimately capitulate. Then I thought about Edna's *cri de coeur*. The message had been recorded two days earlier, but although I was bursting with curiosity I postponed my response for a couple more days.

She was living in the Oliver Messel suite at the Dorchester and I telephoned her there. Edna answered in a quavering voice with overtones and undertones of hysteria.

'Look,' she said, 'something horrible and vile and dirty has happened and I must talk to you.'

---

13 This 'autobiography' would be published as *More Please*.

19

The Nadir

The Dorchester Hotel, that great landmark on Park Lane, whose advent in 1931 had been extolled by Michael Arlen, was a little more sedate than it is now. The lobby and the long and luxurious coffee room were not then thronged with abdominous Middle Eastern caliphs and businessmen in their Brioni suits and Breitling watches, being attended by their Mayfair houris and odalisques. When I went to visit Edna that evening there were only a few men in suits loitering in the lobby, possibly security men protecting some resident sheik.

I ascended to the seventh floor and made my way down a short corridor to the double doors of the suite of rooms which had been decorated by the famous theatrical artist, and friend and Caribbean neighbour of Noel Coward, Oliver Messel. A

German butler admitted me and somewhat nervously I sat and awaited Edna's entrance. It was less theatrical than I had foreseen. She looked a wreck. Clad in a voluminous Dorchester bathrobe, her face impastoed with a thick green facemask eroded by tears, she staggered into the room and collapsed into a large armchair upholstered in green moiré silk.

'Hello, Edna,' I said, passing her my handkerchief, for already more tears were carving fresh ravines for themselves in the green landscape of her face. I had decided to say very little and let her do the talking.

'You think I'm awful don't you, Barry?' she began. 'You don't like Wanda and you never have and you don't like me writing my autobiography because I happen to know that you're writing one as well.'

'I have started,' I admitted.

'Well,' said Edna, with a muculent sniff, 'they're more likely to believe my story than yours, Barry, but what does it matter? I'm broke.'

I looked around the opulent suite. 'Surely not flat broke, Edna,' I exclaimed.

'Oh, this,' she said, extruding another flow of tears. 'The publisher is paying for this until I finish the book. After that it's back to Moonee Ponds, or whoever will have me.'

'Just a minute,' I interjected. 'You made a lot of money. I know you did, because I got ten per cent of it, and Wanda must have made you a great deal more with that Toyota commercial and that musical you did at the Haymarket.'

'It's all gone,' sobbed Edna. 'You must have been in Australia when that show came and went. Critics hated it. Little Charles Spencer in the *Telegraph* said I was finished, and even that sweet Nicholas de Something panned me, as nicely as he could.'

'Don't tell me Wanda doesn't want you any more,' I said with, I confess, mock commiseration.

'Well, she does and she doesn't,' Edna said. 'In the time since you and I split up I made some nice money, and luckily Wanda invested it with a wonderful man in America at something international.'

Whenever I hear the word 'international' attached to a company – and in particular, an investment company – I suspect the worst.

'Wanda said he's very choosy. He doesn't accept everyone's investment. It's really like a private club.' At this, my suspicions deepened.

'But I can't touch the money, Barry,' Edna lamented. 'It's almost as if I haven't got it.' I liked the sound of this even less, but I held my peace.

The butler discreetly interrupted us with a plate of Middle Eastern nibbles, pita bread, hummus and meatballs, possibly left over from some Arabic repast down the corridor. When he had retreated I probed Edna on the subject of her new agent.

'What did you mean,' I asked the lachrymose woman in the bathrobe, slumped in the chair opposite mine, 'when you said Wanda does and doesn't want you?'

Edna picked up a falafel ball in her fingers and put it down again. 'She's a bit spooky,' said Edna. 'She's more than a bit spooky, actually.'

'Spooky?' I asked, suddenly feeling hungry and devouring an entire meatball dipped in yoghurt. 'She has *proclivities*, Barry, and she tried them on me.'

'Proclivities' were phenomena which Australians discovered somewhat later than the rest of the world, but having discovered them they pursued them with extraordinary ardour and energy, as if making up for lost time. I would have thought that Wanda Smellie's very appearance would long since have announced the nature of her proclivities, and the agent had never been shy in mentioning the existence of her female partner.

'It was a while ago now, Barry,' Edna began, deciding to nibble cautiously at her falafel after all. 'Actually, it was during rehearsals for my musical at the Haymarket. Wanda had talked me into that show in the first place and there was a whole cast and a famous director and an orchestra and beautiful sets, but something was wrong.' She paused, and with a pristine napkin pressed to her lips, she spat out her falafel with a grimace. She looked at me with eyes that were almost supplicatory.

'I missed you then, Barry. I wished it was just us doing a show together with me as the star and you, well, as a wonderful warm-up person.' I attempted to look modest, flattered, self-deprecating, tolerant, humble and not enraged.

'Without asking me, Wanda had been talking to the Australian Arts Council, looking for sponsorship, and she had struck a deal behind my back in which that monster Les Patterson was to open my show.'

I had not heard that name for a long time and I assumed that he had either died of alcoholism or venereal disease or that a new Australian government had banished him to Limbo. Nor had I read any of the adverse reviews of Edna's big flop. Needless to say the Australian press had ecstatically reported her failure, but in the quotes I had read, 13,000 miles from the Haymarket Theatre, Sir Les Patterson's presence in the cast went unmentioned.

'What did he do?' I asked her.

Edna's lips curled in distaste. 'Oh, what do you think? He'd had a few sherries of course.' Having 'a few sherries' was an old-fashioned Australian euphemism for drunkenness.

'He slobbered,' Edna continued with mounting distress, 'he tried to sing, and he even sprayed the front row with his horrible drool. There were stains on his suit and everyone could see that ghastly bulge in his trousers made by his tummy banana.' With this, Edna introduced me to a new and repellent metaphor for the virile member. Perhaps it was a coinage of her own?

'He absolutely lost the audience before I even went on stage, and Wanda thought he was funny.'

'Perhaps she thought he was attractive?' I offered lamely.

'Not her,' said Edna, with a sudden bitterness. 'It's me she finds attractive.' Once again Edna raised the napkin to her mouth and I feared she might actually vomit.

'I was in my dressing-room after the first night and Les had been particularly revolting. A few VIPs had even left and Princess Alexandra in the Royal Box didn't even look up, I was told. I was undressing and I couldn't stop crying and Wanda came in and gave me a hug.' Edna gagged slightly as she articulated the word. 'It was a hug from hell,' she said. 'You know she's much shorter than I am, Barry, and she pushed her horrid little face into me, round about here.' Her fingers fluttered in the direction of an erogenous zone. 'I just remember saying, "What do you think you're doing, Wanda?" and she said something sickening like, "You know you want me, Edna".'

It was a spectacular scene, one out of Balzac perhaps? Or was Edna Colette and Wanda Willy?

'What did you do?' was all that I could feebly ask.

'I wrenched myself away. "Don't touch me!" I screamed, and she said — I can barely believe it — "I thought you were a happily unmarried woman?"'

I was getting very hungry indeed and had polished off most of the meatballs. I noticed that Edna's tears had given way to indignation.

'I won't tell you what else she said, Barry, but I realised that I got mixed up with a very troubled woman. I know that in Australia there are a few ballet dancers and Qantas stewards and a few young men in the window-dressing business with *proclivities*, but you can count them on the fingers of a few people's hands.' I tried to grasp this oddly calculated statistic. 'One thing we can be proud of is that we don't have women like Wanda or the whole fabric of our society would fall to pieces.'

Gravely, I agreed. It seemed the wrong time to mention Valmai's proclivities. 'But that was a while ago now, Edna,' I pointed out, 'and you're still with the Talent Factory.'

'The next day she had pretended that nothing had happened,' resumed Edna. 'She must be pretty used to the rejection of healthy, clean-living women. I suppose she is lucky to have found one of her kind to live with . . . I met that creature once.'

'Wasn't that Fran, the LA lawyer?' I asked.

'That's her,' said Edna. 'A lawyer who disobeys the laws of nature. If it didn't make me sick it would make me laugh.'

I made a few enquiries about Edna's Haymarket show. It had been called *Edna – The Spectacle* and it was an ambitious attempt to tell Edna's story from housewife to superstar. It opened with a song and monologue by Les Patterson which, though funny to some, alienated all of the women in the audience who had hoped for a cosy evening in Edna's company. This seemed to me a grave miscalculation.

Just as the audience was recovering from the shock, it was presented with a period setting in 'the olden days', an almost mythical period in history where a large cast milled around in frock coats, crinolines and the motley attire of yesteryear, while a ragged child called Edna attempted to steal a gladiolus from a flower seller who looked remarkably like Eliza Doolittle in *My Fair Lady*. The child gets caught and its headscarf is ripped off to reveal a little mop of mauve hair. There followed a courtroom scene in which Edna is sentenced to transportation to Australia as a juvenile offender, and the courtroom set, which was apparently brilliantly designed, transforms into a sailing ship.

Little Edna, in chains in the hold, then sang a touching lament, 'Why Am I Mauve?'

> *Why am I mauve, what is it I lack?*
> *Wherever I rove I'm always lilac*

That was all that my informant could remember and it was, I was told, affectingly performed, but the audience still had to wait a long time before the Dame Edna they all knew and had waited for finally appeared on stage.

In hearing the description of the show and from reading old press clippings, I gathered that the music by James McConnel and the lyrics by Kit Hesketh-Harvey were witty and original, but that Edna herself seemed vagrant and lacklustre. She had been upstaged by her own show.

'Wanda pushed me into that production,' lamented Edna unconvincingly. 'How could it have made its money back with all those sets and orchestra and such a big cast? Those Talent Factory types are just rock and roll people. They thought it might be fun to have their name on a classy show in the West End. I was a human sacrifice, Barry.'

I took all these crocodile tears with a grain of salt but the hour was late, or very early, and I told Edna that I would come back to the Dorchester tomorrow for a second instalment of her jeremiad. Edna became hysterical.

'Don't go yet, Barry, don't go,' she said in a piteous voice, clawing at the lapels of my jacket.

I realised then that Edna wanted me back. For all my incompetence, I had never made sexual advances towards her and for some reason it was inconceivable to me that anyone else would either, male or female. She was just not that kind of woman.

'What are we going to do about your money, Edna?' I asked. 'You must have *something* left?'

'The tax man's got it,' she said. 'That Ian Smee was a crook and you should have warned me, Barry.'

'You found him, Edna!' I exclaimed indignantly. 'You trusted him. I always thought he was sleazy.'

'Well,' said Edna calmly. 'His fancy schemes cost me everything. I had to sell my Andy Warhol and my Lempicka and I'm lucky I'm not in jail. This book I'm writing is my last hope of scratching back a few pence for my fare back to Australia. I'm sick of fame, I'm sick of being a megastar, I'm sick of being myself.'

And with that, one of the world's most gifted, most mesmeric and most exasperating women rose up from her chair and flung herself at my knees.

'Handle me, Barry,' she sobbed. 'Help me forget what's happened and handle me, handle me again like you handled me before!'

With two gorgeous Ednaettes

Dancing Dame

Sir Les Patterson – diplomat at large

A hard act to follow

OPPOSITE: Edna composes herself

A trusting relationship

OPPOSITE: Disillusioned

Mutual admiration

20

Proclivities

I still felt a twinge of genuine feeling for Edna. We had worked together for so long, and from time to time during our professional estrangement I had missed her exasperating but diverting presence. However, we had been apart for long enough for me to have experienced an exhilarating freedom. It was a chance at last to do, as the saying went, my own thing. Now, with both my parents dead, I needed to reconsider my life and what was important. I needed to turn to a fresh page.

I continued to write my book for Fanny which was described as an autobiography, but I was secretly ashamed of it because I had cravenly obeyed my stern editor's injunction and fictionalised the Dame Edna story. I hoped Edna would never read it and discover herself to be a mere figment of my imagination!

Fortunately she read few books, and the only volumes I could ever remember seeing in her possession were by Virginia Woolf, Danielle Steele and the English feminist and saphist Jeanette Winterson.

It was clear there had been an embarrassing and possibly acrimonious falling out with Wanda Smellie – even if it was one-sided – and I feared that the legal department at the Talent Factory, overstaffed and hopelessly inefficient as it probably was, might not release their client without a struggle. If I were to accept Edna back, I wondered what it might cost me and what other problems would come with her. The tax penalty was one, and Edna's sudden poverty, a not unrelated circumstance, was another.

A quick enquiry in London told me that the rights to Edna's book were owned *in toto* by the Talent Factory's literature department. They now held her copyright worldwide in perpetuity. Worse than this was the problem of Edna's mental health. As she had crouched, sobbing, at the Dorchester I had looked down at her face without make-up and, without her signature 'face furniture', I had witnessed again that strangely familiar countenance that I had observed off and on throughout our acquaintance. It was a face *I had seen before*.

Of course, I dismissed this as a fanciful illusion. I could read Edna's face better than I could read the features of most people I knew, and in idle moments, on the phone or in restaurants, I could sketch her likeness in caricature, on menus and memo pads. Audiences, it seemed, found her familiar, too, and they responded to her seldom generous observations as though to an eccentric, but much loved relative: Aunty Edna. Yes, her face *was* familiar, over-familiar.

For the time being Edna was mostly locked in her hotel suite with the telephone off the hook and room service meals piling up and putrefying in her vestibule. A 'Do Not Disturb' sign hung permanently on the door and the housekeeping staff were banned from entry. Was she becoming a reclusive female version of Howard Hughes, I wondered, letting her fingernails grow to grotesque lengths and bottling her urine? The only people she seemed to be communicating with were me and, at long distance, her son Kenny. It was only then that I thought of Joan.

Joan Rivers was already one of the world's most celebrated comediennes. Her fame in the United States had spread to England and she had already made a couple of appearances on Edna's TV talk show, *The Dame Edna Experience*. The two women had really 'clicked' and Edna had displayed a rather uncharacteristic compassion when Joan's husband, Edgar, had committed suicide. I think Joan was one of the few women in the world that Edna envied, apart from Mother Teresa and Princess Diana, for Joan had her own line of jewellery which she sold with huge success on television. Joan also had an enormous house in Bel Air which I think Edna deeply coveted. Whenever she was in Los Angeles she was an honoured dinner guest *chez Rivers* and there was always a little group of Edna's Hollywood friends and admirers like Vincent Price and Coral Browne, Roddy McDowall, Swifty Lazar, Angela Lansbury and Warren Beatty.

In this company Edna shone; the housewife from Moonee Ponds was almost old Hollywood, if the lights were dim enough. Joan had been to see the show at the Haymarket, had sent flowers and applauded vigorously, and she had remained loyal when audiences diminished. When Lord (Jeffrey) Archer, the production's faithful backer, reluctantly pulled the plug Joan had sent messages of hope and condolence. It was natural I should think of her when Edna was at the nadir of her despair. A fax came by return:

Dear Edna,
You are loved in America and those London critics are shits.
There's a great little theatre in San Francisco. Do a couple of
weeks there and you'll be a blast! The Village People are sure to
come.
Love Joan

And so it was that an extraordinary adventure began: Dame Edna's American career. The Village People did come, or what was left of them, and they brought their mothers. Edna thrived in a smaller theatre with a new public and I took a great vicarious pleasure in her resurrection. It was just as well that, before we embarked for the United States, I had dissuaded her from striking back at some of the critics who had attacked her last London venture.

When a few unfavourable reviews or downright hostile notices greet a theatrical offering in which you have made a large financial and emotional investment, there is a temptation, sometimes irresistible, to lambast the critics. It is true that not many critics are terribly smart and few have the temperament and talent of an artist, even a mediocre artist. However, in my own experience, I have looked back on devastating criticisms – mercifully few – and, to my annoyance, often found them to be right. If Dame Edna could have foreseen her Broadway success, which followed so closely upon her dismissal from the West End, she would have summoned her journalistic detractors and embraced them.

It was a new life in San Francisco, and we had a producer from Broadway and a generous backer. The fellow who ran the little theatre off Union Square was rather a rough diamond who failed to take his sneakered feet off the desk when Edna first entered his office, and whose manners tapered off from there. It didn't matter. Edna rented a large apartment on Russian Hill with a view of the Golden Gate Bridge and Alcatraz, and she was fêted by the social lions and lionesses of San Francisco such as Denise Hale, Ann Getty and Merriwether McGettigan. Everyone came to the show: Michael Tilson Thomas, Armistead Maupin and Amy Tan. It became the 'thing' to do. Edna's two-week engagement became four months, the show transferred to the Booth Theatre on Broadway, and within one year of her London debacle, Edna had won a special Tony Award. Soon after came the Drama Desk Award for an Outstanding One-person Show and the Outer Critics Circle Award.

The devastated woman I had seen holed up in the Oliver Messel suite at the Dorchester Hotel was gone. As I sat in black tie at one of the many award ceremonies in New York where Edna routinely stepped up to accept some ugly bauble, I marvelled at the transformation. It was as if her year 'in the wilderness' had not existed. She herself seemed to have completely forgotten the miseries of her recent past.

'It wasn't that bad, Barry,' she said. 'The trouble with you is that you always see the glass half empty and not the glass half full.' It was an infuriating cant phrase that Edna was currently using to death.

Kenny had flown to America to design his mother's new wardrobe, and Edna had also imported Madge, who had been exiled to New Zealand long before. When I saw Madge again she seemed much smaller and more desiccated than I remembered. I wondered how she had put up with the treatment Edna had dished out to her over the years, but she mostly seemed to accept her subservient role without complaint. It was as if she had some secret: some hidden knowledge that enabled her to withstand the taunts and indignities to which Edna subjected her. She still wore that horrible fawn polyester dress with a cardigan the colour of an overcooked brussels sprout.

It was hard to know why Edna needed the presence of her New Zealand bridesmaid, unless it was to impress the torpid and apparently depressed little Kiwi widow with her new-found grandeur. But every now and then I observed on Madge's lips a faint smile. It was not a smile of martyrdom, for it had about it a faint hint of the triumphant, confirming my view that she was not as downtrodden as she seemed. I went to a big dinner given for Edna by Stephen Sondheim and observed Madge Allsop chatting excitedly between Christopher Walken and Nathan Lane. At the other end of the table, Edna, her benefactor, having caught sight of her bridesmaid having a good time, glared in disapproval.

Meanwhile, Kenny was beginning to make a name for himself. He had long since graduated from the fashion school in Melbourne and relinquished his job as a part-time waiter at Smail's Place. I was not certain, however, if the connection with Clifford Smail had been entirely severed, and I became more certain that Edna's favourite son might have chosen a path in life in which women, apart from his mother, played a negligible role.

'He's looking for "Miss Right", Barry,' Edna frequently announced when I asked about Kenny. 'He has grown into a lovely boy and he is going to break a few hearts, mark my words.'

I had little doubt that he would, but the hearts he would break might not be in bodies which Edna would find acceptable.

The dresses Kenny designed for his mother were becoming more extravagant than ever before, and he told me that he had received enquiries from other stars like Meryl Streep, Faye Dunaway and even Elizabeth Taylor. On the night of the Tony Awards Kenny was in attendance, and it was certainly not Miss Right who accompanied him. Clifford Smail had changed since I had last seen him, looming over my table in the restaurant in a blood-stained apron. He was a man best described as stolid, in contrast to the slim undulating figure of Kenneth Everage.

He still wore his thick beard but his head was shaved in the style of Bruce Willis, and the diamond (was it bigger?) in his left earlobe glinted fiercely. Clifford must have been one of the first of the shaven-head-brigade who were soon to become ubiquitous.

'How is your mother, Edna?' I ventured one day when we were having lunch at Sardi's famous theatre restaurant, where a caricature of her had been recently unveiled.

'It's nothing like me, is it, Barry?' she said, glaring at her cheerfully exaggerated likeness on the wall. 'I would never wear that necklace he has given me, and my nose is more classical. What were you saying?'

I repeated my enquiry about old Mrs Beazley.

'I think I spoil her,' said Edna, returning to her *raviolis al sugo*. 'You know my old home at Moonee is a museum owned by the National Trust?'

'I had heard something about it,' I replied, 'but all of that happened while you were . . .' I strove to find a tactful form of expression '. . . while you were letting Wanda Smellie guide your career.'

Edna grimaced at the thought of her last agent. 'That woman had a funny smell, Barry, and it wasn't just her name that put the idea into my head. Fancy a woman wanting to play doctors and nurses with another woman anyway! What's that all about?'

'It's called . . .' I wondered what impact the word 'homo-sexuality' would have on my luncheon companion. It would probably destroy her appetite. I chickened. '. . . It's called something medical,' I finally equivocated. 'It's apparently more common than we think, but it's not as obvious as the male version.'

Edna made a gagging noise. 'Euchhh!' she exclaimed. 'It's rife in New York, I believe. Young men from broken homes *passing through a phase* and then deciding to keep on passing through it as many times as possible.'

I declined to tell her that her Broadway producer was gay, his assistant was gay, the publicist and his entire staff were gay, that half of her audience was gay, and that her favourite stage doorman Ted needed a woman like a fish needed a bicycle. My suspicions about Kenny – and Valmai – I also kept to myself.

'Well,' Edna continued, 'my home is a big tourist attraction in Melbourne, especially with the Japanese. Our former enemies come by the bus load and shuffle from room to room. Everything is exactly as it was when you first started popping in, though there are ropes across the chairs now and a sign on the fridge door in Australian and Japanese saying "Do not Touch". They've turned our old garage into a cinema and they're running all my TV shows in a loop in five languages.'

'But your mother, where is she?'

'Oh, she's still there, Barry. The sweet people at the National Trust included her on the inventory along with the other furnishings and fitments and utensils. They've put a little window in the door of her room so that tourists can peep in at her. Thanks to me, Mummy is quite a celebrity. We decided not to let the public file through her room. She deserves privacy, even though she doesn't know if she has it or not.'[14]

'Does the National Trust feed her?' I asked, with undetected irony.

'My very word,' said Edna, using a phrase I hadn't heard for years. 'She's living off the fat of the land, although she doesn't know that she's a tourist attraction, and that there are postcards of her available at the souvenir desk. Mummy probably likes the idea of people coming and going, and seeing those yellow slant-eyed faces pressed against her little window.'

There were still intermittent rumblings from faraway London where Wanda Smellie, Edna's bitterly disappointed suitor, was trying to make trouble. Edna's book, *My Gorgeous Life*, had done well but it looked as if the royalties would somehow be swallowed up in litigation and 'hidden' costs. Moreover the Talent Factory, I was delighted to learn, was on the skids. All of its notable rock star clients had left and audits were being demanded. There was talk of impending bankruptcy, in which case all of their assets, and some of Edna's, would be placed in receivership. This was news I thought it better to withhold since Edna seemed, in spite of her success, emotionally fragile.

'Do you know why they love me, Barry?' she said to me once. 'It's because I'm vulnerable. I pride myself on my *vulnerability*.'

14 At the time of writing, Gladys Beazley is still alive!

It was probably the most outrageously inaccurate epithet that could ever be applied to Dame Edna. It was exactly what she was *not*, and never had been. Still, she had her ups and downs like most divas and I began to wonder if she might not be that new thing that people were talking about: 'bipolar'. It was becoming a fashionable excuse for every sort of erratic and irresponsible behaviour. It might even be something Edna might like to have, if she knew of its existence. It would go well with vulnerability.

'Sometimes I think I'm too *sensitive*' was another of Edna's favourite phrases.

The New York season ended triumphantly and Edna, a stranger to false modesty, revelled in her newly discovered popularity 'across the pond'. I knew she was tired – I was, too, merely being in her propinquity – but she seemed in no way the woman on the brink of a nervous collapse that she had been at the Dorchester. It was time for us to go back to London before a long American tour started the following spring, though I wondered why she did not feel that a visit to her mother, who must have been incredibly old, might have been a more appropriate act of filial devotion. The maintenance of Norm's obelisk might also have been another priority.

About a week after the curtain fell on her last New York performance I noticed that she seemed edgy. I put it down to adrenalin withdrawal. She was also reading something with a brown paper cover concealing its title, and she delved into this volume at every opportunity. Far from giving her pleasure, it seemed to increase her perturbation. One lunchtime at La

Goulue on Madison Avenue, when she was away in the rest-room, I saw the object of Edna's intense perusals poking out of her black Hermès Birkin. Naturally I had a quick peek. Edna had been studying *The Joy of Gay Sex*. I wished I hadn't cheated. I felt the disappointment of a parent when its child discovers that Santa Claus does not exist. I wished that Edna could have gone on living and working without this glimpse of an alternative universe.

We had only been back in London a few days but by this time the demise of the Talent Factory had been widely pub-licised. The police, the fraud squad and probably the Inland Revenue office had incriminating video footage of Talent Factory executives, including Wanda Smellie, hauling files and documents out of the back door of their building in the middle of the night and stashing them in vans.

One night I had a call from Edna which I will not easily forget. The voice on the phone was very quiet and controlled, which meant that she was not quiet or controlled in the least. Edna had not gone back to the Dorchester but was staying more humbly in a small flat in Hill Street, Mayfair.

'I'll come over in the morning, Edna,' I had said to her. 'It's nearly midnight now.'

Again, almost in a whisper this time, she begged me to come. 'It's a family health problem,' she said. 'It's desperate.'

I threw on some clothes and got to her building at about 1 a.m., praying that this was not a wild goose chase.

'Kenny has proclivities,' she said as soon as I came through the door. 'He's a very sick boy.'

To my amazement I noticed that Edna was smoking and I had never seen her do this. In the past we had been discreetly approached by cigarette companies asking if Edna could smoke in one of her shows, or even decline a cigarette. Presumably it didn't matter to them either way, so long as it connected her to the habit as a user or rejector.

Edna expelled a long cloud of smoke and thumped down into an armchair. 'Look, when we were talking about Wanda Smellie's proclivities I got to thinking and I bought a few publications. They were horrible, unclean things and I've binned them. I only hope that they don't find their way into the hands of kiddies or senior citizens.' I frowned and studied the dull mushroom carpet of this thirties apartment.

'Last night,' continued Edna in a dry quaver, 'I went to Langan's restaurant and that horrible slob who runs it, Peter Langan, told me Kenny was there at another table. I went over to surprise him and found him—' Edna paused and emitted a kind of visceral yelp. 'I found him with that Smail person, and they were holding hands across the table.' Edna's quaver became a sob, and she was soon convulsed in tears. 'My son Kenny is a poofter,' she wailed. 'What have I done to deserve this?'

There was no doubt about Edna, she could bring any subject back to herself with an expertise like no other.

'*I know what they do*, Barry,' she whispered hoarsely. 'I read it in a ghastly book with illustrations. I know how they operate now. You wouldn't believe it.'

I rose and went through the motions of comforting her,

putting my arm around her shoulders and offering her a hand-kerchief. After a loud emunctory blast, she said, 'When Kenny was a baby I don't know how many times I held up his chubby little ankles and dusted his botty with talcum powder and soothed his rash with zinc cream.'

Where was this leading to, I wondered.

'Do you want to know what he's doing with it now, Barry? Do you? *Do you?*'

'No, no, Edna, I don't and, well, he may not . . . er . . . that's to say it could be Cliff who . . .' I broke off in shame and confusion.

Edna sat there pale and wide-eyed as though she had had a glimpse of hell. 'All of that zinc cream, all that talcum . . . and for what?'

21

Madge

I was reflecting on this dramatic scene as I strolled down Piccadilly a week later. Edna had told me that she had not approached her son and his friend during their amorous *tête-à-tête* in the restaurant but had quickly turned away and fled, sobbing, into Stratton Street. I think she had decided not to confront Kenny about his – and what was then beginning to be called – 'sexuality', but to go on pretending that he may have just been looking for Miss Right in the wrong places. Denial was not yet a popularly known condition.

I turned into Duke Street on my way to a picture gallery to examine a licentious engraving by Fragonard, and on the spur of the moment decided to call into Fortnum's Fountain for a coffee. Immediately I spotted Madge Allsop sitting alone at a corner table with a pot of tea and a cake stand of petits fours. It is possible she was wearing a hint of make-up and I perceived that perhaps, long ago, she might have been pretty, in a faded way, like an old chintz cushion left too long in the sun.

She welcomed me to her little table and we embarked upon the first conversation we had had in many years. 'Do you like London?' I ventured, for want of anything to say.

'Edna is not a well woman,' replied Madge, ignoring my question.

'What makes you say that, Madge?' I asked, surprised. Without Edna looming over her like a vulture, Mrs Allsop seemed to have undergone a personality change. I suddenly saw a rather shrewd little woman across the table.

'She's not well *in herself*,' reiterated Madge, using the famous Australian phrase. 'Mind you, she was always kind to me at first when we were both at the same wee school in Moonee Ponds. She saved me from a horrible bully called John Bromley who used to give me Chinese burns and shout "Say fish and chips, Madge, say fish and chips" and I would say "fush and chups" like we say it in New Zealand and everyone would laugh, even Miss Maddox the teacher, and I would cry and Edna would say, "Chin up, Madge" and she didn't know it but no one had been nice to me since I came over from New Zealand on the *Wanganui* and I know her wee moods and when to keep out of the way and there's no harm in her really, Barry. She changed a bit after I married Douglas Allsop and Doug was the sweetest, loveliest, gentlest person you could ever meet and he was a New Zealander himself so he never asked me to say fush 'n' chups and she came on our honeymoon and she was there when Douglas had his wee accident in the mud pool and she invited me back to Australia and then there were the TV shows and all her famous friends and you looking after us until that Wanda woman came along and Edna changed and dropped me like a hot cake and all her other friends as well, including you, and now she's found out she made a big mistake and I think she was lonely when Norm was alive and in some ways marriage is the worst loneliness of all when you come to think of it and she probably won't even miss me if I go back to New Zealand, but there was something else that happened a long time ago . . .'

Ever since I had known her, Madge had carried taciturnity to the point of being marginally mute, but now the flood gates seemed to have opened. As she paused momentarily for breath I noticed that she was overcome by some curious emotion. Her eyes had filled with tears.

'Yes, Barry,' she continued, composing herself at last, 'something happened years and years ago and I feel I owe Edna something. However she treats me, I owe her something.'

'I don't see what you could possibly owe her,' I said with a surge of sympathy for this little old lady who had been so consistently abused and publicly denigrated by Edna.

'Take my word for it, Barry,' Madge resumed, 'I might explain the whole thing to her one day but it might tip her over the edge. I have written it all down though – all of it – and I want you to read it, but only after I've gone to my wee reward. It was meant that we should bump into each other today, Barry. The Celestial Beings meant this to happen.'

I had forgotten that all New Zealanders believe in flying saucers, aliens and extraterrestrial creatures. Madge rummaged in her battered Air New Zealand bowling bag and produced a slightly soiled envelope addressed to me.

'It's all here,' she declared, 'but promise you won't open this until I have fallen asleep in the arms of my Maker. She must never know until I'm gone.'

I presumed that 'she' was Edna. I put the envelope in the inside pocket of my jacket and pressed Madge's hand. 'I promise, Madge,' I said, realising that the old bridesmaid was very lonely and probably completely off her rocker. 'But I think I may have to wait a very long time before I can open this envelope. You look as fit as a fiddle,' I added, with what I hoped was an expression of sincerity.

'Don't flatter me, Barry, just do what I say,' said Madge, fixing me with a long conspiratorial look and signalling to the waitress. 'I'll pick up the wee docket.'

The late-night telephone call from Vanessa came as a surprise. 'I didn't think you were really talking to me, baby,' she said in a voice that sounded the richer for a few drinks.

'I'm always pleased to hear from you,' I replied, or words to that effect.

'I'm freelancing a lot now,' she said, 'and amongst other things I'm working on the *Book Programme* on the BBC.'

'I hope you're making some of those writers look better.'

'Christ,' replied Vanessa, 'I had a tough one today. That's why I'm ringing.'

'Now, don't be indiscreet, Vanessa,' I replied. 'Salman is a sort of friend of mine.'

Vanessa laughed. 'No, it's not Salman. But some women, not me, do find him sexy.'

Suddenly, I had an urgent need for Vanessa to find me sexy, too. 'Who was it?' I asked, trying to distract myself from the joys of being Vanessa's guest.

'Wait for this,' replied Vanessa. 'It was Valmai Everage, Edna's dykey daughter.'

'On the *Book Programme*!' I exclaimed. 'Edna's daughter? Are you sure?'

'She's written a tell-all book and guess what it's called?'

I sat slumped by my telephone, trying to get a grasp on what was happening and already trying, without success, to imagine the effect this news would have on Edna. She hadn't mentioned Valmai in a long time and I had simply assumed the woman was living in a rural district on the outskirts of Melbourne with her 'partner', making pots or running a female-friendly B & B.

'What's it called?' I asked, weak with anxiety.

'*Edna Dearest: The Confessions of a Superstar's Daughter.*'

Panic-stricken, I almost yelled down the phone: 'Edna must never find out about this! Don't tell a soul, Vanessa!'

'Listen, baby . . .' My friend seemed to be laughing, 'the book is printed and the *Book Programme* goes to air next weekend. Valmai will be signing copies in Hatchards any day. She's even got herself a big agent. It's that Smellie woman we met out at Channel Nine.'

I felt as if I was sliding into a nightmare. So Wanda Smellie was going solo and still pretending to be an agent, and she had even hijacked Edna's daughter. What a deft act of revenge on her ex-client it was, though I could not imagine what grievance she might have to justify this. I dreaded to think how Edna might react to this news, on top of her discoveries about Kenny and his proclivities.

'Thank you, Vanessa,' was all that I could say, though the nature of the information she had imparted hardly deserved gratitude. 'Could we meet up soon for lunch or something?'

'Be my guest, baby,' said Vanessa. I winced.

The next morning, after a sleepless night, I tried contacting Wanda, but to no avail. Then I called my editor Fanny and decided to tell her the bad news.

'What can we do, Fanny?'

'You'll have to tell Edna immediately,' came the pragmatic advice, 'and soon, before that book hits the shops and the publisher sends out review copies. It can't have happened yet, or we would have heard. I'll call you back.'

Fifteen minutes later Fanny was back on the phone. 'I've got a number for that Smellie monster, but no one will tell me where Valmai is hiding out, or anything about what's in the book except that it's not a hymn of filial gratitude and adoration.'

I scribbled down Wanda's number.

'Incidentally, Barry,' Fanny said, 'did I ever tell you that Wanda once made a move on me at the Groucho Club? She's not a nice lady.'

It was an advantage speaking to Valmai's literary agent on the telephone and to be out of range of her annihilating breath. Her words, however, were no less lethal.

'I have nothing against Edna *per se*,' insisted Wanda, who seemed to have a new-found passion for Latin tags. 'I don't see any *prima facie* reason why I can't represent a talented young female writer who just happens to paint a truthful picture of an ex-client.' I had stopped trying to understand what the hell she was talking about after '*prima facie*' but at least I knew I would never hear the words '*mea culpa*' from her lips.

Wanda continued forcefully, but in English. 'Val has written a fucking brilliant book about a lonely and abused childhood, and if you want my opinion, you've got a typical homophobic attitude to Valmai's gender choices.'

'Oh, she's got choices, has she? Then why couldn't she have chosen a better agent?'

'She came to me, Barry, and I have been helping her edit her material. I thought it might have been a book for Blooms-bury or Virago, but it's bigger than that so we went to Harper-Collins and they're over the moon. When *Edna Dearest* hits the marketplace, no one will give a shit about that book you're doing with Fanny.'

'You are foul mouthed in more than one sense, Wanda,' I replied, surfing on a wave of rage and adrenalin. 'Where is Valmai now, you appalling cow?'

'She's *in situ*, here with me,' hissed Wanda. 'She needs me and what I can offer her. She doesn't need you or any other male chauvinist bastard!'

On that unedifying note, my conversation with Wanda Smellie came to an abrupt end.

I had no choice but to tell Edna. Standing in the small elevator as it rumbled upwards to Edna's sixth-floor flat in Mayfair, I wondered what mood she would be in. Her emotional state had become unpredictable and I had to remember that she was no longer a young woman. I never really thought about her age or even tried to calculate it, which I suppose is the highest compliment one can pay any actress.

When she opened the door she was wearing a turquoise leotard and white socks. 'I'm in the middle of pilates,' she said, 'but go into the kitchenette and make yourself a nice smoothie. You'll find soy milk in the mini fridge and there's a jar of spirulina on the kitchen table. Use the vitamiser.'

I had no idea what pilates was or, for that matter, how to make a smoothie but I guessed that they must both have been the latest thing. Edna's reference to a 'vitamiser', instead of a blender, would have been lost on anyone who had not lived in Australia in the fifties. It was an endearing lapse.

In the middle of her sitting room, which was rather dinky, Edna had installed an apparatus that was not unlike a rack in some medieval torture chamber, or was it a Procrustean bed?

Were Pilates and Procrustes the same person I wondered? Edna was not alone. There was a tall Asian-looking instructor with a lot of black hair manipulating her in the other room, and as I muddled around in the kitchen scattering green spirulina dust, trying to make myself a drink with the unlikely constituents Edna had recommended, I wondered when the coast would be clear and I could deliver my bombshell.

Messily, I put a couple of scoops of the viridian powder into the glass vessel, added a chopped banana and a few dates I discovered in the fridge, and poured in half a carton of soy milk. But my mind was on other things. The seduction of Valmai by that vile agent, for one thing. All her life, Edna's daughter had shown serious signs of delinquency and I had known for some time her partiality to members of her own sex. Was she, like her brother Kenny, 'passing through a phase'?

Edna had been a far from perfect mother and it would be unusual if Valmai did not suffer from what had been called 'abandonment issues'. I had once, bravely, pointed this out to Edna before one of her extended trips abroad, but Edna pooh-poohed the idea. 'That's ridiculous!' she had snapped. 'I've abandoned her hundreds of times before and it didn't make any difference. She's just sulking and her father spoils her.'

I rammed the black plastic lid onto the blender and pressed a red button. There was a tremendous roar and the whole kitchen seemed to shudder. The lid flew off and a thick ejaculation of slimy green smoothie sprayed in all directions until I managed to hit the stop button.

While I was still mopping up the aftermath of this viscous eruption, I heard the front door slam and, for better or worse, my moment had arrived. As soon as she saw me Edna burst into peals of laughter.

'You look like the Incredible Hulk,' she shouted. 'I wish Takao could have seen you before he left just then. The Koreans have a wonderful sense of humour.'

I glanced in the mirror over her buffet and saw that quite a lot of bright green smoothie foam clung to my shirt front, upper lip and eyebrows. My heart sank as I realised how quickly this mood of levity was going to change.

'Sit down, Edna,' I said, scrubbing my face with a hand-kerchief, 'something serious has happened.'

Edna was still laughing. I had to get on with this.

'Valmai's in town.'

Edna sat down and stared at me.

'Valmai is in town,' I repeated, 'and she's got a book coming out which we are not going to like.'

'But Valmai couldn't even write a note to the milkman!' exclaimed Edna. 'And I'd know if she was here, I'm her mother. What's all this about, Barry?'

'It's about Wanda Smellie. She's got Valmai in her clutches and she's somehow, probably with the help of a hack journo, managed to get a book out of her.'

Edna seemed to be in a daze. Was she on heavy medication, I wondered? It was as if she had not heard anything I had just told her.

'What did you think of Takao, my pilates instructor? Did

you think he was . . . could he possibly have . . . proclivities?' she asked.

'Forget about proclivities, Edna!' I barked. 'He probably has – who hasn't for Christ's sake? – but we're talking about your daughter, Valmai, who is about to do a great deal of damage. At least Kenny and Clifford are only leaping into bed and not leaping into print.'

'That was completely uncalled for, Barry. He's got rid of Clifford, anyway,' added Edna triumphantly. 'I told him that he was breaking my heart, but I decided not to mention the zinc cream and talcum powder, not at this stage anyway.'

I listened to these ravings with the patience of a saint.

'It wasn't the horrible thing I thought it was anyway, Barry, when I saw Kenny and Cliff in Langan's,' Edna went on. 'Kenny was actually saying goodbye because Clifford was going back to Australia. That restaurant experience was a big step up the ladder for Kenny, I think, and Clifford sweetly taught Ken some of his culinary secrets: his signature drizzle, for instance.'

'It sounds delicious, Edna, but where is Kenny drizzling at the moment? You might need his help.'

'He's staying in Pimlico with a nice architect, but I'm not worried about that. Brian has children apparently, and he's a regular church-goer.'

I realised that I was grinding my teeth, my head was throbbing and my fingernails were biting into my palms. 'Edna,' I persisted, 'we have to do something about Valmai's book. It's no good approaching Valmai. I'm trying to find out if someone I know has a contact at HarperCollins.'

'I do,' said Edna brightly. 'Rupert might help.'

'Who's Rupert?'

Edna looked coy. 'Just a boy I've known for years. He's quite big in the media world these days. I knew him when he was a youngster in Melbourne delivering our papers in the morning on his bike. He'd throw a rolled-up copy of the *Sun News-Pictorial* over our front fence every morning and I'd always give him two and six at Christmas. I had a feeling then that he'd go a long way, and not on a bicycle.'

'Well, if ever you needed to call in a favour, now is the time, Edna,' I said. 'All those two and six pence might have just bought you a way out of hell, and hell it will be if your daughter's revelations come out. Are you still in touch with this man?'

'My very word, Barry. We exchange Christmas cards and he writes me nice letters in ink. Who does that these days, except Prince Charles? I only wish that they were both better friends.'

'Please do it,' I exhorted her, 'and do it now. I won't be far away and I'll be on my mobile.' I held up the rather large black instrument with its telescopic aerial and chunky plastic buttons. 'I'll be waiting for your call, Edna.'

22

Edna's Fête

I had left Edna in a chirpy, almost caffeinated mood. The potentially devastating effects of Valmai's revelations seemed not to concern her, as I had expected they would. What I'd anticipated was meltdown, wild panic and nervous collapse. Her 'contact' in the publishing world seemed like a nebulous solution. Did she know this mythical figure? Was she really acquainted with the powerful tycoon who had, long ago, delivered her morning newspaper?

At times like these I began to wonder if Edna herself was a real person. She was so unlike any rational being I knew.

And I began to worry about myself. Since Edna and I had become reconciled, I had been totally at her beck and call. Anything that I did, or hoped to do, was subservient to her needs and desires. I had found myself mixed up in her financial affairs, mercifully without penalty, I had quarrelled with her termagant of an agent and become somehow enmeshed in her family life: namely her children's romantic perversities. Everything else in my life was on hold, seemingly forever.

Again, as I walked along South Audley Street, past Harry's Bar and the expensive shops, I imagined my life without Edna. Whenever I saw her it seemed to be in connection with some terrible drama, and in speaking to her, in placating her, in attempting to reason with her, I had to modify my personality to get through to the woman. The world found her irresistible, clever and even motherly, but to me she remained an impenetrable enigma. If things went on this way much longer I would be used up; I might even lose my own identity in the struggle.

Days passed, and to keep my sanity I concentrated on my own book, with a lot of encouragement from Fanny. It was like writing a novel because she had insisted that, for commercial reasons, I should keep up the fiction that 'Dame Edna' was a clever theatrical parody of my own invention. I was eager to learn further news of Valmai's book but Fanny had discovered nothing on the grapevine. I assumed I would be hearing the worst at any moment.

Every day I scanned the 'Londoner's Diary' in the *Evening Standard* which always carried literary gossip, but there was nothing. My phone didn't ring and I was certainly not going to call Edna. What did it really matter, anyway, if Valmai Everage, in cahoots with Wanda Smellie, did her worst? It might even increase the public's interest in *my* book but, to my dismay,

I realised that Fanny's company was only publishing my work because it was all about Edna, my gaudy, garrulous nemesis. Would I ever get back to being me?

I delivered the last two chapters of my book and went to Greece. I had been to the island of Spetses before and loved it. It was only two hours in a catamaran from Athens. I could hire a kayiki and a boatman for the day and sail to the other side of the island for a swim while the boatman snorkelled across to the rocks to gather my lunch of sea urchins, or we'd visit small and unfrequented coves. Across the sparkling aquamarine water, the rocks and little beaches seemed to be decorated with beautiful white shells and fragments of sun-bleached coral, though as one swam closer to the shore these glistening objects turned out to be lumps of styrofoam, ragged sheets of plastic and nondegradable plastic bottles: the indestructible flotsam and jetsam of that popular dumping ground, the Aegean. But swimming in Greece is still like swimming nowhere else on earth, and I have liked the Greek people ever since I was a university student in Melbourne[15] when we would all have an incredibly cheap dinner at the Amonia Café in Lonsdale Street.

One didn't always have to take a boat trip because there was a perfectly good concrete beach in the town itself where, every year, I would find my friend Simon Gray, the playwright, and his wife Victoria. Simon told me that there was a new arrival in the house where they were lodging, a fortune teller called

15 The second-biggest Greek city in the world.

Patrick who had advertised his presence on the island and was receiving a large number of curious and credulous customers. I met the soothsayer informally one morning at the beach and he seemed a very agreeable, unnoticeable little chap. He was from Essex and had a bald head and a mahogany tan. He probably cruised the Greek islands in the summer with his swimming trunks, espadrilles and crystal ball.

I was always susceptible to intimations from the future, however transmitted, and having hitherto only employed the talents of a Queensland sibyl, I made an appointment with Patrick and staggered up the hill that evening after my siesta to see what Fate had in store for me. Simon had just had a long reading from which he emerged amused, but with a couple of dents in his scepticism.

'Your turn,' he said. 'He's pretty expensive at thirty quid an hour but he's rather convincing. He reckons I've had about fifty-seven past lives. He'll be interested in you because you have three or four lives going on at virtually the same time so presumably he will have two or three hundred past lives to discuss with you!'

I can't remember much about Patrick's predictions except that I found him, as had Simon Gray, oddly plausible. I suppose one can't help liking someone a little who is prepared to sit down and talk about you for an hour flat. However, he did say there was a woman dominating my life and that I had to free myself from her somehow. When pressed for a description of this succubus he was elusive, but he seemed to think she was a malign influence. I knew very well who she was.

Every day during this short vacation I would walk down the narrow cobbled street in the old town and buy the *Herald Tribune*, and whenever possible a copy of a two-day-old *Daily Telegraph*, scanning the latter for any news of a Dame Edna scandal. But there was nothing; not a whisper.

Back in London, with the fortune teller's words still ringing in my ears, I sat down by my answering machine to listen to the messages. There were twenty-seven calls and one of them, four days old, was from Edna. She sounded very put out that I was not there to answer the telephone because she had received an offer from some women's museum in Denmark to hold an exhibition of her clothes and memorabilia – programmes, posters, photographs and, of course, famous eyewear. She wanted me to negotiate with the Danes and she wanted a large consultancy fee for Kenny as designer of most of the clothes. She was still talking excitedly when the tape ran out.

It was odd. Ten days ago there had been a major crisis with Edna's hostile daughter about to bring out a tell-all memoir, aided and abetted by a vindictive agent. What had happened in the interval? I would have to drag myself up to that rented flat in Mayfair if I wanted an answer, but it was the last time I would ever do so. My mind was made up. This time it was divorce.

Edna received me in a jubilant mood. She was wearing something very red and ornamental by Versace, whom she had met through Elton John. The swirling patterns on her dress, reminiscent of the colour scrolls and arabesques on an old-fashioned merry-go-round, clashed with the timid floral décor of her flat. She immediately bestowed a cool little kiss on both my cheeks in the lady-like fashion she had only recently adopted, and her favoured *modus operandi* for checking for the newly healed sutures of plastic surgery. It seemed too self-consciously 'continental' for a Melbourne girl from the wrong side of the tracks. Indeed, any sort of kiss from Edna felt a little strange; she was not a woman given to physical intimacies.

The sitting room was full of flowers, not gladioli however, which Edna had recently decided were rather 'common' and suitable only for flinging at her audience. Instead there were big arrangements of China blue hydrangeas. I wondered if she knew they were Proust's favourite flowers? It seemed a dissonant conjunction: Edna and Marcel.

'You remember Kenneth, don't you, Barry?' To my surprise Kenny had emerged from the kitchen carrying a platter of nibbles. 'They look so yummy, Kenny!' Edna exclaimed. 'Sun-dried tomatoes and arugula have always been my favourites.' Edna pronounced arugula 'arooogala' with a sensuality she reserved for food and clothes. I doubted that sundried tomatoes or arugula could have been her favourites for very long, since no Australian of her generation would have considered eating tomatoes that had been left out in the sun or consuming a raw vegetable that was more weed than lettuce.

Kenny had certainly grown up since I had seen him last. He was taller and quite good looking with his startling blue eyes, and his mullet coiff was dyed a rather sulphurous yellow. He wore jeans which had been artfully distressed by the manufacturer, a sleeveless black mesh singlet and a leather metal-studded wrist strap.

'Hi,' said Kenny. He had a habit of waving little greetings with his wrist pressed to his hip and fluttering his fingers. I had noticed for quite a while that the American salutation 'Hi' had been appropriated by Australians and English alike, but it always sounded faintly anomalous.

'Hello, Kenny,' I said. 'What's going on?'

Edna interrupted. 'We're having a little cocktail party and Kenny's making the canapés.' She pronounced them 'can-apes'. 'You have popped in at exactly the right time, Barry.'

Kenny gave me a friendly smile beneath his moustache. 'Can I fix you a Bellini, Baz?' he enquired, using the irritating diminutive.

'I don't drink, I'm afraid,' I replied, 'but if there's a cup of tea I'd love one.'

'We've only got Earl Grey,' said Edna haughtily. 'I hope that will do?'

I remembered the old days with a pang. Then it would have been Robur tea, or Bushells or, at a pinch, Griffiths, which was advertised beside roads and railway tracks all over Victoria with 'Five miles to Griffiths Tea'. In those more robust days, no Australian would drink perfumed tea.

The doorbell rang and I realised this was neither the time nor the place to raise any of the serious matters I hoped to discuss, but at least I would get to meet a few of Edna's new friends.

'Kenny's staying here with me for a while, Barry,' said Edna.

'It's so lovely having family around.' I nodded and glanced into the hallway as Kenny opened the front door, admitting an enormous black man in black tie. I saw the two men give each other an affectionate little hug.

'Jason's here, Mum,' Kenny cried.

'Jason's the help,' explained Edna, using the American genteelism for servant. 'He's adorable,' she added as Kenny and the adorable help disappeared into the kitchen. It was now or never, I thought. Edna was straightening a picture. 'Do you like my new Hockney, Barry?' she asked. 'I just bought it. It's from his second Californian period and it's an artist's proof.'

'How's Valmai?' I blurted out. 'Is she coming tonight?'

To my amazement Edna laughed good-naturedly.

'Poor little Val,' she said. 'I think she's had an attack of the sulks, poor lamb, since they pulped her book.'

'Pulped it? I hadn't heard.'

'Oh, it's old news now, Barry,' said Edna, plumping a cushion. 'The publishers decided her effort wasn't up to scratch and it just kind of . . . went away.' Edna accompanied this information with a wave of her hand, to illustrate the vaporisation of *Edna Dearest*. 'You wouldn't have heard about it. We kept it out of the press, naturally. Poor little Val was just going through a spooky phase.'

I wondered who 'we' was. Perhaps Edna herself and the man who had once delivered her morning paper? The doorbell rang again and Jason emerged from the kitchen to admit the first guest.

'Valmai is probably disappointed,' Edna resumed *sotto voce*, 'and that Wanda woman went bananas, but one day she will realise it was all for the best. Lucian, darling!'

I knew Lucian Freud slightly but I wasn't sure if he remembered me. He gave me a tight ascetic smile. Edna he did seem to know, but it was hard to tell what he thought of her. He may have seen her as a possible subject for portraiture, spatchcocked on a tousled bed, grey thighs akimbo.

As the room filled up with people, the word 'pulped' kept passing through my mind on a loop. How powerful Edna had become, I thought, and what a huge distance she had placed between her present incarnation as society hostess and the timid frump I had met half a lifetime ago in Moonee Ponds. I overheard Nicky Haslam telling Barbara Black that he had known Cole Porter at the Waldorf Towers, and he also managed to mention Cecil Beaton and Noel Coward in the same sentence. Joan Collins and Christopher Biggins seemed to be laughing a lot at a private joke and possibly wondering why they were there, or how soon they might politely leave for somewhere else. Ed Victor, the celebrated literary agent, was fawning over his new friend and client Conrad Black, the Canadian tycoon. The future Lord Black was fawning in turn over his hostess.

'Hello, Possum!' he said whimsically, bowing and kissing Edna's hand. The room was becoming crowded and everyone was eating and drinking, thanks to the vigilant Jason and Kenny who fluttered attentively. I perched awkwardly beside another man on a small regency-striped sofa in the corner. How did Edna know all of these people, I wondered, and how did they know her? Perhaps they were all here in the expectation of meeting someone else. She was no longer a social novelty in London but I suppose she was what some people would describe as a 'one-off'; a collector's item. Andrew Logan and Zandra Rhodes seemed to know her intimately, and leaning on a stick, Lord Snowdon, the Queen's ex-brother-in-law and a famous photographer, greeted her effusively.

The incongruous figure beside me on the sofa appeared to be very tired and detached from the noisy gathering. 'Excuse I, mate,' he said, nudging my elbow. 'Isn't that Lizzie Minnelli over there?'

'Yes,' I averred. 'But she prefers to be called "Liza",' I added pompously.

The man was drinking Foster's beer, 'necking it' from the bottle. 'Gee,' he said, 'Mum seems to know everyone.'

This must be Brucie, the rarely mentioned son. I recognised the dandruff farmer I had only met twice before, most recently in the back of a limousine on the way to view Norm's obelisk. I introduced myself.

'Very nice to meet you, mate,' said Brucie, shaking my hand.

The word 'mate' sounded rather friendly coming from him, although in Australia it is often given a hostile inflection.

'You've done a lot for Mum over the years. You've probably seen more of her than the family has.'

'I'm afraid that may be true, Bruce,' I shouted, for the noise in the room was almost deafening. At that moment I saw Andrew Lloyd Webber and his wife enter with Tom Stoppard. 'Your mother seems to be on close terms with everyone.'

Brucie took a pull on his beer bottle. 'Everyone except Joylene.' Seeing my puzzled look, Brucie elaborated. 'Joylene's my wife but Mum never liked her. It was a religious thing basically. Even though her family didn't go to Mass much, Mum always found fault. I shouldn't have made this trip alone, really, but Joylene said that even if Mum had sent two tickets she wouldn't have come.'

'Have you seen your sister Valmai?' I asked at the top of my voice.

'I spoke to her on the phone but she's pretty pissed off with Mum, and she's bloody well turned lezzo. I suppose I'm telling tales out of school.'

'I had heard she made some gender choices,' I replied tactfully, 'but so, I think, has your brother Kenny.'

'Tell me about it!' asserted Brucie. 'Ken bites the pillow big time, but Mum won't wear it.' He looked almost anguished. 'Listen, mate, you could be a poofter, too, for all I know, but imagine what it feels like to have a brother *and* a sister batting for the opposite team. A bloke begins to wonder if it's in the genes – that he might be a pillow-biter himself underneath.'

I looked sideways at the lean, almost scrawny man in jeans, boat shoes and a fawn zip-fronted pullover. He was no longer in his first youth and wore a pair of cheap glasses, crudely repaired with a Band-aid. I noticed, as he nervously drew on his cigarette, that he chewed his fingernails.

'Mum hasn't introduced me to any of this mob here tonight, mate. Basically, she's probably a bit embarrassed that I'm here.' I realised he had picked up the buzz word 'basically' and would be flogging it to death. 'Basically, she thinks I've let her down in business. She's bankrolled me in a few things that have gone pear-shaped, but it was never my fault, basically.'

'What things?' I asked, noticing that David Tang had just arrived with the Duchess of York on one arm and Kate Moss on the other. David was an infallible guide to the A-list.

'Isn't that Fergie?' enquired Brucie, as if he'd just spotted Mother Teresa.

'You were talking about Edna assisting you financially,' I prompted.

'Oh, there were different businesses of mine that she helped with. The dried fruit mail-order business was a non-starter, but when Joylene and myself opened our Spa and Wellness Centre in Wonthaggi[16] I was sure we were on to a winner. Joylene's a certified therapist and she does the organic coffee enemas, but that's a tough one to sell in a small place like Wonthaggi.'

'Almost anywhere, I would have thought,' I ventured.

For the first time a small but tragic smile crossed Brucie's lips. 'The customers generally fall asleep, but their bums are awake all night and staring at the ceiling.' I could see it was a jest he had made successfully many times before. 'Well, Baz,' he continued dolefully, 'basically we blew it, and Mum said she could see it coming and that she wasn't throwing any more

16 A town built on black coal reserves, Wonthaggi was used by the Victorian government in response to the disastrous New South Wales coal strikes at the turn of the century. It currently has a population of 6600.

good money after bad, particularly after the Afghan restaurant, the Aboriginal dating service, the macadamia furniture and the pre-loved, gently used and autoclaved marital aids.'

Second-hand vibrators would have been a specialised market at the best of times, I thought. How had Brucie sold some, if not all, of these enterprises to his mother?

'Right now,' said Brucie, 'I'm working on a pretty exciting project I've got in the pipeline: almost drinkable designer water. I'm relaunching Moonee Waters – Moonee Ponds sits on a subterranean aquifer. The ponds are just the tip of the iceberg. They haven't been tapped for years.'

By now it had become almost too noisy to talk, and I felt very sorry for this man, orphaned by his mother's success.

There was a hacking cough – a terrible cough – close at hand and I recognised, without even looking, the bronchial eruption of Kenneth Jay Lane, that charming and dapper purveyor of fake jewellery to the rich and famous. I liked him and rose to have a few words with him when Edna interrupted.

'You know Kenny, do you, Barry? He's my other Kenny.'

Lane lit a cigarette as though his next cough depended on it.

Edna leant in close to my ear, 'I saw you chatting with Brucie. He's a brilliant boy but he takes after Norm – no initiative and no drive – and he married a little gold-digging RC. They hadn't been married seven months before little Craig came along. Need I say more?'

I saw that Brucie had moved from the couch and had sidled up to Sarah Ferguson, staring rather rudely at her homely freckled countenance. He held out a paper napkin and I heard him say, 'You don't know me from a bar of soap, Your Majesty, but is there any chance of an autograph? It's not for me, it's for the wife, she's a big fan.' The Duchess of York politely assented to this request but had to find her own pen since none was proffered. Cringeing at the gaucheries of my fellow country-men I moved away, just as I heard Edna's eldest son spelling out 'J-O-Y-L-E-N-E'.

There was a tinkling from the baby grand piano and I saw that it was Jools Holland at the keyboard. Nicky Haslam leant on the instrument and began to sing 'Mad About the Boy', looking a bit too obviously in the direction of Jason the waiter, who was trying to move people into the dining room where a buffet of shepherd's pie was on offer. It was a very successful party and it went on, with people coming and going, until almost midnight, by which time Jools and Nicky had launched into a selection from *Call Me Madam*. For me, the whole event was an amazing and unmissable spectacle: London's homage to my friend Edna.

And yet, come to think of it, I had called at the flat that evening unannounced. I hadn't been invited. Was it possible – could it be? – that my friend Edna wasn't really a very nice person after all?

23

Uncle Vic

I telephoned Edna the next day to thank her for the party and she sounded, unsurprisingly, a bit flat.

'Yes, it was lovely wasn't it, Barry, and I'm glad you popped in. I hadn't invited you because it was mostly for friends and not business. I don't think it's good to mix them, do you?'

I wondered how many people there were actually friends of Edna's. I could name at least half a dozen I'd talked to who had never met her before in their lives. 'I'll remember that when I have my next party,' I said rather lamely.

After all these years she still had the infallible knack of delivering an insult with a lovely smile.

'Did you meet Seth Foxson last night?' she asked. 'He's that brilliant shrink from Finchley who's having an affair with my new literary agent.'

I didn't know that Edna had a new literary agent, nor was I aware that she knew a psychotherapist. Even the term 'shrink' sounded alien coming from her, but then she was becoming alien.

'What about him?'

'Well, Barry, he thinks it would help if I saw him a couple of times a week. He can help me address a few issues.'

So, Edna had started 'addressing issues' had she? I was very curious to know what they might be.

I had to call by her flat later that day to discuss the details for the Queen's birthday party at Buckingham Palace. It was to be a huge event in the Royal backyard, and only the top artistes and musicians of the day had been commanded to perform. Edna was one, and it was a tremendous honour.

Kenny was out at the gym, a popular rendezvous for young men like him and one which afforded them an opportunity to indulge their two favourite pastimes: flirtation and narcissism. Edna seemed, understandably, a little hungover and preoccupied. She was also annoyingly *blasé* about the exciting Royal Command Performance.

'Why do you think this Foxson fellow can help you, Edna?' I asked her.

'He thinks I need medication, Barry, because I have too many ups and downs.'

'But ups and downs are part of life,' I protested. 'You don't want drugs to iron you out and turn you into a vegetable, do you?'

'I have to tell someone about Uncle Vic,' Edna said with a tremor in her voice. She stood and walked across to a pointless little desk in the corner of the sitting room. She was lighting a cigarette, a very rare indulgence and a sure sign of nervous agitation, and when she returned to the couch I saw her hand was trembling as, like an amateurish schoolgirl, she puffed on the thin Cartier filter.

'Vic was my mother's favourite brother,' Edna began, 'and he often used to come around when we were kids. He always gave us lollies and he used to take me down to the park and push me on the swings . . .'

There was a long pause while Edna took a few more puffs. I felt she was trying to hold back a tumultuous emotion.

'He pushed the swing in a funny way, pushing me from the front and sending the swing higher and higher.' I wondered where this was leading. 'Well, every now and then, as he pushed the wooden seat, his hand slipped up along my leg, under my frock near my front botty, and he kept laughing and saying, "How's that, Edna, how's that?"'

Edna again paused, this time to extinguish her cigarette and blow her nose.

'I knew there was something wrong, Barry,' she continued. 'I didn't know what, but I was frightened, and I can still feel that horrible hand where no uncle's hand should ever be.'

'Did you tell your parents?' I asked.

'Of course not. They worshipped Vic and they were always

proud of the number of Japs he'd killed during the period of hostilities. But at afternoon tea, when we were all sitting around the table, he gave me a funny look, trying to work out if I'd said anything. I can still see that look now, Barry. It's . . . it's horrible, and the whole thing affected me for years.'

'Your marriage?' I asked, gently probing.

'Oh yes,' exclaimed Edna, with a dry and bitter laugh, 'Uncle Vic affected that all right. There were things, intimate things, Norm wanted to do but I wouldn't let him. Perhaps if Uncle Vic hadn't existed I might still have stopped Norm from doing them, whatever they were. You see, I never really found out what they might have been because Norm was too shy to ask, but if he had I would suddenly have become very sleepy . . . Very, very sleepy.'

Edna seemed to be nodding off. The trauma of these disclosures, no doubt combined with the drugs that this Foxson quack was giving her, was plunging her into what might now be called 'a dark place'.

'Why are you worrying about all of this now, Edna?' I asked with real concern. 'The incident on the swings was nasty, but not as serious as other things that might have occurred.'

'But how do I know they didn't happen?' Edna exclaimed. 'What if I've blacked it all out? It's happened to plenty of other women, and it's always an uncle, haven't you noticed? Dr Foxson wants to put me into his clinic and do a proper assessment. He thinks I might be heading for a breakdown.'

'Have you told this to anyone else?' I asked.

'Only Judy, my new literary agent,' replied Edna, dabbing

her eyes with a Kleenex. 'She was a bit hard-hearted and said I had to put it in my next book. In fact, she got quite excited and said the only way for a showbiz autobiography to become a bestseller was to include something about a deviant uncle. "Avuncular molestation", as she called it, is very common and it sells books, she said. But that doesn't kill the pain, Barry.' Edna's voice broke and she burst into a flood of tears.

It seemed useless to persist with words of reason and sympathy. Something had brought all of this to a head and Edna's sudden rise to fame might have triggered a pathological reaction. I distrusted Foxson. I remembered him now, at the party with his corduroy clothes, a natty beard and that giveaway of the phoney, a grey ponytail. He had obviously latched onto Edna to do a major job of psychiatric empire-building.

I tried to change the subject to the more pressing matter of Edna's starring performance at Buckingham Palace. It was to be on the following Friday night and she would need to spend an afternoon at rehearsal.

'Why should I give up all my time?' she whined peevishly.

'Because everyone else is, Edna,' I replied crossly. 'Paul McCartney will be there for most of the day, Peter Gabriel will be there as well, and Ozzy Osbourne, Eric Clapton, Shirley Bassey and Elton John, just to name a few.'

'I know, I know, of course I'll be there. What's the matter with me, Barry? Could I be cracking up?'

'Don't talk like that, Edna. That old rogue with the ponytail, Dr Foxson, has put the wind up you. Didn't you tell me the other day that your gynaecologist said you were at the height of your powers?'

'But everything has fallen apart,' lamented Edna. 'Kenny and Valmai both have that terrible illness, Brucie wants more money to squander on that little Roman he's married to, and I've just heard from New Zealand that Madge is only hanging on by a thread.'

I was shocked by the last piece of news. 'Poor Madge,' I said. 'I didn't know she had gone back home. What's the matter with her?'

'Oh, she's always crying wolf, but I know she's got restless-leg syndrome, a deviated septum, and something called Crohn's Disease. That doesn't surprise me.'

I was genuinely appalled at Edna's pitiless indifference.

'It's just as well I cut her out of my will ages ago,' she went on brutally. 'It would be a pity for good money to go to some distant niece of her late husband Douglas. Isn't Dame Nature wonderful, Barry, the way she arranges these things?'

Edna seemed considerably more cheerful despite her catalogue of woe. 'A car is going to pick you up on Friday morning, Edna,' I said. 'I have all your costumes so you can choose what dress you're going to wear on the day. I have a friend from the BBC called Vanessa who will help you get ready.'

Edna looked sceptical. 'Not that hussy you used to have in tow I hope, Barry? I don't think I want her touching my face. She had funny feet and they were a bit on the grubby side as well.'

The royal event was to take place in the garden behind Buckingham Palace (a large garden – comprising more than forty acres). By chance I had seen the Queen a few days before at a private view at the Royal Academy.

'Will it be very noisy?' she asked me.

'Very noisy, Ma'am,' I replied. 'In fact, you might still be able to hear it at Balmoral.'

'Oh dear,' replied the monarch, 'I'm a bit worried about my lawn with all those people.'

It was a touching moment – the Queen had suddenly been displaced by a suburban housewife.

Vanessa and I got to the Palace early. It had seemed simpler, more expedient, and more relaxing for me to stay at her place in Pimlico, and I had wangled a special pass for Caleb so he could see the Queen, if only backstage on a television monitor. Security was intense but, in the British style, unobtrusive. A small village of tents had been pitched in the large park at the back of the Palace as canvas dressing-rooms, green rooms and dining areas for the performers and the army of technicians. A big stage had been erected and there were bleachers against the back wall of the Palace for special guests, with a flag-draped Royal Box for the Queen and her family.

A mood of high excitement prevailed all morning as things were made in readiness for the biggest spectacle of the decade. It was anticipated that there would be an audience of 16,000 people stretching from the gates of Buckingham Palace right down the Mall to Trafalgar Square. The television audience would exceed 200 million viewers worldwide.

'You look like shit,' said Vanessa. 'You shouldn't have exerted yourself so much last night.'

Caleb was crying. He didn't like me, and I hated him. I'd never met his father, who was some TV presenter, but from looking at the child I could imagine the oafish features of his other parent. He was very spoilt by his mother who let him wander freely into the bedroom, sometimes at awkward moments. 'Who's that funny man?' he would ask, and I suppose, on reflection, it accurately described what he saw.

'I can't say I'm feeling great, Vanessa,' I replied. 'I'm worried about Edna. She's making a fool of herself with that Finchley shrink and she's more flaky than usual. She might even be going slightly bonkers. The whole thing is getting to me.' I looked at my watch. 'Where the hell is she anyway? The limo should have dropped her here forty minutes ago.'

Vanessa, always pragmatic, recommended I call Transport. I could hear Peter Gabriel rehearsing his rock version of 'God Save the Queen' which he was going to perform that night, spotlit on the roof of the Palace.

Transport, when I finally got through, told me the car had been waiting in Hill Street for over an hour and there had been no response to doorbells or phone calls. I rang off and felt sweat cascading down my back. Where was she? What had gone wrong? Christ! The obvious had not occurred to me in the first minutes of panic but now I telephoned the flat myself.

Kenny answered almost immediately and I heard loud vocal music in the background. Kylie Minogue?

'Oh sorry, Baz,' he said, 'I tried calling you but I must have had the wrong number. Mum's in hospital. She's on some new tablets and she got up in the middle of the night and ate everything in the fridge. I got home from a club at about four in the morning and she was up and talking to herself nineteen to the dozen. I think she thought she was in a playground and on a swing or something, and she was making very funny noises. It was weird so I rang that Doctor Foxson and he came around, gave her a shot and took her off to some clinic.'

I felt I was going to faint. Kenny gave me the name and number of a private hospital, St Rita's in Marylebone.

Vanessa looked very concerned. 'What is it? What's she done now?'

'That bastard of a shrink has knocked her out and shoved her in a bin. What'll we do?' I asked.

'It's simple, baby,' said Vanessa who, to my annoyance, seemed to be laughing. 'Send on her understudy!'

'And who might that be?' I snapped. Caleb was pulling at my trousers with very sticky fingers.

'You, baby.'

'Me?'

'Who'll know? We've got the gear here, I've got the make-up, and *voila*!' She opened her case and produced a mass of purple hair. 'The wig! Edna's not going to disappoint Her Majesty tonight.'

'How do you happen to still have that wig?' I asked,

incredulous. I had to sit down. It was all too much, too much.

'I saved all the stuff from our last gig in Australia, but after I flogged those bloody photos I didn't think you'd want to see me again so I kept the wig as a souvenir. Aren't you lucky that I'm sentimental?'

'I'm surprised it didn't find its way onto eBay,' I said unworthily. Relief and gratitude in my case sometimes come out as sarcasm.

It was a long time since I had been 'Edna', but I knew I could pull it off. All I had to do was get out there on cue, and introduce the Queen who was arriving about a third of the way into the show after the noisier rock bands had played their thunderous and heard-one-you've-heard-them-all ditties.

I rehearsed a few Ednaisms in my head as Vanessa painted my face and lacquered my nails with some indestructible varnish. Caleb was asleep on a couch, thank God.

We could hear the murmur of the huge crowd from not far away, and soon it was roaring like no crowd I had ever heard before as the bands began their hugely amplified banging and twanging. Thirty minutes later 'Edna' sat before the mirror in a long, pink jersey silk dress embellished with silver scrolls, one of Kenny's finest achievements. I wasn't there any more, but wherever I was, I wasn't feeling all that well. Too many coffees perhaps? Too much exertion on the previous night with the elastic Vanessa? One thing was certain: there had been too much Dame Edna and her infernal problems and complications.

A young man in a yellow jumpsuit wearing a headset and an

anxious expression put his head around the corner of my makeshift dressing-room. 'Five minutes, Dame Edna, she's nearly here.'

I was on.

After a short totter in the unfamiliar high heels along a boardwalk and up two flights of metal steps, a microphone was thrust at me and a firm hand at my elbow guided me over the tangle of cables into the blinding light. It was all on such an enormous scale, with an audience stretching out forever, that I didn't feel nervous; it didn't really feel like a show at all. Then a tremendous surge of sound from the audience told me that the monarch was on her way to the Royal Box, and I could just see her in the distance, picked up by a spotlight.

'The birthday girl has arrived!' Edna announced, and there was an even greater roar from that vast congregation. I don't know what else Edna said, but it was brief and it produced a couple of satisfying tsunamis of laughter. I was soon tottering back the way I had come, no longer with those helpful hands to assist me. I had done my bit, or Edna had, and I could get home as best I could.

'They loved it!' said Vanessa. 'They loved you, and it was short and sweet. Paul went on a bit too long, I thought.'

I sat down and took a deep breath, then I stood up feeling giddy. I sat down again and I felt a terrible wave of fear and loneliness overcome me. Should I breathe more deeply, or not breathe at all? I fought to stop myself from fainting and wondered if this was what a heart attack felt like.

'Are you all right, baby?' asked Vanessa, looming up very close to me.

I couldn't bear anyone to be near me, yet I had a fear of dying alone so I clutched her hand. Yes, I decided I was certainly dying and not in the manner, or attire, in which I had hoped to quit life. 'Better get a doctor or get me to hospital, but don't make a fuss.'

Vanessa looked scared to death and I was frightened she might bolt. 'I'll get someone from backstage,' she said.

With the last of my strength I implored her not to do that. The last thing I needed was a newspaper headline 'Dame Edna Collapses at Palace, Steals Queen's Thunder'.

'Just get me quietly into the car and to a hospital. No one must know,' I whispered.

Obediently, Vanessa grabbed Caleb and her make-up kit, and as I leant heavily on her arm we made it between the tents to the parking bay. The chauffeur was there and looked at us with alarm.

I remember little else so I must have passed out, which was better than the fear of almost certain death, but before I did I recall asking where we were going.

Ness said she had found the name and number of a hospital in my suit pocket. They were expecting me.

24

A Nun's Story

It was a white ceiling, and the wall was white as well, with a framed print of a cheerful regatta by Dufy. A nun in a white habit stood beside my bed. I felt a sharp pain in my right arm, just above the elbow, which must have woken me. The nun was taking my blood pressure and the pain in my arm had been caused by the contracting cuff attached to her puffer.

'You'll live, Edna,' said the kind nun with a smile. There wasn't much of her face visible; she was well-wimpled. 'We'll have to get you into the bath. You've been like this since they brought you in last night.'

I tried to speak but my lips felt like crumpets. I must be full of sedatives, I thought. I tried to remember what had happened to me.

The nun must have seen my expression of agonised enquiry. 'Nothing's the matter with you, Edna, it was just a case of hyperventilation. If the girl who brought you here had any sense she would have given you a paper bag to breathe into. She probably panicked.'

'Where am I?' I asked, but the way the nun smiled back told me that I must have made an incomprehensible noise, or none at all.

'I'm Sister Lo, and I'm a big fan, Edna.' She was peering at me intently. 'It's nice to meet you in the flesh. We've got a woman downstairs, one of Dr Foxson's patients, who is in a very bad way. She thinks she's you!' The nun burst out laughing and her gold crucifix bounced on her substantial starched white bosom.

I had never seen a nun laugh before, except in *The Sound of Music*. I hoped she wasn't going to start singing. I was starting to feel quite a bit better now I knew that I was not due to die immediately, but whatever drugs they had given me had completely immobilised me, and given me a fuzzy irresponsible feeling.

'Bath time,' announced Sister Lo, getting down to business. She pulled back the covers and hauled my legs over the side.

'Oh, Edna,' she exclaimed, 'you are naughty going to bed in your pantyhose!' She went off into further peals of laughter.

Groggily perched on the edge of the bed, I saw a reflection of myself in the glass of the Dufy print. It was Edna by Francis Bacon. The make-up was smeared across my face and my eyes were black and purple smudges. My mouth, still caked with lipstick, resembled a terrible wound and I observed that my fingernails were still lacquered a bright crimson. I must have arrived in an appalling state the night before and been shoved into bed without even a perfunctory sponge bath.

'Good morning, Doctor,' said the nun. 'She's just going to have her shower. We hate looking like the Wreck of the Hesperus[17] don't we, Edna?'

I tried to explain that I was me and not her, but I felt all over like my mouth felt after a dental injection. I recognised the doctor who stood at my bedside; it was Foxson, the Finchley ponytail. He wore a rumpled suit jacket, jeans and an open-necked shirt; the tie-less look affected by middle-aged men wishing to appear youthful. He smiled at me as if pleased that my appearance confirmed his most pessimistic diagnosis. He opened his briefcase and I saw him snapping an ampoule, preparing to fill a hypodermic needle. I cowered, whimpering at the end of the bed, clutching at Sister Lo.

'Don't worry, pet, Doctor knows best,' she said. 'It's only a little shot to calm you down. Doctor wants you nice and quiet for a week or two.'

Foxson looked almost vengeful as he grabbed my arm and stabbed it with his instrument. His face was very close to mine.

---

17 Used to denote a dishevelled appearance, the term originates from a poem by Henry Wadsworth Longfellow in which a proud sea captain ignores advice about a storm approaching, and then must tie his young daughter to the mast of the ship to prevent her from being swept overboard. The ship founders and sinks and the girl's body is found later, still strapped to the broken mast.

'It's for your own good, chum,' he said, and I caught a whiff of garlic from last night's cannelloni at some Hampstead trattoria. 'You're a pretty sick chap.' Turning to the nun, he said, 'Get the patient cleaned up quickly before the Largactyl kicks in. I'm going downstairs to see Dame Edna.'

I remember little more than stumbling around in the shower, a lot of shampoo and a black man, probably a male orderly, lifting me back into bed. When I awoke, or returned to consciousness, it was Tuesday morning and I learnt later that I had slept for forty-eight hours. Vanessa was sitting in the plastic chair in the corner of my room looking at me curiously.

'Is that you, Nessie?' I asked. I could speak again, it seemed, but in a woolly voice. On the floor, playing with Lego, there was a child with the face of a middle-aged television presenter.

'Shit, I was worried about you, baby,' Vanessa said. 'I thought you'd had a heart attack or something but I found the name of the hospital in the pocket of your suit. You were having such a panic attack after the show at Buck House, we got you in here immediately, or Doctor Foxson did. What a dishy guy he is, incidentally!'

If I had been more articulate I would have quickly and eloquently expressed a contrary view of this money-grabbing ghoul who treated hyperventilation as if it were schizophrenia.

I peered at my visitor. Vanessa looked particularly attractive this morning in her gored jeans and faded 'I'm With Stupid' T-shirt. Even in my bedridden state she could still inspire what D. J. Enright called 'a brief but distinct convulsion'. I hoped she had left her camera at home. Shots of me laid low in a loony bin might still fetch a good price and Edna might have to go back to her illustrious contact to keep me out of the papers.

'Do you like the glads?' asked Vanessa. 'I brought them in yesterday but you were asleep. That nice nun put them in a vase.'

There were flowers on the little ledge in my room, a very large vase of gladioli, if they could be described as flowers. They were more like saplings. I stared at them with a faint nausea. A large black woman entered the room brightly and placed a tray on my lap. Lifting the metal lid she exposed a brown cartilaginous mess with a scoop of rice on the side. There was a quivering, yellow dessert and a mug of tea. With a shaky hand, I attempted a sip, having to hold the cup awkwardly to avoid a chip on the rim. I am not overly fastidious, but a chipped hospital cup induced visions of instant *E.coli*. I had a flashback to my childhood. I had poured myself some milk out of the fridge into a cup by the sink and, as I raised it to my lips, my mother had rushed into the kitchen and snatched it from my hand, dashing the milk everywhere. 'Not that cup, Barry . . . That's the *gardener's* cup!'

'Excuse I? Are you decent?'

A familiar figure stood in the entrance to my room, snapping me back to the present. It was Edna, looking surprisingly formal in a black Chanel suit.

'You poor thing, Barry. We are a couple of crocks, aren't we? Or we were. Thanks for understudying me at the Palace the other night. Now you know how hard I work. Isn't it ironic? I get rushed to hozzie and then you.' Edna had begun to say ironic a lot, as had everyone. It was thought to be a new word for coincidental. 'Thanks to that wonderful Seth Foxson, I've never been better. In fact, I am checking out now. The car's waiting.'

She glanced, with more than a hint of disdain, at Vanessa and the BBC presenter on the floor. Her gaze travelled from the top of Vanessa's head down to her long, salty, barely-shod feet.

'What a tiny room they gave you, Barry,' she said. 'Just as well you've only got one bunch of flowers. I've given all my bouquets to the poor little possums in Intensive Care and I'm afraid some of them may last longer than the patients.' Edna helped herself to a grape from a bowl of fruit on the nightstand.

'Seth Foxson is a genius,' she said. 'In the few days since my crisis he's helped me realise that I never really loved myself – I only liked myself very much indeed. Seth gave me the courage to go all the way. I *adore* myself now. Doesn't it show?' Edna, her back pointedly turned on Vanessa, spread her arms and beamed expansively.

'Loving yourself so much must have been a novel experience,' I said, with a sad attempt at satire.

Edna then launched into a breathless chronicle of impending, or conjectural, triumphs. 'People are at last beginning to see me as an actress, Barry – I mean, *actor*,' she hastily corrected the sexist lapse. 'You have been wonderful in nurturing my career as a comedienne, but you never addressed my other talents.'

I had wondered for some time when Edna would start addressing things other than envelopes. Gender issues couldn't be far down the track.

'Sam Mendes wants me for his new production of something called *Phedre* at the Yankee Stadium in New York,' Edna continued. 'The Americans say I'm the only British star who could sell it out.'

Supine, I could only squeak my congratulations.

'Then,' continued Edna, beginning to glow and expand, 'because the MAC cosmetic people love my skin, they want me to be their new face. Move over Liz Hurley, Isabella Rossellini and that other woman!'

'Do we get any free samples?' interrupted Vanessa impudently.

Ignoring her, and now riding on a tidal wave of self-esteem, Edna carried on, 'George is going to publish *The Compassionate Camera.*'

The room raised its eyebrows.

'It's my collection of photographs of amputees,' Edna explained. 'The book will be so big and heavy, they're going to sell it with a special lectern like they have in church.'

'Couldn't they abridge it, like its subjects?' I asked, attempting a jest and failing.

But Edna, on a roll of hubris, continued, '. . . and Heather Mills is writing the introduction.' She had saved the most dramatic news until last. 'Guess who's going to be the new ambassador to Washington? Moi!'

Amongst Edna's many recently acquired expressions, 'moi'

was perhaps the most irritating. She had probably picked it up from her hairdresser.

Edna perched on the edge of my bed. She seemed infinitely more friendly than usual, due no doubt to the fact that I was, for the time being at least, a write-off and practically sectioned.

'You know who I mean by Nancy Pelosi?' Edna had always prefaced a major name-drop with the usually superfluous phrase, 'You know who I mean by', such as 'You know who I mean by Michael Jackson?'

'Yes, I think I do,' I replied. 'In fact, I believe I introduced you to Nancy in San Francisco.' I was feeling better after a slug of contaminated hospital tea.

'Well,' continued Edna, 'she's invited me to the White House for tea with the Obamas. Michelle wants Kenny to design her new wardrobe and Nancy has hinted that I could land a wonderful job as Presidential Life Coach. They're a sweet couple but they need grooming.'

Vanessa seemed to be snorting into a Kleenex. Had I been out of circulation so long that all these spectacular developments in Edna's life had passed me by? Or were they just fantasies?

There was no sign of Caleb. Probably gone to the loo, I thought.

'Did your son Kenny design that suit?' asked Vanessa sweetly.

'Of course not!' said Edna, barely looking at the young woman. 'It's just an old Chanel – it's the only black thing I've got, in honour of poor little Madge. You know she passed away last week?'

I was shocked and saddened. 'Poor Madge. How?' I asked.

Edna gave me a beatific smile. 'Oh, Barry, it was merciful. She should have gone years ago and I sometimes suggested it. I think she was in a facility in New Zealand, or perhaps South London. We'd rather lost touch, I'm afraid.'

'In that case,' interrupted Vanessa. 'You'd better read this.' She produced a long sealed envelope from her handbag. 'It's quite old, I think. I found it in your pocket, Barry, when I was looking for the name of the hospital. There's a whole office crammed in those pockets. How often do you wear that suit?' She handed it to Edna.

'What does it say that can't wait?' snapped Edna, thrusting the envelope back. 'I haven't got my reading glasses, only these.' She indicated her spectacular, gem-encrusted face furniture. For the first time since I had known her, I noticed that her glasses were lensless.

Vanessa read the inscription on the envelope. '"For Dame Edna – to be read on the event of my death, from Marjorie Allsop".'

As Vanessa tore open the letter, Edna said, 'She's probably left me something – poor old thing, probably something I gave her once. I hope it'll be easy to get rid of. She never had much of her own.'

Vanessa began to read:

Dear Edna,

When you read this I will be gone, to a nice wee place I hope. We have known each other a long time and all that time I have kept a secret. If I had got it off my chest long ago, I might have had a happier life but they would probably have put me in jail.

I always looked up to you from the first time we met at Moonee Ponds Grammar, after they sent me over from New Zealand. Then you married Norman and you seemed to find happiness, even though the poor wee lamb was an invalid. But you were always cheerful and you had the lucky gift of being able to laugh at the misfortunes of others.

I know I'm no oil painting, and I never was, even when I was dolled up none of the boys ever asked me to dance, and something in my organism told me that it would be a miracle if I ever married and had a wee family, and yet Edna, I loved children and longed to have a bubba of my own. I even thought of adopting one, but not an African one like the fashion is now, a real one like your precious little Lois.

You never knew this, and I know it would have sickened you if you had, but once, when you were out, I tried breastfeeding Lois, but her little bubba-gums hurt my chests too much, and judging by the little one's screams it didn't work in the way nature meant it to. But we bonded all the same.

You were always so busy, Edna, and so creative, and I was just the babysitter. Then one weekend you and Norm decided you would go to Wagga Wagga with wee Lois in her carry-cot.

I knew that your aunty had a bach[18] on the outskirts of Wagga and that you would be staying there. When you had gone I couldn't get Lois out of my mind. I had winded her so often and changed her wee nappies and I had worried about her lazy eye, her impetigo and the rash in her navel. Her cradle cap worried me, too. I spent many hours pouring olive oil into it and scrubbing it with a toothbrush — my toothbrush, I might add.

I went up to Wagga on the train the next day and checked in at O'Shaughnessy's Family Hotel[19] wearing an assumed dress. That night, round about mozzie time, I went out to your aunty's house and hid in the lantana. I saw you go on to the veranda and sit in the old cane chair with Lois at your chests, something I longed to do. You then popped her down under her net and went inside. I must have waited for nearly an hour, my wee heart thumping. The moon came up and I suddenly worried about Lois. You hadn't winded her. If I could only hold her little mottled body over my shoulder and pat her little quilted back. In a minute I was on the veranda, trying not to slap my muddied jandals[20] too loudly on the deck. Seconds later, I lifted the gauze and her eye met mine. She knew me, she smiled and a wee white trickle flowed from the corner of her mouth.

Heaven forgive me, but I was off into the night with your precious wee daughter in my arms. A mad part of me must have

18 New Zealand for country shack.
19 Now the Royal Wagga International Conference Centre Resort and Spa.
20 New Zealand thongs or flip-flops.

planned it all, for I had bottles and rusks in my tramping rucksack and we were on the night train to Melbourne. I felt she was meant to be mine. You never met Del and Adrian Mannix, did you, Edna? They were old friends from Palmerston who had settled in Pascoe Vale. They had been trying for a family for years, without success, and I loaned them Lois. I said she was mine due to the fact that I had accidentally tried for a family myself one night with a fellow who came to fix the washing machine. The law wasn't as strict then and Del and Adrian fell in love with Lois as soon as they saw her.

Over the years I would visit them when you thought I was going to church or doing that macramé course, and as Lois grew she called me Aunty Madge. Del and Adrian believed my story and to this day, Lois has no idea she is your wee bairn, Edna. I did a wicked thing and I feel sorry for the koala community because the suspicion fell on them when Lois disappeared. Perhaps the muddy footprints of my jandals gave the police that idea.

As you know, I married Douglas years later but he passed away on the honeymoon before we had a chance to try for a family. I never told him about Lois.

Oh, Edna, I have carried this guilt for so long and I tried to make up for it by helping you even when you were sometimes slightly horrible to me. You would be proud of Lois now. She has grown into a fine woman is now a qualified psychiatric carer since her advanced studies at Our Lady of Dolours Nursing College. I have gone to my reward but please forgive me.

Your loving friend,

Marjorie Allsop

Edna's face was ashen. 'If that woman were alive now, she'd be turning in her grave,' she whispered hoarsely after a long silence. 'She's a criminal and New Zealand has produced more than its fair share of them!'

Caleb ran into the room, closely followed by Sister Lo.

'Look who I found being a naughty boy in the ward, pestering patients for sweeties,' said the nun. 'I think some of the other sisters have been spoiling him, haven't they you scallywag?'

Suddenly the nun became aware of the subdued atmosphere in the room. Edna still sat rigidly at the end of my bed, staring at the wall, speechless.

I broke the silence. 'Have you met Dame Edna, Sister?' I asked. 'She's been in observation downstairs but she's just been discharged.'

The nun looked from me to Edna and back again. 'Oh! Oh ... I'm so sorry,' she stammered. 'I thought *you* were Edna, Barry. I mean I didn't know that she was a real ... er ... woman.'

'Don't I look like a real woman?' barked Edna. 'What's been going on here?'

'I don't know what's real and what isn't,' said the nun.

Join the club, I felt like saying. If this scene had taken place in a work of fiction, I wouldn't have believed it.

'But if you really are Dame Edna,' said Sister Lo, 'I feel I know you, I know you very well. My Aunty Madge always talked about you when she came to see us.'

'And who is Aunty Madge, prithee?' interjected Edna, lapsing into the archaic.

'She was a sweetheart,' said the woman. 'She was an old friend of my parents, but unfortunately she's just passed away.'

Edna's powers of divination, her second sightedness, seemed not to have deserted her. 'What is your real name, may I ask, nurse?' Edna could not bring herself to address the nun by her sacerdotal title.

'You don't know me from a bar of soap, but I'm Sister Lo. Actually,' she added with a smile, 'I'm Lois Mannix and I love your work.'

Even Caleb on the floor fell silent in response to the eerie hush that had descended on the room.

'Lois?' exclaimed Edna. 'LOIS!' Then she gave out an almost bestial cry which I feared might have been audible throughout St Rita's, and fell bawling across the bed.

'I don't want to believe it!' she screamed. 'I *won't* believe it. What have I done to deserve this? I've been a nice person all my life. I'm kind, I'm caring, I'm an icon, I'm almost a saint. I've won the Golden Rose of Montreux, a Tony and a Tony nomination amongst other things. How could Dame Nature let this happen?'

'What are you raving about, Edna? Isn't it wonderful you've found your long lost daughter?' I protested rather ineffectually.

Sister Lois still looked bewildered.

'I gave birth to a Catholic, Barry,' croaked the prostrate Edna, pointing a jewelled and trembling finger at the astonished Bride of Christ. 'Two gay children and a Roman Catholic!'

Sister Lois went over and quietly closed the door into the corridor.

I think we will not return to that hospital room. I think that just now we are not wanted there. I think it would be best for us to go quickly and quietly away, leaving the child and its mother, the nun, the megastar and the man in the bed. At the end of the corridor we will descend in the lift to Admissions, past the chapel and the pharmacy and the large holy mosaic next to the hospital florist, with its chrysanthemums, carnations, drooping tulips and sympathy cards. Out in the street, thunderous with traffic, we may take one last look over our shoulder at the red brick clinic where neither we, nor anyone else, is wanted now.

APPENDIX

*Miscellaneous jottings,
doggerel and ephemera
saved from Edna's shredder.*

Edna's Lexicon of Taste

(circa 1965)

COMMON	NICE
Washhouse	*Laundry*
Yard	*Lawn*
Runners	*Sand shoes*
Ham and beef shop	*Delicatessen*
Veranda	*Porch*
Sweater	*Jumper (pullover)*
Blood nose	*Nosebleed*
Tea	*Lunch (dinner)*
Pictures	*Theatre*
Smokes	*Cigarettes*
Rubbish	*Garbage*
Passage	*Hall*
Lollies	*Sweets (confectionery)*
Ice chest	*Fridge*
Carpet sweeper	*Hoover*
To pull the chain	*To flush the toilet*
Kettle	*Teapot*

COMMON	*NICE*
Till	*Cash register*
Fly paper	*Mortein*
Meat safe	*Cool cupboard*
Shoes (boots)	*Footwear*
Writing pad	*Compendium*
Strides	*Slacks*
Bathers, togs (trunks)	*Costume (bathers)*
Stove	*Oven*
Googies	*Eggs*
Chooks	*Fowls*
Quilt	*Bedspread*
Paper shop	*Newsagent*
Haircut	*Trim*
Stockings	*Lingerie*
In-laws	*Relations*
Boarding house	*Guesthouse*
Hose	*Sprinklers*
Sitting room	*Lounge*
Briquette	*Mallee root*
Sleep-out	*Spare room*
Sideway (down)	*Drive (up)*

COMMON	*NICE*
Face washer	*Flannel*
Pillowcase	*Pillowslip*
Radio	*Wireless*
House	*Home*
Beer	*Ale*
Photo	*Painting or 'original'*
Shopping list	*Order*
Pretty	*Attractive*
Next door	*Neighbour*
Carpets and lino	*Floor coverings*
Soldier	*Serviceman*
Pudding	*Dessert*
Serviette	*Napkin*

Edna's Good Housewife Rating Guide

MARKS

1 **If you are a smoker, do you**

   a) smoke whilst cooking   (0)

   b) put cigarette in ashtray whilst cooking   (2)

   c) refrain from smoking in the kitchen   (5)

2 **When tasting the soup, do you**

   a) take a clean spoon each time   (5)

   b) put the spoon back into the pot   (0)

   c) run the spoon under the tap before using again   (2)

3 **When you are serving food, do you**

   a) never touch it with your hands   (5)

   b) sometimes help it a little with your fingers   (1)

   c) wash your hands before touching it   (2)

4 If you own a 'Fler' wooden salad bowl, do you

a) scrub it out with hot water and soap after use   (5)

b) refrain from washing it at all in the French style   (0)

c) wipe it over with a little olive oil on a clean cloth (1)

5 When pouring milk at the table, do you

a) puncture a hole in the foil top of the bottle   (0)

b) use a jug   (5)

c) take the foil top right off   (2)

6 When you have cleaned the table for a meal, do you

a) give it a good wipe down   (5)

b) flick the crumbs away onto the floor   (0)

c) sweep off the mess with a little broom   (2)

7 When washing cutlery, do you

a) make sure all the egg is out of the fork prongs   (5)

b) put it into a bowl of hot water   (4)

c) wipe it clean on the teatowel   (0)

8 After washing dishes, do you

a) cover them with a clean cloth   (1)

b) dry them up and put them away   (5)

c) run them through with fresh water and leave   (1)

9 When emptying the tea leaves, do you

a) tip them down the sink (3)

b) dispose of them down the lav (0)

c) pour them down the gully trap (5)

10 With rubbish in the kitchen, do you

a) leave it lying on the bench or in the sink (0)

b) put it wrapped into the tin (5)

c) throw it straight into the tin without wrapping (2)

11 After emptying your rubbish tin do you

a) leave it as it is (0)

b) put fresh paper on the bottom (1)

c) scrub it with disinfectant and repaper (5)

12 While rinsing out teatowels, do you

a) change the water twice (2)

b) rinse them until the water is clean enough
to drink (5)

c) wash them until the water is free from soapy suds (2)

13 When your hands are wet, do you

a) dry them on your apron (0)

b) wipe them on a hand towel (5)

c) use a teatowel for drying them (0)

14 **With the kiddies' potty do you**

a) keep it in the kitchen (0)

b) keep it under their bed (1)

c) keep it in the lav (5)

15 **When rubbing through your smalls, do you**

a) use the laundry for this purpose (5)

b) use the kitchen sink (0)

c) use the bathroom basin (2)

5 and under: Disgraceful
6–20:   Acceptable
21–70:   Good

How things have changed, today, Possums!

Ode to Garden City

*Typical of Edna's many occasional verses, usually penned in the limo
on the way to the venue. This was for a new Brisbane shopping mall.*

I've always been a housewife like Mrs Brown or Mrs Smith,
Then I became a Megastar, an icon and a myth.
It's amazing in the circumstances I've remained so modest.
Considering that I've been 'Damed', and one day I'll be
    'Goddessed'!
I've accepted far more honours than any woman has before
But I must confess I've never been a 'Figurehead' before.
Yet Garden City Shopping Centre here at Mount Gravatt
Said: 'Edna, we need a Figurehead, and you're exactly that.
You're the human face of progress, you're the retailer's ideal,
You're glamorous, you're feisty, but more than anything you're
    REAL.'

I know my limitations, Possums, I don't stay up all night bopping
And I love my friends and family, but above all I love shopping.
I drink a scrummy caffé latte, every day about eleven.
Then I head for Garden City which is my idea of Heaven.
I'm not a spendthrift glamourpuss, I don't give in to greed.
But here in this amazing place is everything I need.
There's a seafood store to die for, with lobsters, prawns and bugs,

There's wedding dresses, baby clothes, there's cabbages and rugs.
There are clothes galore on every floor and gifts for all occasions
And quaint exotic food stores, for our gorgeous little Asians.
You name it, Possums, it's all here, and if you want some proof,
Explore with me this Aladdin's Cave, beneath one wondrous roof.
There's a dentist and a doctor in this great retail adventure,
In case your veins need knotting, or you cough and break a denture.
So it should be pretty obvious – even to a dunce –
That with facilities like this, you can have both ends fixed at once.
No wonder tots are goggle-eyed, no wonder seniors cry:
'Please wheel me around Garden City, once before I die.'

Brizzy is famed for landmarks – though some have not fared well.
Remember Dreamland, Baxter's, and the old Bellevue Hotel?
But the Breakfast Creek Hotel's still there, the Storey Bridge
    survives,
And what you've torn down won't concern the under forty-fives.
But Brisbane folk have woken up – and here's the nitty-gritty–
They've demanded a new landmark – its name is Garden City.

There's just one disappointment, from shop to shop we roam:
That awful anticlimax, when the time comes to go home.
If I become a politician, though I fear I'm far too pretty,
I'll fight to make each Aussie home a Bonsai Garden City.
And in case you girls are wondering, as I stroll around these stores,
It's Civic Pride I'm flushed with, and not the menopause.
Now I'm off to have my hair done, or a slimming lunch instead.
You've got to keep your head and figure – if you're a Figurehead!

Gladdy Song

Inspired by the music-hall song 'I've Got a Lovely Bunch of Coconuts',
Edna penned this rousing audience-particpation song in 1964 for her
show Excuse I.

Roses are red
Violets are blue
I love all flowers whatever their hue
I am no stranger to the hydrangea
And I've got an eye
For bonsai.
But though I love pansies
Violas and phlox
Azaleas, delphiniums, dahlias and stocks
And the smell of wisteria gives me hysteria
I must admit I'm a bit in favour of one flower
I love the best
It's not a sunflower, I wonder if you've guessed:

Chorus:
I've got a lovely bunch of gladdies
There they are a standing in a vase
Big ones, small ones, some as big as your thumb
Give them a twist, a flick of the wrist
There's lots of different ways of arranging them!

Just remember all you mums and daddies
There's lots of flower power to be had
All you need is a lovely bunch of gladdies
And you'll never be sad so long as you wave a glad.

Singing:
Wave a wave a glad the flower of Australia
It's much better than a rose, a daff or a dahlia
When you're feeling melancholy
Take a grip of your gladioli
And you'll never be sad so long as you wave a glad.

Edna distributes gladdies to the audience:
Now you've all got a lovely bunch of gladdies
See them all a waving in the aisles
Pink ones, red ones, some a lovely maroan [sic]
Think how lucky you are to have a gladdy all your own
The world's made up of lots of good and baddies
So who cares if we all go a little bit mad:
All we need is a lovely bunch of gladdies
And we'll never be sad so long as we wave a glad.

We've got a lovely bunch of gladdies
Watch us hold them high above our heads
Left, right, left, right, any way we please
There's nothing like a lovely gladdy waving in the breeze
It doesn't matter what your whim or fad is
You can do it in the nude or fully clad
All we need is a lovely bunch of gladdies
And we'll never be sad so long as we wave a glad.

Alternate Gladdy Song

(1970 version)

(tune: 'When You Wore a Tulip')

If you wave a gladdy and they wave a gladdy
And I wave a big pink glad,
Then we all, holus bolus, waved our gladiolus
'T would be a sight to cheer the sad.
There's no vision more holy than massed gladioli
They're Australian through and through;
So keep your courage and trust up
Give your gladdies a thrust up
And your dreams will all come true.

The language of flowers
Has magical powers
Just grip firmly on to your stalk;
If you've only a slip of one
Tremble the tip of one
And your gladdy will be ready to talk;
I could wave mine for hours, and say it with flowers
So join in all you mums and dads
There's such comfort and solace
In the Aussie gladiolus
So rise up and tremble your glads.

Ode to the Barnardos

A fund-raising tirade delivered by Edna a quarter of a century ago to raise money for the Barnardo's Homes, and their great benefactor, the couturier Bruce Oldfield.

When Bruce first ran his chilly tape
From my slender ankle to naked nape

I asked him: 'Of all the girls you've dressed
Tell me frankly, Possum, who's the best?'

Yet I doubt if his answer would give you a shock
As you gaze at me now in this stunning frock

But I must be as generous as I am able
To those poor runners-up in the Oldfield stable

You all look gorgeous, you've all done your best
And it's not my fault I'm better dressed.

But tonight's event is no mere charade
Of glamourpusses on parade

And though I'm an actress and 'chantoose'
I've been given a job to do by Bruce

He said: 'Edna, please write a few talented verses
To make those silly old tarts put their hands in their purses

It's within your powers as a megastar
To remind us all how lucky we are.'

So as we gobble our champers and avocados
Let's think of the work done by Dr Barnardo's

And let me tell you my secret for satisfied living:
It's giving and giving and giving and giving

What a relief to know your donation
Won't be squandered away on administration.

I think of young Bruce as though he's my son
But if I get too emotional my mascara might run

So welcome to this Barnardo's beano
(To think I almost wore my Valentino!)

But a spooky voice inside my head
Made me slip into this instead

And darling Bruce would get such a shock
To spy me in a rival's frock

But isn't this Oldfield number bliss?
I know women who'd kill to dress like this

But Bruce's top clients all agree
It's an honour to be upstaged by me

But all the Barnardo's boys and girls we know
Are the real stars of this glittering show

With our generous help their feet will be planted
On the road of life we took for granted

So turn your minds, Possums, from food and sex
The fashion tonight is big fat cheques!

All Things Bright
and Beautiful

With the exception of the second verse this is sung to the traditional hymn tune. It was featured in Excuse I, *circa 1964.*

When I get home from a day in a city street
I pop on the kettle, though I'm nearly dropping on my feet
Make a nice cup of tea
Then I switch on my favourite channel.
It's the best time for me
As I flick off my flyaway panel.

When I get home from a night at a flesh and bone theatre
If you call it a treat looking up and down each street for a meter
I think of songs from the old shows
As I powder my nose
And I think of an old hymn that time will never dim for me
Before I met my Norm, it was the only hymn for me.

All things bright and beautiful
All creatures great and small,
All things wise and wonderful
Australia has them all!

Our famous ballerinas
Joan Sutherland their star[21]

---

21 Some mistake, surely – B. H.

Our Hoover vacuum cleaners
Our Violet Crumble bar;
A cloth all Persil-snowy
For an Austral picnic spread
Where hums the humble blowy
And beetroot stains the bread!
All things bright and beautiful
Pavlovas that we bake;
All things wise and wonderful
Australia takes the cake!

Our great big smiling beaches
The smell of thick Kwik-tan
Our lovely juicy peaches
That never blow the can;
Our gorgeous modern cities
So famed throughout the earth
The Paris end of Collins Street
The Melbourne end of Perth.
All things bright and beautiful
Though cynics sneer and plot
All things wise and wonderful
Australia's got the lot!

The Farex that we scrape
Off those wee Australian chins,
The phenyl that we sprinkle
Inside our rubbish bins;
The wives of our great statesmen
Who stand by and inspire,
The wives of TV idols
Especially Dolly Dyer!

All things bright and beautiful
Our wonderful wealth of natural mineral resources,
All things wise and wonderful,
And our even more wonderful wealth of different brands
    of tomato sauces

Australia is a Saturday
With races on the tranny
Australia is the talcy smell of someone else's granny
Australia is a kiddy
With zinc cream on its nose
Australia's voice is Melba's voice
It's also Normie Rowe's[22]
Australia's famous postage stamps
Are stuffed with flowers and fauna
Australia is the little man
Who's open round the corner;
Australia is a sunburnt land
Of sand and surf and snow
All ye who do not love her
Ye know where ye can go!

All things bright and beautiful
All creatures great and small
All things wise and wonderful
Australia has them all!

22 Australian crooner of yesteryear.

Audience with Dame Edna – September 1980

The lyrics of one of Dame Edna's most successful songs, set to music by Laurie Holloway. It includes a reference to Bianca, the then spouse of a popular crooner and friend of Dame Edna's.

A cheering crowd at my stage door
An audience crying out for more
That's what my public means to me
The loyal fans who queue for hours
The cards, the telegrams, the flowers
That's what my public means to me
You need to have a pretty humble attitude
When you see little faces looking up grotesque with gratitude
But from tiny tots to grannies
I love all your nooks and crannies
That's what my public means to me.

The Queen's birthday honours list
A lovely Cartier on my wrist
That's what my public means to me
A limousine, a sable coat,
The lump that's rising in my throat
That's what my public means to me
Superstars may come and go but there's no other
That folks identify with their own mother

There's even people in this room
Who wish they'd sprung out of my womb
That's what my public means to me.

The David Hockneys on my wall
The Royal visitors who call
Yes, Possums – that's what my public's done for me
All those requests I get to stay
With famous folk in St Tropez
For that's their idea of fun for me
But they can keep Roman Polanski and Bianca
It's for the company of nobodies like you I hanker
You're my shelter from the storm
You're all as precious as my Norm
That's another thing my public means to me.

And now the time has come to part
I've got an ache inside my heart
That's what my public do to me
Though little know-alls squirt their poison
I can feel my eyelids moisten
When I think how my public still stays true to me
I may be forced to live in a tax haven
But I know I'm home when I see all those gladdies wavin'
And how could I forsake them
When they raise their stalks and shake them
That's what my public means to me.

Springtime for Edna

This piece of ephemeral journalism — a completely fictitious rendering of the facts — was written for a now defunct English magazine.

Funnily enough, it if hadn't been for spring my wonderful mother would still be living at home. I was going through an old box-room a few Septembers ago (I'll never get used to your spooky EEC idea of springtime in April) when I discovered that my old darling had been living under our roof for ages in a cocoon of motherly Melbourne memorabilia.

Our local Twilight Home sent their van around almost immediately after my phone call and the driver — a delightful chappy — assured me that it wasn't a bit unusual for conscientious Australian spring-cleaning families to stumble across the odd senior citizen. In those days Norm (later Lord Everage) was still living at home and although he had already felt a few tell-tale twinges his slippered feet had still a very long way to shuffle along the road to international Urological Stardom. He was a tower of strength — so firm, yet gentle — as we bundled my blinking oldster cuddling a hastily packed bundle of bygones off on her new adventure. When I saw her peaky little face peeping through the grille of the fast receding granny-van and turned to help Norm and the children stoke our incinerator,

I thought how much Mummy reminded me of a cuddly Australian marsupial which had just scratched its way out of hibernation.

It's incredible what does come to light when spring erupts in the Antipodes and I don't think I'd have the strength to cope with it alone now that Norm is more or less the property of Science.

Can you imagine yours truly, sickle in hand, hacking my way through a sea of glads to get to the front gate to collect my fan mail? Come spring, that was always Norm's job and the brave old possum used to risk life and limb every morning as he battled his way through the sticky stalks to my chock-full box. You spoilt EEC softies can't imagine what perils lurk in the suburban shrubbery. Sometimes my beauty sleep would be interrupted by a hoarse cry from the front lawn, and the family knew that some venomous marsupial or creepy-crawly, rudely roused from its long snooze, had successfully penetrated my husband's slumber suit. This was in the years before Australian laboratories perfected our internationally acclaimed spider-repellent pyjama bottoms.

Deadly funnel web spiders, or 'webbos' as we affectionately call them Down Under, can be a darned nuisance in the mating season, and it's not fun jumping out of bed in the middle of the night for a glass of water only to find, too late, that your favourite slipper is the honeymoon suite for a hairy pair of wooing webbos.

It's happened to my old friend and bridesmaid Madge Allsop more than once, foolish wretch. Being a New Zealander, she

335

never picked up the sensible Australian habit of shining a torch inside her mules before her nocturnal excursions, and it's a miracle she's alive to tell the tale.

Ever since Madge first moved into my mother's old room, the screaming sirens of the Suburban Serum Service wailed to a halt outside our front door night after night, making sleep in Humoresque Street an impossibility. Many is the time the Webbo Squad have hacked down our front door to find Madge repulsing the advances of an amorous wombat or grappling with a killer blowfly on heat.

A top Sydney toxicologist told me once that my bridesmaid probably attracted more than her fair share of scary intruders because of some secretion or other exuded during periods of excitement. Yet, it's sad for my poor old playmate that, what attracts lower forms of life, seems to have the opposite effect on the human beings she rubs up against.

Personally speaking, I find spring days in Australia more perilous than the hours of darkness. It's a nightmare trying to dissuade EEC visitors from jumping in for a swim at one of our award-winning, internationally acclaimed beaches. The low-flying shark-spotting choppers induce a false sense of security, as do the crowded ranks of blood transfusion units at the water's edge. But although our sharks very rarely venture far inland during the mating season, they are often inclined to mistake the pale torsos of EEC swimmers for scaly soulmates. Unfortunately, Australian rape laws have yet to be amended to provide adequate compensation for the innocent victims of underwater molestation.

Our bird life is arguably the most articulate in the world and our parrots and cockatoos – or 'cockies' as we affectionately call them – chat away non-stop like a cross between Clive James and Germie Greer. A tendency to talk about the first thing that comes into their heads is another gorgeous Aussie trait that gets our cockies into a lot of hot water when springtime comes around.

Quite frankly, I used to insist that my little ones wore earplugs when they got anywhere within range of our feathered friends. For a few weeks every year the Australian air is blue with the raucous conversation of foul-mouthed budgies. Hence the term pornithology, I suppose.

I am a bit of a bluestocking underneath, as you probably know. In fact, if I'd lived in Bloomsbury in the olden days I would have given old Virginia Woolf a good run for her money. Be that as it may, whenever I feel the sap rising I more often than not start whistling a tune or two from *The Rite of Spring* – in my book, one of Stravinsky's most delightful shows.

The other day, as I peeped from my Dorchester penthouse across Park Lane Street at your gorgeous Hyde Gardens, there was no doubt about it, Possums; something was definitely trying to poke itself up between the deckchairs. There were daffs and crokes all over the place, and as winter wanes I know it's time I started waxing. Wherever I happen to be, spring is the time when I tackle these famous limbs with my preferred depilator.

In the old days, of course, it was a simple abrasive mitten and it's a spooky coincidence that as I write these words I can hear prickly old Madge buffing herself up in the bathroom with the Black & Decker floor sanding attachment I gave her last Chrissy.

I always get a bit downier at this time of year and my wonderful son, Kenny, and his sympathetic flatmate, Clifford Smail, used to always supervise my annual polishing with a saucepan of cosmetic wax bubbling away on the hot plate. Now Megastardom demands that I take myself off to a little Mayfair clinic and it's marvellous to think I will be able to wear those sleeveless frocks and shorter skirts that suit me so well in the sickly EEC sunshine.

Dame Edna's bulging archives contain much more of this meretricious material – B. H.

Acknowledgements

The author wishes to acknowledge the assistance of his publisher Matthew Kelly, who pressed him to this unappetising task; his attractive secretaries, Meredith and Nicola, who were available at all hours of the day and night; Angela, his legal adviser; and Natalie, who graciously supplied the writing materials.

Some of the photographs in this book came from the Arts Centre, Performing Arts Collection in Melbourne – of which the author is patron. Both publisher and author thank the Arts Centre and its staff (especially Janine Barrand, Patricia Convery and Sandy Graham) for their assistance in locating and providing material.